WHO WAS *THE REAL ELVIS*?

You could ask his wife Priscilla, whose divorce left him with an emptiness that so many other women tried unsuccessfully to fill.

You could ask the doctors who prescribed the "medicines" that he desperately took to cure his pain.

You could ask all the people to whom he gave such incredibly lavish gifts—and from whom he demanded so much to keep him going in a life he both hated and loved.

You could ask the millions of fans who jammed the most successful concert tours of all time as they watched Elvis turn himself inside-out in performances never to be forgotten.

Above all, you could read this fascinating story.

ELVIS
The Final Years

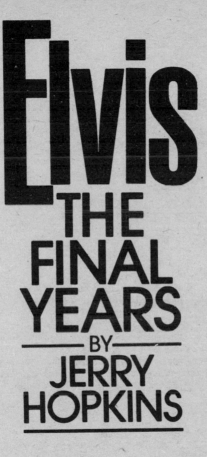

Elvis
THE FINAL YEARS
BY
JERRY HOPKINS

B
BERKLEY BOOKS, NEW YORK

ELVIS
THE FINAL YEARS

A Berkley Book / published by arrangement with
the author

PRINTING HISTORY
PBJ Books edition / August 1981
Berkley edition / September 1983

Acknowledgments

Approximately seventy-five individuals were interviewed for this book. Most of them hadn't been interviewed by anyone else before. Many gave me exclusive access.

One of these was Colonel Tom Parker, who never really gave me an interview, providing instead what took the form of low-key, rambling monologues. To him I offer my special thanks for allowing me to clear so many fences merely by dropping his name.

Others deserving deepest appreciation include Grelun Landon, Jerry Schilling, John Wilkinson, T. G. Sheppard, and John Bakke, for their unstinting time and support.

More who gave their time and shared their memories included:

—In Memphis: Ginger Alden, Jo Alden, Jackson Baker, Melissa Blackwood, Pat (Medford) Booth, Bill Burk, Marian Cocke, JoCathy (Brownlee) Elkington, Maurice Elliott, Maggie (Smith) Glover, Lowell Hays, Jr., Milo High, Marion Keisker, George Klein, Howard Massey, Mike McMahon, B. P. (Buddy) Montesi, Bill Morris, Dee Presley, Kang Rhee, Billy Ray Schilling, and David Stanley.

—In Los Angeles: Bob Abel, Bill Belew, Tony Brown, Joan Deary, Pat (Perry) Gerson, Rick Husky,

Jerry Knight, Malcolm Leo, Frank Lieberman, John O'Grady, Marty Pasetta, Gerald Peters, Mario Sanders, Sol Schwartz, Gary Smith, Myrna Smith, Andy Solt, Sam Theaker, Linda Thompson, Del Trollope.

—In Las Vegas: Bruce Banke, Sam Belkin, Gene Dessell, Joe Guercio, Marty Harrell, Bill Jost, Henri Lewin, Artie Newman.

—In Nashville: Chet Atkins, Mae Axton, Jerry Carrigan, Betty Cox, Bobby Emmons, Steve Goldstein, Larrie Londin, Joe Mescale, Pete Peterson, Diana Shepard, Shelby Singleton, Bobby Wood.

—In Honolulu: Phil Arnone, Ron Rewald, Eddie Sherman, Kalani Simerson.

Another large debt is owed to RCA Records, whose Los Angeles office opened its files, provided a desk, a telephone, and the unlimited use of a photocopy machine, as well as a complete set of Elvis's records.

A number of previously published books about Elvis also were consulted, occasionally for direct quotation or information, more often for confirmation of material obtained in interview. They included: *Elvis: What Happened?* by Red West, Sonny West and Dave Hebler as told to Steve Dunleavy; *Inside Elvis* by Ed Parker; *My Life with Elvis* by Becky Yancey and Cliff Linedecker; *I Called Him Babe* by Marian J. Cocke; *Elvis: Portrait of a Friend* by Marty Lacker, Patsy Lacker and Leslie S. Smith.

Contents

Elvis is not John Doe. This situation cannot be compared to anything else. It is certainly not a normal life, traveling and all that. But it is a nice abnormal life.

—Linda Thompson
People Magazine, 1975

December 19–21, 1970

It may have been the most unusual weekend in Elvis Presley's life, although it was so typical, too. It began in Memphis on Saturday, December 19, 1970, with a fiery family fight. It was Elvis's father Vernon's job to write the personal checks and when he came at Elvis with a handful of bills, shaking his head the way he always did, Elvis mumbled, "Fuck . . . here we go again."

"Elvis . . ." Vernon began, "somethin' here we gotta talk about."

"Yeah . . ."

"Lookit, Elvis, I know you don't like me sayin' anythin' about your money, but I just got these in from California and I wanna check 'em with you. There must be a mistake, because this one's from Kerr's and it says you charged $38,000 in guns there this month."

"Christmas shoppin', daddy. That's all."

Vernon merely shook his head and shuffled the bits of paper around. He knew the next one probably was accurate, too. "This other's from the Mercedes place in Hollywood. Says you bought six cars there last week for eighty thousand . . ."

"Those are the big presents, daddy. One's for 'Cilla, 'nother's for Sheriff Morris . . ."

"Now, Elvis, how many times I got to say it? Vegas

pays you real good and the Colonel says now you're tourin' again, there's gonna be good money there, too, but we just not makin' that kinda money these days to spend so much as this and . . ."

Elvis had heard it all before. His daddy had grown up poor in Mississippi, a sharecropper and sometime ditchdigger who went to jail for forging a check to buy groceries. That was during the Great Depression, when Elvis was three years old. Only the Internal Revenue Service had bothered to count the millions of dollars that Elvis had earned in the years since.

By the time Elvis appeared on the Ed Sullivan show, from the waist up, in 1956, soon after "Heartbreak Hotel" was released, the lines were drawn: Elvis was adjudged a threat, by parents and teachers and ministers, and by this declaration the generation gap was defined. Elvis's daddy and the parents of all his followers came from a security-conscious generation, veterans of that terrible Depression, while Elvis's, coming out of the 1950s, was freedom-seeking and believed in testing authority.

For many, then, Elvis was the original Fonz, the archetypal greaser or rocker who became a model for a rebellious age. "They all think I'm a sex maniac," he told an interviewer at the time, speaking of his critics. "They're just frustrated old types anyway. I'm just natural."

Yet, Elvis was not a rebel, not really. He enjoyed the role, it was clear, but it was also apparent that he hated it. He was genuinely hurt by the criticism he got in the fifties. It embarrassed him in front of his doting mother, who'd taught him to call everyone "sir" and "ma'am," a habit he maintained until his death.

It wasn't surprising, then, when Elvis became a rather bland figure, a patriot willing to gamble his career to serve two years in the army, a loving son who wept openly at his mother's death, a performer who returned to civilian life a crooner of ballads and opera

("It's Now or Never"). He sought approval in established areas, becoming an innocuous actor who ambled good-naturedly through dozens of sappy but wholesome Hollywood musicals, and then went where only the most established stars performed, Las Vegas.

Never was there any rough edge, a drunken fight, an arrest, a sex scandal, such as was the case in the careers of Sinatra and Brando and most of the younger rock stars of the 1960s. He didn't say he was bigger than Jesus, as Beatle John Lennon did; Elvis worshipped Him, openly, and recorded albums of gospel songs. He also took an apolitical stance, refusing to reveal his conservative beliefs for fear of offending. He generously supported dozens of charities and hundreds of needy individuals.

Thus, Elvis became two-dimensional, inoffensive, a slate upon which nearly everyone could scratch his or her fantasy. And it was a slate you could wipe clean afterward, changing your fantasy at any time, without fear that Elvis would do anything to make that dangerous.

In the 1950s, Elvis seemed to be rebelling against the establishment. In the 1960s—the Hollywood years —he was embraced by the establishment. And as the 1970s began, he *was* the establishment. A lot of people could identify with that kind of success. But not his daddy.

Elvis glared at his father and finally said, "Daddy, it's only money. There's more where it came from. . . ."

"But, son . . ."

Elvis gritted his teeth and growled, "Daddy, I don't want to talk about it!"

Usually Elvis tried to keep his temper in check, but tonight Priscilla joined Vernon; she hated his wild spending, too. When Elvis wanted, he could be the model of Christian patience. His fury also was legendary. When the gates to his Graceland estate weren't opened promptly enough by his gatekeepers—most of whom were relatives—he was famous for ordering the limousine driven *through* the gates. How many times had he angrily humiliated the guys who worked for him? How many television sets had he shot out with his derringer? There were many things that aroused his ire and being told what to do was one of them.

"Lookit, goddammit," he said, "it's my fuckin' money and I can do whatever in goddamn hell I want with it!"

When the shouting had stopped and a taut silence had constricted the room, Elvis aloofly stalked out of the mansion, wearing a purple velvet suit and cape, gold belt buckle, amber glasses; carrying a jeweled white cane and a .45 caliber pistol in a shoulder holster. He then drove one of his cars to Memphis International Airport and for the first time in his life, he bought a ticket on a commercial airline and flew to another city *alone*.

Elvis had never done anything like this before. Why, at the age of 35 he'd never even been in a bank. (No need to: When he was young, he was poor; when he was older he had people to take care of such things.) Surrounded by salaried lackeys for nearly fifteen years —even through his army duty in Germany—he was effectively isolated from ordinary life and society. And now he was on his way to Washington, boarding not a chartered jet but a commercial airliner to sit with Real People.

His destination wasn't selected randomly, or in anger. There was purpose and determination in making this flight and Elvis had planned it for some time, although only John O'Grady knew about it. O'Grady was a tough ex–narcotics cop, now a private detective who had been hired a year or so earlier by Elvis's attorney, for help in a paternity suit. Sometime after that, O'Grady says, he started Elvis collecting police badges.

"I was a cop for twenty years, a sergeant in charge of the Hollywood narcotics detail. I knew when people were doped up and Elvis was strung out on pills. Now, I'm not saying he didn't have prescriptions for those pills, but he was strung out. If you know what to look for, the eyes, the slurred or speeded-up speech, I mean, twenty years and I *knew*, so I figured if he started carrying badges around, maybe he'd stop taking that shit. I was in Hawaii talking about industrial security at a cops' convention in 1969 and I met John Finlator, the deputy U.S. narcotics director. Elvis said he wanted a U.S. narcotics badge to add to his collection. I set up a meeting. I thought it might help."

Of course, Elvis had his own reasons for meeting the nation's number two narc. He carried a pistol almost everywhere he went these days—sometimes even to bed, stuck into the waistband of his custom-made silk pajamas or in the pocket of his robe. He and some of his boys had deputy sheriffs' badges and permits to carry sidearms in Memphis, courtesy of his friend Sheriff Bill Morris, and in Palm Springs, where he owned another house. Elvis believed that if he had a federal badge it would allow him to go armed everywhere in the United States.

There was another reason he wanted the badge. For Elvis, the word "drugs" meant heroin, and he often talked with his friends about how that, along with communism and Communist sympathizers like Jane Fonda and Rap Brown, constituted one of the country's most insidious threats. "He talked with other performers in Vegas," says Jerry Schilling, one of Elvis's closest friends the last eleven years. "They were junkies, and after he talked to them they stopped taking drugs. I know that sounds far out, but it's true. I personally know of two individuals who stopped taking heroin. Elvis figured if he had a federal narcotics badge, he could maybe scare some other entertainers into kicking dope."

Elvis reported to the American Airlines check-in counter in Memphis, where he was sold a ticket and whisked into the V.I.P. lounge and then boarded on the flight to the Capitol separately. Thus he didn't go through the security check for weapons and his pistol wasn't discovered. He also was traveling under the name John Burroughs, a name he'd used for years for personal mail and telephone calls. In Washington, he hailed a taxi to the Washington Hotel. What happened on the way was one of the stories Elvis would tell and retell about the weekend. "He had the driver stop at one of those ghetto donut joints on the way to the hotel," says T. G. Sheppard, another friend. "He had his diamonds on his fingers and he had his gun and one of the people·there says, 'Allll-visss Presley—lookit them diamond rings on you hands, man. Lord have mercy!' And Elvis says, 'Yeah, man, an' I'm gone keep 'em too'; and he pulls the .45 outta the shoulder holster. He'd laugh when he tol' this story. He had the deepest laugh I ever heard. He laughed all the way down to his soul."

Once at the hotel, Elvis made a number of calls to Los Angeles, as well as plans to go there. Why is not clear. His meeting with Finlator was set for Monday morning and he may simply have become lonely, and so flew to California because it was the place where he knew he had friends, outside of Memphis. Or he may have been caught up in the James Bond-ish nature of the whole thing and this was the way he played it. Elvis loved spy movies and Clint Eastwood was one of his favorite movie stars; he enjoyed bringing such drama into his own life any way he could. His erratic behavior also could be explained by illness or drugs.

First he called Gerald Peters, a fiftyish Englishman who'd recently begun chauffeuring Elvis around in Los Angeles. When the operator told him "Mr. Burroughs" was calling, and there was no response, Elvis broke in and whispered, "Sir Gerald . . . it's me. . . ."

Elvis told Gerald he was in Washington and said he was coming to Los Angeles. Twenty minutes later he called to say he'd changed his mind and thirty minutes after that he called another time to say he was arriving on Trans World Airways flight number 85, arriving at 1:17 A.M. He swore Gerald to absolute secrecy regarding his present whereabouts and plans and then called Jerry Schilling.

Jerry was a big, good-looking former football player for Arkansas State University who'd worked for Elvis off and on for about five years, first as a movie stand-in and then as a personal bodyguard. Following Elvis's instructions he called Gerald and together, in secrecy, in the middle of the night, they drove to the airport to meet The Boss.

The picture Jerry paints is executed in a mix of bold and subtle strokes. One-thirty in the morning and there's Elvis exiting the plane still wearing his cape and purple velvet suit, a stewardess on each arm. Jerry also notices that Elvis's face is swollen up . . . and then he sees that Elvis is carrying, besides the cane, a small cardboard box. Jerry looked into it and counted a toothbrush, small complimentary-size toothpaste and soap, a little washrag.

"What's that?"

"Well," he said innocently, "I had to get some stuff for traveling."

Elvis had Jerry call a doctor to meet them at his home and then, on the way in from the airport, they took the girls home. It was then that Elvis told Jerry the story about what had happened in Washington when he told the airline ticket agent he was boarding with a pistol. The agent followed him onto the plane.

"I'm sorry, Mr. Presley, but you cannot fly on this plane with a gun."

Elvis angrily left the plane, fairly running down the staircase. The pilot, who was watching, followed him and ran along behind on the tarmac, calling, "Mr. Presley, please come back. This is the pilot, please accept our apology. . . ."

Elvis finished telling the story as they rode up the drive of his sumptuous estate in a rich section called Holmby Hills. The doctor was waiting at the gate. Elvis told Jerry his swollen face was a reaction to a penicillin shot. It's not clear if this is true; when and under what circumstances did Elvis get such medication? Was it a reaction to one of the prescribed drugs he took regularly? Years later, his physician would say Elvis frequently suffered severe allergic reaction to several drugs. Whatever the cause of the problem, the doctor in attendance this night in California gave Elvis a shot of his own and Elvis slept for eight hours.

At noon Sunday when he woke up, Elvis hollered for Jerry and when Jerry came running, he said, "I want you to come to Washington with me." He didn't tell Jerry why.

"Aw, Elvis, look, I just took this job at Paramount and if I go to Washington tonight I'll miss work tomorrow; this is important to me. . . ."

"Don't worry about it. I'll charter you a jet."

"Elvis, there's no way I can make it there physically and get back to work in time."

Elvis looked down at his feet, a little boy toeing the ground, and said, "Okay, I'll go by myself."

Jerry sighed resignedly and began making arrangements for the trip. He called the Washington Hotel and reserved two rooms—yes, they remembered "John Burroughs"—and then booked two seats on a flight leaving about ten o'clock that night. Now Elvis was traveling under another alias, Dr. John Carpenter, the name of the character he'd portrayed only a year earlier in a film called *Change of Habit*. On the way to the airport, Gerald stopped at the Beverly Hills Hotel so Elvis could cash a check for $500. Jerry and Elvis had had no cash between them and Jerry assured Elvis that "you can charge plane tickets and hotel rooms and meals to credit cards, but you really can't travel properly unless you got money for tips and incidentals." Elvis looked at him as if he didn't know what he was talking about, but nodded his approval.

By now, Elvis had been gone from Memphis for more than twenty-four hours and his family and friends were frantic. At first they thought he'd merely gone for a ride to cool off following the fight. Then they began to make casual inquiries. Joe Esposito and Charlie Hodge, two of Elvis's hired hands, both started calling around the country. Gerald was one of many who got calls: "Uh, by the way, you haven't heard from Elvis, have you?" Gerald of course said no.

When Elvis boarded the plane in Los Angeles, every seat was full. Christmas was only five days away and in 1970 that meant every plane heading east from California was carrying soldiers on leave from Vietnam. About half the passengers on the flight were in uniform. Elvis, seated on the aisle, struck up a conversation with several of the men. It was late, but the mood was up, people were in the aisles laughing and talking.

"Elvis and I settled down," Jerry says, "and pretty soon he tells me he's going to write a letter. Now, I think Elvis in his whole life only wrote about three or four letters. He tells me he's going to Washington to get a federal narcotics badge from John Finlator and he is writing a letter to the President of the United States, President Nixon. He asked me to proofread the letter."

In the letter Elvis expressed freely his ideas about Jane Fonda and communism and especially drugs, showing concern about the role popular musicians and singers played in this. He said he wanted to do something positive and wanted to talk to Nixon about that. He told the President he was staying at the Washington Hotel under the name John Burroughs, gave his room number, and suggested he call his personal public relations man, Jerry Schilling, to make an appointment.

"Well, first of all," Jerry says, "there was a lot of

grammar and stuff that probably could've been changed. But I knew where his heart was in the letter and I liked it the way he wrote it, so I said, 'Elvis, it's perfect the way it is.' "

Jerry returned to his book after reading the letter, and Elvis started talking to another GI. After a few minutes, he poked Jerry in the ribs. "Jerry," he said, "where's the money?"

"I got it, it's safe . . . why?"

"Jerry, give it to me."

Both men were whispering. Jerry said, "Elvis, this is our expense money. You can't . . ."

Elvis said, "Jerry, this soldier's going home for Christmas and I want to make it a good one for him and his loved ones."

"Elvis, we won't have any money for tips and . . ."

Elvis gritted his teeth and said, "The guy . . . just . . . got . . . back . . . from . . . Vietnam." So Jerry gave him the $500 and Elvis gave it to the soldier and said, "Merry Christmas."

The plane arrived in the Capitol Monday, December 21, at 6:30 A.M. Elvis had eaten a half-box of candy that someone had given him and again his face was swollen. Jerry saw Elvis to the waiting limousine and called the hotel, telling the desk to get a doctor. Elvis said he wanted to go to the White House first.

"Elvis, it's six-thirty in the morning. Let's check with the doctor first and clean up. . . ."

"Godammit, Jerry, we're going to the White House now!"

They rode silently to 1600 Pennsylvania Avenue as Elvis took out his pen and covered a portion of the envelope containing his letter: "Personal—For the President's Eyes Only." Driving to the guard gate, Elvis got out of the car and, extending his hand with the envelope, he said, "Sir . . . ?" The guard looked right through him, as if Elvis didn't exist.

Elvis glanced back at Jerry as if he didn't know

what to do, as if his feelings were hurt at not being recognized. Then he remembered his mussed clothing, shoulder-length hair, and tinted glasses.

"Oh," he said to the guard, "uh, uh, I'm Elvis Presley and I have a letter for the President and . . ."

The guard snapped to and smiled broadly, apologizing when Elvis explained his mission. The guard said he'd see the letter was delivered as soon as Nixon was in his office. The limousine then took Elvis to the hotel.

After the doctor left, Jerry asked if he could call Memphis. "Elvis," he said, "you've been gone for two days and I'm very worried about your father and Priscilla. They must be going crazy. I gave you my word and you know me, I'm not going to break it. But can I call down there and say you're with me and you're okay? We don't have to say where you are . . . and I've got to get back to my job, so I'd like to have Sonny come up here." Sonny West was another of Elvis's full-time bodyguards.

Elvis agreed and told Jerry to stay at the hotel to take the President's call. He then left the hotel alone to take the limousine to John Finlator's office, leaving Finlator's number with Jerry.

Finlator was expecting "Mr. Burroughs" and, leaving a wake of startled secretaries and intermediaries behind him, Elvis was ushered quickly into the deputy director's office. Elvis got right down to business. He said he wanted to donate $5,000 to Finlator's department. Finlator was startled by the offer, graciously refusing it, explaining that his department was funded by the taxpayers, so Elvis already was a contributor.

At first Elvis thought Finlator was reacting the way others did when he suddenly gave them expensive rings and cars. So he did what he usually did. He laughed and said, "It's okay . . . really . . . I want to do it." Elvis knew from experience that most people refused a magnanimous gesture at first, but always accepted eventually.

John Finlator wasn't like the others and he said no again. Elvis wasn't certain how to handle this rejection, so he told the deputy director how he'd already talked two entertainers into getting off heroin in Las Vegas.

"And, uh, uh . . . if I had a badge from your department, sir, I'm sure I could do more good work. Sir, that's why I'd like you to give me a badge."

Finlator said he'd be pleased to arrange for an honorary badge.

"Uh, no sir, that is, it's important to me to have the real thing."

So saying, Elvis then produced his deputy's badges from Memphis and Palm Springs.

Again Finlator was struck dumb and again he turned Elvis down. It was impossible, he said. There were regulations. It was not a choice. It was out of his hands.

"Elvis was depressed when I got him on the phone in Finlator's office," Jerry Schilling says, "and before I could say anything, he said, 'Jerry, I can't do any good here, I'm coming back to the hotel.' I interrupted him. I said, 'Why I'm calling, Elvis, is the President wants to see you right away.'"

Amazingly, the letter had reached Nixon and he cleared twenty minutes in his schedule. Elvis told Jerry he'd pick him up in the limo and before leaving asked Finlator one more question.

"You won't mind if I ask the President for the badge, will you, sir?"

Finlator chuckled and said no, go ahead, because that was the only way the department could give him one.

When Elvis returned to the hotel he found Jerry waiting and Sonny checking in. Together they went to the White House, where they were met by Egil "Bud" Krogh, Nixon's top enforcement officer, later convicted as one of the Watergate conspirators. When they told him they were armed, he advised them to leave their pistols in the car. Except for one. This was a gold-plated commemorative World War II Colt .45 that Elvis had picked up while in Los Angeles as a gift for the President. This was given to Krogh, who checked to see that it was empty, whereupon Elvis finally was sent into the Oval Office.

Jerry and Sonny were disappointed when Elvis left them behind. Krogh explained that it required more security if more than one person went in.

"Well," Sonny said, "I know Elvis and he'll ask the President to let us in."

"It doesn't matter if he asks or not," said Krogh. "It's out of the President's hands."

"Well, Elvis is a pretty hard guy to say no to."

At that moment the interoffice telephone buzzed. It was the President, asking that Jerry and Sonny be allowed in. At the same time, Elvis appeared at the door and said, "Come on in, guys, I want you to meet the President."

Elvis was grinning broadly, as excited as a small boy. As soon as Elvis met Nixon he explained his need for the federal badge and Nixon told Krogh to take care of it.

Jerry and Sonny hesitated at the door to the President's office, clearly nervous about entering. Elvis laughed and said, "C'mon, c'mon . . ." For years afterward he would retell the story of this meeting and always tease his bodyguards about their timidity.

Nixon came forward and shook their hands stiffly. "Elvis, you got a couple of pretty big guys here. It looks like Elvis is in pretty good hands with you two. You guys play football?"

The small talk continued for a few minutes as the White House photographer snapped several pictures, one formal shot of Elvis and Nixon, other more candid shots around the President's desk. Then Elvis said, "Mr. President . . . you know that Presidential button you gave me?"

Nixon started and said, "Oh yes . . ." and pulled two

more lapel pins from a drawer, coming around the desk
to hand them to Jerry and Sonny.

"Uh . . . sir . . ." Elvis said. "They've got wives, sir."

The President started again, returning hurriedly to
his desk to get two brooches.

Nixon then walked the trio to the door, patted Elvis
awkwardly on the shoulder and told Krogh to take the
boys on a tour of the house. The badge arrived twenty
minutes later.

It was a weekend of such exquisite paradox—only
three days, a drop in life's bucket, yet a Saturday-
through-Monday gem nonetheless, one which revealed
much about Elvis and his world. Western civilization
was full of boys who never grew up, especially in the
United States. Elvis was one of these, a full-sized
grown-up who had a fight with his father and reacted
by running away from home. And what did he do next?
He played cops and robbers in Washington. Flying
alone for the first time, indulgently eating a half-
pound of chocolates, refusing to take no for an answer
from authority figures (the Washington ticket agent,
John Finlator), writing the President of the United
States and expecting a meeting to result, believing that
whatever you wanted you got, openly sharing his pos-
sessions (guns and money)—in almost every move he
made, Elvis showed himself to be an eternal child,
trapped in a cocoon of his own spinning, innocent,
naive, protected, and more than a little spoiled.

In the afternoon, Jerry returned to Los Angeles, to
report to work at Paramount the following day without explanation (who'd have believed him?), and Elvis
and Sonny went back to Memphis, where Elvis strode
into Graceland and shouted to Priscilla, "Hi, hon, I'm
home."

Late Summer, 1970

In the late summer of 1970, as Elvis completed an engagement in Las Vegas, there was no personality on the planet who could claim greater fame. Before going to this desert city, Elvis had been little more than an interesting curiosity left over from another era, and now he was the definition and embodiment of the word Superstar. Such creatures are rare. It was inevitable that Presley's manager, Colonel Tom Parker, would put this phenomenon on tour.

People had been after the Colonel to do this for years, ever since the Beatles did for the sixties what Elvis had done ten years before that. After all, hadn't the Beatles said Elvis was their inspiration? Hadn't John Lennon said, "Before Elvis there was nothing"? But the Colonel wisely rejected all offers, fearing the possibility of failure due to premature release. In no way did he want Elvis to be regarded as another oldie-but-goodie on the comeback trail. When Elvis began touring again, the Colonel wanted him to be bigger than anything else then occasionally available—bigger than Bob Dylan, bigger than the Rolling Stones, bigger than Frank Sinatra. So he gambled on Las Vegas as the place where Elvis could establish his superiority. He gambled and he won. Now, after only three engagements in just over a year's time since Elvis had emerged from relative obscurity in Hollywood, the Colonel, and Elvis, were ready to conquer the rest of the North American continent.

The first meeting with the people who ultimately booked nearly all of Elvis's road shows was held in 1969 before Elvis even went to Vegas, when the Colonel invited two energetic promoters named Jerry Weintraub and Tom Huelett to his office at MGM. Other meetings followed, over dinner, or in the steam room of the Spa in Palm Springs. The Colonel loved the steam room; was able to spend hours in one without wilting, and enjoyed holding meetings in them because those he was negotiating with were unable to match his stamina.

Both Weintraub—who was married to singer Jane Morgan—and Huelett were promoters who had established their names and reputations during the heavy rock years of the sixties, when Weintraub, operating from Los Angeles, booked Eric Clapton and Cream, and Huelett, working in Seattle, handled tours for Jimi Hendrix. Joining forces, they began promoting national tours and by 1969 when the Colonel began considering them seriously they were known as honest, ambitious, efficient, and tough.

Modestly, six widely scattered concerts were set, in Phoenix, St. Louis, Detroit, Miami, Tampa, and Mobile, beginning just two days after Elvis closed in Nevada on Labor Day 1970. It was a sort of test run, a shakedown tour to see how Weintraub and Huelett—and Elvis—worked together. Elvis worried about the audiences. Everyone else worried about logistics. They *knew* the shows would be successful. Tickets sold out only hours after they went on sale. If he and his management had wanted him to, Elvis could've performed in a hundred cities. What caused concern was organization, not appeal.

"It was pretty funky compared to what came later," says Joe Guercio, the orchestra leader who had taken the baton in Las Vegas the previous month and who would conduct for Elvis for most of the next six years. "Most of us were traveling in a Granny Goose airplane. We called it Greyhound Airlines. Oh, it was pretty together, but we didn't know how much equipment we needed and we had different pickup musicians in every town. We were doing a show every day and when you're rehearsing new horns and strings every day, you want to cut your wrists."

"We weren't organized," says Joe Mescale, leader of the Imperials, the gospel quartet that Elvis used as backup singers. "We didn't even know we needed an announcer until we got out on the road. So Al Dvorn, who was in charge of the souvenirs, told *me* to do it. He told me to get up there and tell 'em we got these pennants and teddy bears, it's their last chance to get 'em before we start the show."

These were minor problems and the overall impact of Elvis on tour far outweighed them, in fact swamped them in a tidal wave of what looked like the 1950s revisited. Each of the auditoriums held at least 10,000 persons, who paid $5, $7.50, and $10 apiece to see the show (giving Elvis individual concert grosses ranging up to nearly $100,000). In every city, after the Sweet Inspirations and the Imperials and comic Jackie Kahane performed and Elvis walked out, there was an incredible flash of energy and light as everyone present let out a roar and thousands of Instamatics went off. Long minutes passed as Elvis bathed in the wash of applause and the stroboscopic twinkle of tiny flash cubes, while behind him rumbled the rhythmic thunder of his backup band. There he stood, center stage, his arms outstretched, showing off his jeweled cape, a popular god reincarnate, a sort of comic book hero come to life.

"That first tour was exciting," says Joe Mescale. "We felt like history was being made. It was loose, the organization wasn't together yet, but nobody cared, because it was so darned exciting. When we got to a town, the people were waiting for us. They were at the hotels. They were in the restaurants. They were at the auditorium all day long, waiting."

There was a story that Elvis himself told over and over in the years to come that captured the spirit of the time. "We flew to Mobile and the hotel didn't have any air conditioning, man, and that's a no-no. Gotta have that air conditioning. Anyway, on the way into town we passed a Holiday Inn, so I said, 'Let's go there, to hell with this goddamned sweat-hole.' I got on the phone and called the Holiday Inn and said, 'Ma'am, I'd like some rooms and I'm comin' right over.' I didn't tell her who I was. She said, 'I'm sorry, sir . . . no rooms.' I tol' her she didn't understand and I needed thirty rooms right away. She said, 'I'm sorry, sir, there aren't any rooms. Haven't you heard . . . Elvis Presley's in town?' "

Elvis loved the tour and for days afterward in Memphis he talked excitedly about all the things he'd seen and done, laughing now about the bomb threat in Phoenix and the limousines that didn't show up. " 'Member," he said, "the godawful yellow Merc we got?" Then he told the story about the Mobile Holiday Inn again.

He also fell into a post-tour physical and mental depression and disorientation, caused by a recurring eye problem that later would be diagnosed as glaucoma, and on top of that, the symptoms that come with the regular dosage of chemical stimulants and sleeping potions.

Like uncounted tens or hundreds of thousands of other Americans in the 1970s, Elvis counted amphetamines and barbiturates, more commonly known as "uppers" and downers," among his closest friends. What made this unusual in Elvis's case was that his use of pills was kept so quiet and seemed so shocking when the truth began to leak out, just weeks before they killed him. This was true of much in Elvis's life, however. Just as his mother's drinking was a closely guarded family secret, so it was with some of Elvis's personal habits. It went against southern tradition, which said if you had nothing nice to say, you said nothing; dirty wash was *not* hung out to public view. Elvis also expected uncommon loyalty from those around him. People who worked for Elvis didn't talk —even when they left his employ. On top of that, Elvis's image was so clean, no one suspected there *were* any secrets. Drugs? Nonsense. It was suspecting the Pope was a bigamist. Still, the truth was, Elvis used "drugs."

It was when he was a corporal in the tank corps in the wintry snows of Wiesbaden, West Germany, a decade before, that a sergeant introduced him to stimulants, so he wouldn't fall asleep while on watch at night. Uppers were no strangers to country music; the only strange thing about Elvis's use of them was how long it took him to begin. In the years that followed his army service, Elvis often used the "diet pills" to trim down for his movies, or for the cross-country drives between Memphis and Hollywood.

When Elvis began appearing in Las Vegas, use of these pills increased. By now Elvis was nocturnal. In the International Hotel, and later on the road, his windows were covered with aluminum foil and bedtime was when the sun came up; breakfast was served in late afternoon.

"We lived a fast life," says Jerry Schilling. "Not only Elvis, but the rest of us, too. We lived long hours, slept in the daytime and lived in hotels. We started taking a sleeping pill to make it easy. After a while one wasn't enough. Sometimes for a weight problem or to wake up for an early studio call, we'd take a diet pill. Over a period of time, one diet pill wasn't enough either."

The pills weren't a problem in 1970. That would

come later. Elvis's dependency was growing. There were signs that drugs *could* become a problem in his life, but this early no one worried about it. Drugs were a part of the music scene, as much a part as guitars and girls. No one paid much attention. If anyone thought about it at all, they might have commented on how *few* drugs Elvis took.

A week after returning to Memphis, on September 22, Elvis flew to Nashville for what was supposed to be a week of recording. His eyes began hurting, so the session ended the same day it began with only four songs completed. Two of these, "Snowbird," a faithful copy of the recent hit by Anne Murray, and a sloppy version of Jerry Lee Lewis's "Whole Lotta Shakin' Goin' On," were included in a country album released a few months later, in January 1971, and the other two, "Rags to Riches" and "Where Did They Go, Lord?" were released as a single in March.

With Elvis going home after only one day, that left four days of recording time open for James Burton to record *his* album. Elvis's guitarist and an oldtime southern rocker from the 1950s, Burton had received $6,000 to produce an instrumental album for A&M Records, and so he did, with Elvis paying for the studio time. According to musicians who played the sessions, everyone got ungodly drunk. (The result was released by A&M but it wasn't popular.)

Back in Memphis, Elvis was officially on vacation.

September, 1970–
January, 1971

Never in the history of entertainment had another personality been so completely and relentlessly merchandised as Elvis. As he rested for nearly two months in Memphis following his first tour, the Elvis *"machine"* ground out product and planned for the release of still more of it. The machine was, of course, the creation of that legendary master manipulator, Colonel Tom Parker.

Colonel Thomas Andrew Parker—the title was honorary, acquired in Tennessee—was a bulky, cigar-smoking man who reminded some of P.T. Barnum or W.C. Fields, others of Frank Morgan, better known as the Wizard of Oz. He *was* the man behind the screen, pushing the right buttons, pulling all the proper strings. "The Colonel," as he was always called, was The Manager's Manager, the yardstick by which all other talent managers measured themselves, like Elvis a true legend in his own time. No other manager ·approached him— not the late Brian Epstein, who managed the Beatles; not Gordon Mills, who managed Tom Jones and Engelbert Humperdinck; not Jeff Wald, who managed Helen Reddy; not Jerry Weintraub, who later managed John Denver and booked Frank Sinatra; not anyone. Every one of these managers, and hundreds more— and not just in music, but in film and athletics, and in every other area of entertainment—actively sought to be like the Colonel.

The stories told about him were incredible, dating back to the 1930s when he was an orphaned carnival con man, painting sparrows yellow and selling them for canaries; doubling the admission price to a show and guaranteeing half back if dissatisfied, always paying the 50 percent refund, but so what—before the tent was empty and now it was always full. The stories would go on and on and on.

Colonel Parker brought this same carney huckster-ism to the Elvis career in 1954, when Elvis was 19 and still performing on flatbed trucks and in high school auditoriums, more than a year before "Heartbreak Hotel." The Colonel'd made Hank Snow and Eddy Arnold the Number One country singers and when he saw Elvis, and the itchy female reaction to him, he thought Elvis could make it three for three. When they shook hands on the deal—25 percent for the Colonel, 75 for Elvis—neither of them in their wildest fantasies envisioned what would happen next. By 1970, they both were living legends and famous throughout the world.

Over the years, many came to regard Elvis as some sort of puppet. Surely, they said, Elvis didn't volunteer for all those lame Hollywood musicals! All those tacky album covers! All those awful songs! After all, hadn't the Colonel himself once said about those films, "Anybody who'll pay mah boy a million dollars can make any kinda picksha he wants"?

When I decided to write a book about Elvis in 1969, I wrote Elvis requesting a meeting. The reply came over the signature of Roger H. Davis, an attorney for the William Morris Agency. It said in part: "Mr. Presley and his activities constitute a huge and highly successful commercial enterprise which he and his management intend to exploit in the most advantageous way while simultaneously retaining complete control over any dissemination to the public." Perhaps never before, or since, has a talent agency been so candid about one of its clients.

While it's true, of course, that the Colonel directed the tone of the letter, carefully note the wording, how the phrase "he and his management" gave Elvis top billing. Elvis always came first with the Colonel—on the thousands of Christmas cards that went out each year ("From ELVIS and the Colonel"—with the letters spelling "the Colonel" printed only a quarter the size of the letters spelling "ELVIS"), on the contracts, and on everything else. Although Elvis may have had virtually nothing to say about the opportunities presented by the Colonel—the choices of things to do—it must never be forgotten that Elvis had total, final say on which he'd do and how he'd do it. For example, Elvis agreed to do an NBC television special in 1968 (the Colonel's idea), but rather than sing Christmas carols (also the Colonel's idea), he dressed in black leather and sang "Tiger Man," proving to a huge holiday audience that the substance and strength were still there.

The Colonel usually read Elvis pretty clearly. He knew Elvis wanted the widest public acceptance possible. (What performer doesn't?) That's why Elvis kept his mouth shut about his conservative politics, his fawning over Nixon and Agnew and George Wallace, his fondness for police; Elvis didn't want to antagonize the more liberal segment of the population. That explains the image of the all-American boy—one that Elvis worked hard to perpetuate and the Colonel worked hard to support. The Colonel knew what to tell the press and what not to tell it. He also knew how to keep things out of the newspapers. This was standard for any personal manager. He protected his boy and saluted God, country, and motherhood at every opportunity.

The Colonel also knew Elvis got bored easily and

this influenced the stages in Elvis's career. When movie profits began to drop—Elvis had grown to hate those films—Elvis did the 1968 television show (his first in eight years), and then did Vegas, and when Vegas began to pale, he went back on the road.

It was a classic symbiosis. They served each other's needs precisely. The Colonel was The Manager and Elvis was The Talent. It was true what Grelun Landon, who worked with the Colonel for twenty-five years, once observed: "The Colonel always said the manager's responsibility was business and the artist's responsibility was the performance and never the twain shall meet." Unlike most other managers and performers in recent times, Elvis and the Colonel never even saw each other unless it was to enact business.

There were times when Elvis got mad at the Colonel, of course, yet overall he thought they had a fair exchange. Elvis gave over to the Colonel the power to shape and mold his career—and a million or more dollars a year as the Colonel's quarter interest of his income—in return for a unique lifestyle that allowed him to be pampered and left alone, and for being given a kind of freedom—through protection—that few ever truly know. He lived by night, renting movie theaters and amusement parks after they were closed to the public. He surrounded himself with salaried playmates —many of whom actually lived in the same house with Elvis and Priscilla and little Lisa Marie. He bought anything he wanted any time he chose. (Cadillac agencies in Memphis were famous for opening at 3 A.M. to accommodate one of Elvis's shopping sprees.) He gave away millions of dollars in cars and rings and houses and airplanes. And the Colonel kept the money flowing. People can say whatever they want about Elvis and the Colonel, but it was a partnership that worked for more than twenty years and generated, according to the best estimates, $18 billion worth of product, and it hasn't stopped yet.

"Colonel Parker," says Henri Lewin, the Hilton Hotel vice-president the Colonel negotiated with, "is the biggest manipulator of human resource the world has ever known. He never overexposed Elvis and he never made a mistake."

In the autumn of 1970, the Colonel was in his rabbit warren of offices at MGM in Hollywood, the walls ablaze with Elvis movie posters, the corners cluttered with lifesize cardboard Elvis figures and giant teddy bears. A big deal was cooking in the editing rooms a hundred yards away as Elvis's first documentary, *Elvis: That's the Way It Is,* was being rushed for November release, to coincide with Elvis's second tour.

For the Colonel, coordinating a promotional campaign that included more than one element was a piece of cake. In the past, it was usually a movie and a soundtrack album. Now it was a film and an album and a tour. Every day dozens of calls were made, to Denis Sanders, the documentary's director, and to the publicity offices of MGM. The studio's poster— "FILMED AS IT HAPPENED, 'LIVE' ON STAGE IN LAS VEGAS"—was rushed over for the Colonel's approval. Photographs were selected. Meetings were held with representatives of RCA to make sure there would be an adequate supply of records in the cities where the movie and Elvis went. Press kits were sent to record stores, theater owners, and auditorium managers; in many cases these were followed up with telephone calls.

There were nine concerts in seven days in this second tour and with the exception of Oklahoma City and Denver, all were on the West Coast, so in early November Elvis moved to his home in California. It was from there, on the eleventh, that he left by charter jet for shows in big coliseums in Oakland, Portland, Seattle, San Francisco, Los Angeles, and San Diego. Everywhere the shows were sold out just hours after tickets went on sale, setting new attendance records. At the Forum in Los Angeles, where he performed afternoon and evening shows, 36,000 tickets sold in less than two days, with the more devoted fans camping overnight in front of the box office. Everywhere Elvis was greeted with a roar that sounded like the ocean and thousands of rippling flash cube pops. It was, as one writer put it, the world's best light show, and the Colonel didn't have to pay a penny for it.

No matter what Elvis sang, or did, the audience lapped it up. Elvis was like no other, for with him there seemed to be no foreseeable market saturation point. Even when the "Elvis industry" seemed to be producing at a runaway pace—gone amuck like Homer Price's donut-making machine—still there was an audience ready to consume it happily. Each year, for example, RCA proudly published an updated pamphlet entitled *The Complete Catalog of Elvis Records and Tapes*. In 1970, there were 30 pages of albums, 8-track stereo tapes, cartridges, cassettes, and stereo reels, all of it "available at record dealers everywhere." That meant the stuff still sold sufficiently to keep the material in stock and to give it precious warehouse space, although much of it was of mediocre quality and some of it 15 years old.

What made this even more amazing was that so many of Elvis's records were "repackages," records that were released more than once with only slight changes in the packaging. For example, in August, while Elvis was still in Las Vegas, the fifty songs that the Colonel claimed as million-copy sellers were pressed onto four discs and put in a box with a photo book, confidently called *Elvis' Worldwide 50 Gold Award Hits, Volume 1*. And just two months later, a double album, *From Memphis to Vegas/From Vegas to Memphis,* originally released only a year earlier, was re-released as two separate LPs, called *Elvis in*

Person at the International Hotel and *Elvis Back in Memphis*.

However arrogant this approach to marketing may have seemed—all of it conceived and directed by Colonel Parker, of course—the stunning thing was that it worked. Such repackaged product seldom made the record charts, yet Elvis's loyal audience was large enough—while still others were suckered in, thinking the albums were new—to ensure that each was comfortably profitable. His was an audience that crossed all lines. Elvis spelled legend to longhairs and rednecks alike and if they were fanatically adoring, they were also well behaved. People just weren't arrested at Elvis Presley concerts. Elvis didn't cause riots, only excitement. He didn't bait the police who ringed the stage—when he borrowed an officer's cap for some clowning, he returned it with a polite thank-you. His bumps and grinds still caused female bladders to let go, yet even when he dangled the ends of his fringed and beaded macrame belt between his legs suggestively and curled his lip, the effect was self-mocking. Elvis was sexy, but he wasn't ever threatening.

The tour ended in Denver, where Elvis was feeling high and fit. Elvis and his touring group stayed in the hotel where the Playboy Club was located. "You know what end-of-the-road parties are like," says the Imperials' Joe Mescale. "Well this one was wild, just wild . . . and you can't print any of it!"

The natural high continued in the weeks following as Elvis relaxed in California, watching a lot of television and wandering into Hollywood and Beverly Hills to spend $38,000 on guns and $80,000 on cars for Christmas gifts. It was then that he returned to his family in Memphis, where he argued with his father and Priscilla over money and left in a fit of anger for Washington to meet John Finlator and Richard Nixon.

*　　*　　*

By Christmas all was calm again at Graceland and if Elvis reviewed the year he must have been pleased. Just when he'd begun to tire of Las Vegas, was growing slightly bored, the tours had begun, giving him another opportunity to test his power. And he'd done well. Both tours were short, only sixteen shows in all, but every concert was a sellout. Travel expenses were high, yet so were the grosses, showing the Colonel that in the American heartland it was possible to make money faster than in Nevada.

Elvis also liked his first documentary, *Elvis: That's the Way It Is*—enjoyed watching it in his Graceland screening room, loved reading some of the more flattering clippings that were forwarded to his home. Said Howard Thompson in the *New York Times:* "The powerhouse drive that used to flail about wildly is shrewdly disciplined and siphoned until it explodes into his extraordinary sense of rhythm. Tired? Elvis? He's ferocious. Most impressively of all, he comes over as a genial, reasonably balanced guy. . . ."

Even his albums were accepted graciously—especially the movie soundtrack.

Then to cap it off, only a week before, the President had given him a U.S. narcotics badge.

So on New Year's Eve, just before midnight, Elvis fairly strutted into T.J.'s, a popular Memphis nightclub that he'd rented for his annual party. At the door was Richard Davis, who'd worked as Elvis's valet for seven years. Another former employee, Alan Fortas—he'd been in charge of keeping all of Elvis's cars in running condition—was behind the bar. Ronnie Milsap, the club's regular singer, was on the stage.

"Hey, E," came the greeting over and over that night, "great party, man. Happy New Year!"

Priscilla was on his arm and over there stood his daddy, Vernon, who had his arm around Dee, formerly married to General Patton's personal bodyguard, now *his* wife and the mother of three young sons who'd one day tour with Elvis. Vernon's brother Vester, a guard at the Graceland gates, was trading stories near the bar with Sterling Pepper, another guard whose son Gary, seated at a table nearby, was president of the International Elvis Presley Fan Club. At another table sat George Klein, president of Elvis's high school class and now a popular Memphis disc jockey. Red West was there with his wife Patty, and so was Billy Smith, another cousin. Jerry Schilling and his brother, Billy Ray, were over against a wall, talking with Sheriff Bill Morris.

Elvis stood near the edge of the room, his back to the wall. (He hated to have his back to anyone.) He looked around and puffed on his thin cigar and grinned at Priscilla. "Happy New Year, babe," he said. "Believe me, it's gonna be all right."

Elvis was riding a giant wave at the start of 1971. He was 36 years old on January 8, and eight days after that the national organization of Junior Chambers of Commerce held its annual banquet in Memphis and named Elvis one of seven young men of the year.

"I'd tried to get him to take that honor several times, but he wouldn't accept it," says Bill Morris, who was instrumental in getting Elvis's name before the national Jaycees organization. "This would have been the last year that he could have accepted it, because of his age. I talked to him about what the Jaycees were really doing and the effect they had on the leadership of this nation and he finally said, 'Hey, that's keen, I might just do that deal.' It was the first public function that he ever attended."

The place: the Municipal Auditorium concert hall, the same huge room where as a teenager Elvis attended all-night gospel sings. With Elvis at the ceremony were his family and closest friends. When his name was called, he walked briskly to the podium, wrapped in the warmth of applause.

He adjusted the high collar of his dark blue suit and

touched the bridge of his tinted glasses, then grabbed the microphone nervously: "I, I, I'd like you folks to know that I was the hero of the comic book. I saw movies and I was the hero of the movie. So every dream that I ever dreamed has come true a hundred times. And these gentlemen over here . . ."

He looked at the other Young Men of the Year. Ron Zeigler, who was President Nixon's press secretary, was one of them.

". . . these type of people who care and are dedicated, you realize that it's possible they could be building the kingdom of heaven. It's not too farfetched from reality. I'd like to say that, ah, I learned very early in life that without a song, the day would never end . . . without a song, a man ain't got a friend . . . without, without a song . . . so I just keep singin' the song. Good night."

Cloaked again in applause, Elvis returned to his seat.

The speech was perfect. In just 44 seconds he had summarized everything he believed and lived, giving his audience precisely what it wanted to hear. While acknowledging the realization of his fantasies, he acknowledged his co-nominees in a way that included him in a group of young men that was engaged in "building the kingdom of heaven" on earth. Abruptly changing the subject, Elvis then rhapsodized the role of song in his life. He was modest. Humble. The effect was reassuring.

January 24, 1971–
June 8, 1971

Elvis went to Las Vegas on January 24. The threat came the same day by telephone. A male voice told Sonny West, who answered the call, that a madman was planning to kill Elvis during one of his upcoming hotel performances. For $50,000 in unmarked cash, the unidentified caller said, he would reveal the assassin's name. A few hours later a menu from the hotel showroom was found in Elvis's mail and message slot behind the Hilton hotel desk. Elvis's picture on the front of the menu was defaced, a pistol was drawn pointing to his heart, and at the bottom was the message: "Guess who, and where?" When the local FBI agent saw the menu, he shook his head and said, "We have to take this one seriously."

Over the years, Elvis had been threatened many times, dating back to the 1950s when jealous, macho boyfriends took pokes at him for making their girlfriends squeal. This was one of the reasons Elvis had gone into seclusion. As a rule, since then, threats against his life were handled without his knowledge. Those around him believed, rightly, that most were cranks and Elvis didn't need to know about them. This time, however, he was told and, given his love of police adventure, he was caught up in the drama immediately. At the same time, he was terribly frightened; if the FBI was worried, so was he, and as the federal agency made its plans for his protection, Elvis began taking inventory of his personal entourage.

The payroll was smaller than usual, an attempt on his part to pacify Priscilla, who was becoming extremely tired of having so many of the boys around the house all the time. When Jerry Schilling had quit to become a film editor at Paramount, for instance, Elvis hadn't replaced him. Now, in Las Vegas in late January 1971, all he had were a handful of faithfuls, with Jerry coming in on the weekends. So he put in a call to his cousin, Red West, who was working for a recording studio in Memphis, and another to Jerry in Hollywood.

"I arrived there," Red later wrote in his own book, *Elvis: What Happened?*, "and Elvis just stumbled into my arms and hugged me. There was no doubt that he was taking this very seriously."

When Elvis called Jerry, he didn't say why he wanted him instantly, in the middle of the week, and Jerry didn't ask why. He was on the next plane to Vegas.

"There's a very serious threat on my life," Elvis told Jerry when he arrived. "I think the guy is either insane or, I don't know what the deal is, the FBI's been contacted on it and I *need* you. . . ."

Jerry said, "I'm here. Whatever you need."

With Jerry and Red and Sonny, and a part-Hawaiian karate instructor named Ed Parker, Elvis felt somewhat better. Hotel security, doubled whenever Elvis played the hotel anyway, was bolstered even more. FBI agents were positioned strategically throughout the showroom opening night. An ambulance and surgical team were standing by.

Just before going on, Elvis looked around his dressing room. "The hotel's told me I don't have to do this show," he said, "but I'm going to do it. I'd rather die on stage than in bed . . ."

His voice trailed off and he was silent for a moment, then he added, ". . . and I don't want any sonabitch running around afterward saying, 'I killed Elvis Presley!' What I want you to do is if some guy shoots me, I want you to rip his fucking eyes out!"

With that, Elvis stuck a derringer into his right boot and into his waistband he pushed a .45. Then, allowing Charlie Hodge to place his jeweled cape on his shoulders, he strode off to do the dinner show.

"It'd been decided," says Jerry Schilling, "that if Elvis heard a shot during his performance, he would hit the floor and someone would jump on top of him, whoever was closest, while the others went after the gunman. So the show was very tight and stiff, until right in the middle, from up in the balcony a guy hollers, 'ELVIS!' Now, this was very unusual. Usually it's the girls who holler."

At the sound of the strange male voice, Elvis dropped to one knee, peering into the darkness beyond the footlights, as applause from the preceding song died out. Sonny and Red peered over the amplifiers, moving their hands toward the weapons they were carrying.

Elvis remained on one knee in the silence and answered the call: "Yeah?"

"I mean," Jerry remembers, "we all thought that this was *it*. Then this guy in the balcony says, 'Can you sing, "Don't Be Cruel"?' And Elvis jumps up and sings it. And as a rule, he *never* takes requests."

During the following weeks Red cruised the audiences along with the hotel security and FBI plainclothesmen, while Sonny and Jerry and Ed remained on guard on stage. Nothing more was heard from the extortionist, however, and on February 23, Elvis returned to Memphis, where he again went into a post-performance depression and physical decline that would extend into recording sessions scheduled for three weeks later.

There was never anything boring about one of Elvis's recording sessions, because they were so unpredictable. Sometimes he went into the studio and recorded song after song after song—getting thirty-four songs down in just five days in June 1970, for example —and other times he blew it all away very quickly, growing bored himself and getting stoned (usually on sedatives, prescribed by his doctor) or sick, and canceling after only a day or two and mostly fooling around during that time, with nothing much to show for it. The only thing predictable was unpredictability.

The first session was set for middle March in Nashville's RCA studios. It'd been six months since Elvis had recorded any new material and although RCA had enough material to get through 1971, there was talk of another Christmas album and nothing had yet been scheduled for release in 1972. So Harry Jenkins, RCA's "vice-president in charge of Elvis Presley," began urging the Colonel to get his boy motivated and the Colonel, working directly with Elvis and through Elvis's number-one aide, Joe Esposito, began passing RCA's wishes along. Initially, Elvis wasn't excited about the Christmas album: Why didn't RCA just re-release the first one, from 1957?

Eventually he agreed and lackadaisically chartered a jet for the twenty-minute flight to Nashville. There he was greeted by a studio full of familiar faces, including the guitarist he believed he couldn't sing without, James Burton (who made $5,000 a week when he worked for Elvis); the rest of the rhythm section handpicked from the best Nashville had to offer (guitarist Chip Young, bassist Norbert Putnam, drummer Jerry Carrigan, pianist David Briggs, Charlie McCoy on harmonica); and twelve backup singers, including the familiar Imperials from his Vegas and road show, the Nashville Edition, Millie Kirkham (with whom he'd recorded for fifteen years), and three other female voices.

Also present and showing somewhat more nervousness were Felton Jarvis, a big jovial Tennesseean who worshipped Elvis like a brother and "produced" the sessions; the sober-faced representatives of Elvis's song publishing companies and RCA; and half a dozen members of his personal entourage. According to drummer Jerry Carrigan, it was the latter group that pretty much set the mood inside the studio.

"The first couple of times I went to work for him," Carrigan says, "people told me, 'Man, when he smiles at you, you smile back or he'll think you don't like him.' I said, 'I'm not a man that smiles all the time.' They said, 'Well, if he says somethin' funny, laugh, man.' I said, 'Well, if it's not funny to me, I'm not gonna laugh.'

"Well, one night they brought a big quart milkshake cup of dill pickles and sat 'em on the little console. Now I'd seen several guys go over there and get a pickle, man, and they'd eat it. So I went over there and just as I got my hand over the cup, one of his guys went, 'No, no!' I said, 'What?' He said, 'Those are Elvis's pickles! Don't you touch 'em!' Now, no way Elvis would mind me having a pickle. It was these yes-men, they ran his whole life. Charlie McCoy started to go into the restroom and they said, 'Don't you go in there!' Charlie said, 'What?' They said, 'Don't go in there!' Charlie said, 'But I have to go to the bathroom.' They said, 'You'll have to wait—Elvis is in there.' "

The March session lasted only one day, when Elvis recorded four songs, including an old hymn that'd been a hit a few months earlier for Judy Collins, "Amazing Grace," and a song of Gordon Lightfoot's that'd been a hit for Peter, Paul, and Mary in 1965, "Early Mornin' Rain." Elvis sounded tired, his performance of the material was listless (although regarded good enough to be released), and the remainder of the week's sessions were canceled the following day. The musicians and singers were told that Elvis's eyes were bothering him.

The next session began exactly two months later, on May 15. RCA was planning a September release for the Christmas album and now was willing to get the album any way it could. Thus, this week of sessions was programmed with Elvis's assistance but without his fulltime presence. He delivered a "scratch track," a rough tape of the songs Elvis recorded at the piano, which was designed to keep the musicians together, who then went in and laid down the instrumental portions, listening to Elvis's previously recorded voice on earphones. Later Elvis and the backup singers went in and recorded the vocal parts and after that, in June, strings were added in Hollywood.

Not all of the material recorded was done so mechanically, however. One of the Christmas songs, "Merry Christmas Baby," for instance, was a sort of lazy jam that ran for nearly six minutes and Bob Dylan's "Don't Think Twice, It's All Right" *was* a studio jam, running eight minutes and unintended for release but recorded anyway and released after Elvis's death. For these songs, and several others, Elvis *was* present. After the session ended, Elvis also sat down at the piano and played "I'll Take You Home Again, Kathleen." It was a paste-up, patchwork way to work, but not without precedent in recording, and the end result was thirty-five songs, more than enough material for three albums, although typically for Elvis some of the songs wouldn't be released for many years.

Elvis wanted to rerecord two of the songs from May, one of them for the Christmas album, and to record a few more songs for his third gospel album, so two weeks later, on June 8, Elvis made his last spring visit to Nashville. Jerry Carrigan remembers it clearly and unfavorably.

"Everybody was drinkin', man, going outside and smoking dope. Nobody was straight. And there was so damn many people in the studio we didn't have a place to sit. The gospel quartets were spread all over the place, his guys were running around, and Elvis was telling stories, so we'd just wander off, go outside, drink a beer, we'd talk, play us some cards. Then one of his guys came out and said, 'Hey, you're gonna have to come back in, you're supposed to be workin'!' Finally I said, 'Look, you want us to come back in there, you're gonna have to clear some of those people out and bring us some chairs so we can sit down.' So they brought us some chairs and we listened to Elvis tell his stories."

All night they were there and eventually they recorded four songs, and the next night they recorded another four. Elvis was genial, relaxed during most of both sessions, easy to please, usually accepting whatever came out the first or second time. He demanded nothing more than the group's attention. But as the second evening wore on, his mood changed radically, and the Presley temper was revealed.

"One of the backup singers wasn't paying attention," says Carrigan, "and he threw the biggest fit and took the microphone and THREW it down on the floor and STORMED out. He said, 'I've run this damn song fifty times and you all *still* don't know your parts!' "

Elvis's entourage scrambled after him, scowling at the singer who had upset their boss.

"Hey, E," one of them cried after the disappearing figure, "hey, E, let's go get some cheeseburgers, man, I know an all-night place that . . ."

In the studio the producer's voice came over the intercom: "Okay, that's it, wrap it up. . . ."

"What about tomorrow?" someone called.

"That's okay, that's it, the session is canceled, thank you and good night."

Elvis sat slumped in his limousine, head sunk into his high collar, staring through tinted glasses, speeding for the Nashville airport.

June, 1971–
December, 1971

Back home in Memphis, life returned to "normalcy," which meant going to bed at eight in the morning and getting up in the middle of the afternoon to have breakfast at five or six, then rent the Memphian Theater for an evening of movies, or on special occasions rent the Memphis Fairgrounds to ride the roller coaster ten times in a row. By 1971, Elvis's normalcy was, by "normal" standards, downright weird. It was a kind of Alice-through-the-looking-glass life, where nothing made sense to the outsider. Of course it made perfect sense to Elvis. Ask a small child his heart's desire and he might say he wished to banish bedtime and stay up all night. Elvis did that, taking logical refuge behind the argument that fame and its attendant bothersome fans made it impossible to go out in the daytime, or to go to movie theaters and amusement parks when others did. Similarly, when he wanted to buy a small fleet of German sports cars as Christmas gifts, the Mercedes agency was thrilled to open its doors at two in the morning. His favorite jeweler in Memphis, the man in California who designed his flashy costumes, no matter who you were, or where, if you were a part of Elvis's life, the calls came after midnight.

"Hello? This is Joe," said Joe Esposito matter-of-factly at 4 A.M. "Elvis wants to talk to you. . . ."

The guys who worked for Elvis lived with him—lived his lifestyle totally. Because Elvis was a longtime aficionado of karate, they took karate lessons too. When Elvis went on a yogurt kick, they ate yogurt until it came out of their ears. They took the same pills he did. They laughed when he laughed and they walked around on eggs whenever The Boss was uptight. Some might have killed for him. All believed they would die for him.

He drove only when he wanted to, he never placed a telephone call, he let them find girls for his lonely evenings away from home. On tour and in Las Vegas they protected him from unruly fans and potential assassins. Some had special functions. Joe Esposito joined Elvis out of the army in 1960 and was his closest friend and confidant; Joe served as Elvis's liaison with the Colonel, carried his personal checkbook, and organized his appointments. Charlie Hodge also went back to his army days and he played rhythm guitar on stage with Elvis and handed him his scarves and Gatorade; unlike Joe, who held onto his own identity, Charlie was the archetypal go-fer, the puppy-like flack and idolator.

Others had been there even longer. His cousin, Red West, of course, went back to his high school days, as did George Klein who, with his wife Barbara, was among Elvis's closest companions when he was in Memphis; Elvis paid for George's nose job and gave him several cars. The mountainous Lamar Fike was another who'd been around since the 1950s. Elvis called him "the Buddha" and he ran the lights in Las Vegas and Lake Tahoe; the rest of the time he took Elvis's harshest abuse.

"Why are you here?" Elvis often asked. "Tell me, fat-ass, why are you here? What do you do? Did it ever occur to you that you are a worthless fat-ass sonofabitch?"

Lamar could talk back, but never was allowed to

win. There was a time he and Elvis were going to Tupelo with some others and they began trading insults. Lamar called Elvis a no-good singer, Elvis started shooting off one-line jokes of the sort Henny Youngman would tell: "You're so fat that . . ." Finally there was one that broke everybody up: "You're so fat, Lamar . . . your toilet is so big there are whitecaps on the water."

Another time, Lamar fell off the toilet at Graceland and got wedged between the bowl and the wall. Laughing hysterically, Elvis had another one of the boys call the fire department to come get Lamar unstuck. Elvis never let Lamar forget that one.

The other guys would sit around listening to Elvis humiliate Lamar, almost as embarrassed as Lamar himself. Other times the guys would be jockeying for position. When Elvis took one to the store with him and bought him a new .38 with pearl grips, the next day he'd show it off to the others who then would see what they could do to get the first one in trouble. Elvis encouraged this. He deliberately spent more time with a new addition to the personal staff, knowing it would send the longtimers into a fit of jealousy. All of them, even Joe, competed ardently to be what one insider called "the Number One boy of the week."

In talking about Elvis's guys—in the 1960s they were called the Memphis Mafia by movie fan magazines—it's easy to forget that Elvis was married during this time. By the early 1970s, with Elvis returned to the public spotlight, it was his wife Priscilla who wore the mantle of mystery. She attended Elvis's openings in Las Vegas and Lake Tahoe, and many of the closings too, the teased, dyed hair and black eye makeup of an earlier time replaced by her natural colors, dressed simply and expensively. Occasionally she would be seen shopping in Beverly Hills or at some of the nicer Memphis stores. Except for this, little was known about her. This was as Elvis wanted it.

Because she had moved into Graceland when she was fourteen, it was easy for her to turn her life over to Elvis, and the first seven or so years of their relationship, she did exactly what he wished. The daughter of an air force officer, she was only fourteen and wearing a ponytail and bobby sox when they met in 1960 in Germany, shortly before Elvis was released from the service. Her parents allowed her to move from Germany to Memphis, and into Elvis's Graceland estate, after Elvis's aunt and father did some talking for him. They said she'd be treated like a princess, enrolled in the very best schools, and so on. And so she was, but in the process she led a highly sheltered and submissive life. In time, however, this changed. She attended a finishing school, studied ballet, design, and modeling. And she became something Elvis never became: an adult.

It became harder and harder for her to accept some of Elvis's demands. When they'd married, he'd let most of the guys go, but now that he was appearing publicly they seemed to have drifted back into their lives again. Joe Esposito and his wife, and Charlie Hodge, actually lived in Graceland with them. It wasn't that she disliked any of these people. She merely wanted privacy and space.

She also began to want an identity apart from being "Elvis's wife." A pleasant and unusually attractive young woman with an exploitable name, she'd often been asked to consider an acting career. She found herself more and more interested in design. Little Lisa Marie was three. A nocturnal lifestyle didn't seem to fit any of this.

Outwardly, the relationship was good; both parties acted according to long-established guidelines: Elvis was protective and Priscilla feathered the nest. When Elvis saw a photographer with a telescopic lens standing on a hill overlooking his Los Angeles home, for example, he pictured a rifleman on the same hill and, fearing for his wife and child, sold the house. Just before they moved into the new one, Priscilla redecorated it with the kind of big, bulky furniture that Elvis liked.

Although Elvis and Priscilla agreed on most things, there were important areas where they didn't. Permitting Lisa Marie to stay up until ten or eleven o'clock and then sleep through much of the day like her daddy might be acceptable now, but what about when she reached school age? Priscilla also believed that Elvis spoiled the child.

Priscilla thought Elvis spoiled himself, too, believed he was too free with his money. When they argued about it, she objected most fiercely to his giving gifts to strangers. Friends and family, she understood, but when strangers were given cars and jewelry, it made her mad.

Most significant was her concern about Elvis's recurring "illnesses" and the "medicine" he took to relieve the many symptoms. But whenever she brought that subject up, he got defensive, or said he didn't want to talk about it or, more winningly, played the wounded little boy.

If trouble seemed to be brewing inside the Graceland gates, outside Elvis's stardom was rushing through the skies, gathering momentum. In February 1971, Elvis was named the world's top male singer for the twelfth time in thirteen years by Britain's weekly *New Musical Express*. This wasn't particularly surprising, for in England Elvis held a godlike position. What was more noteworthy was the attention he began to get in the U.S. In the months following his being named one of the Young Men of the Year by the Jaycees, that part of Highway 51 that ran past his Memphis house was renamed Elvis Presley Boulevard, and while he was appearing in Las Vegas he joined Frank Sinatra, Duke Ellington, Ella Fitzgerald, and Irving Berlin as a recipient of the prestigious Bing Crosby Award, recognition granted by vote of the national board of trustees of the National Academy of Recording Arts & Sciences, for his "outstanding creative and artistic contributions of long-lasting duration in the field of phonograph recordings." In music, there was no higher honor.

He also set records in Nevada. In Tahoe, he played the Sahara, a club too small to afford Elvis and still ask a reasonable price for tickets, so several other hotels chipped in to meet his price, knowing their business would benefit from his presence; all existing showroom attendance records were shattered when 3,400 persons attended the dinner and midnight shows on Saturday, July 17. A month later, back in the International in Vegas, they packed in 4,428 people in two shows, a figure that will never be topped because fire safety laws were broken to achieve it. (The room only seats 2,000.)

The International Hotel in Las Vegas had changed hands since Elvis was there in February. "My first meeting with Colonel Parker was five hours after Mr. Hilton took over the hotel," says Henri Lewin, the German-born Hilton vice-president. "I came in at noon and had a meeting with Colonel Parker at five, so you can imagine how important he was. Tom Jones, Engelbert Humperdinck, Barbra Streisand, they are all great stars. But there is only one who when you announced his name he is sold out for the duration of the engagement. Never before and never again do I think that will be possible.

"Colonel Parker flew in right away from Palm Springs. He had in his contract a clause that if the hotel should be sold it would be up to Elvis and the Colonel whether or not they would extend the contract to the new owner. The Colonel said, 'I did business with [Kirk] Kerkorian [the former owner], I liked him, and I have no reason not to trust that you will be as good, or better.' This time we assured him we would be as good. Later the Colonel made it better.

He accepted the same contract. It was not renegotiated. That was later, the renegotiation."

Elvis and the Colonel were perfect for Nevada. This was a state—more of the mind than of geography—that understood carnival, and by 1971, Elvis was America's best-known and most easily exploited sideshow act, a performer who demanded superlatives, personified exaggeration, attracted the bizarre and extreme.

For months ahead all rooms in the hotel were reserved. Every day lines started forming before breakfast for the dinner show, with friends spelling each other for trips to the bathroom and meals when they remembered them. Everywhere one looked there were the cheap trappings of Presleyana—the scarves, lapel pins, pennants, and styrofoam hats, declaring it an "Elvis Summer Festival"; attractive girls in short skirts selling overpriced souvenir picture books, middle-aged women in rhinestone butterfly glasses selling giant teddy bears (for charity); and trolling the banks of slot machines, packs of women seeking a familiar face, a Vernon Presley, perhaps, or one of the loyal bodyguards. Twice a night they filled every seat, paying $15 apiece to let their steak go cold and squeal and pray for a kiss. After the show they went to the powder room to exchange their soiled panties for fresh; ". . . we never stocked women's pants except for an Elvis engagement," a powder room attendant said.

"I watched the audience as he walked out on stage," says Bill Jost, the showroom's assistant maitre d', "and so many had their faces in their hands. They'd sit there and cry. It was almost biblical, as if the clouds had parted and down a shaft of light came the angels."

Jost's analogy is not extreme, for it was with this engagement that Elvis made his entrance to the rumbling, heraldic score of Richard Strauss's "Also Sprach Zarathustra," better known as the theme from the movie *2001: A Space Odyssey,* used in that picture's dramatic sunrise scene. This was followed by a drum roll of controlled frenzy and an audience reaction of uncontrolled frenzy, as Elvis strode quickly onto center stage, a tall, handsome figure in a suit of black and white and gold appliqué.

"Waaaallll," he sang, "it's all right, li'l mama . . ."

Still Elvis wasn't as thrilled with Vegas as he used to be. After all, fifty-six shows in twenty-nine days is no performer's idea of fun, even if he's being paid more than anyone else in town. It was doubly hard to take because now he stayed in his penthouse suite of rooms, afraid to venture out in public. Only six months before he had FBI agents crawling all over the hotel looking for an assassin, an experience he remembered clearly and uncomfortably.

Yet, Elvis did enjoy himself, often laughing out loud at the antics of his most ardent fans. For example, when he sang "Teddy Bear," one of his 1950s hits, at the Colonel's suggestion he tossed several stuffed bears into the audience, always causing dozens to crash and dive for them, knocking over tables and drinks. By the end of the month, he was trying to heave them into the balcony, winding up and tossing them with a drum roll provided by Ronnie Tutt. Then he'd walk offstage and bring back a teddy that was fully six feet tall and about as big around as the portly Colonel himself. This one he rolled into the audience near the stage and with a signal to the band, began the next song, seemingly oblivious to the pandemonium he caused. Elvis barely could contain himself as two and sometimes three songs later, the fans sitting near the stage still were wrestling and tugging and screeching for possession of the big bear.

This was typical behavior for Elvis. A man of boyish extremes, he would do anything for a laugh, so long as no one was hurt. Joe Guercio, the orchestra leader, tells a story about the time when he began to work for Elvis in Las Vegas. "The first day, Glenn D. [Hardin, the pianist in Elvis's backup band] and I didn't get along. I didn't want to make any waves, no way. The hotel was nervous because God was arriving, you know. This was where the job was. Keep him unhappy and you know where you wind up. The second day, Joe Esposito said, 'What's it like to work with Elvis?' I said, 'It's like following a marble falling down concrete steps.' Next day I come into my dressing room and I couldn't get the door open. I finally push it open and there musta been 3,000 marbles on the floor and a sign on the mirror: 'Follow the marble . . . me.' From that day on it was like I was one of the gang."

In Vegas in July 1971, Elvis hosted parties in his room to amuse himself. At one of them, circumstances gave Elvis a chance to play one of his favorite roles. The Imperials, the gospel quartet that sang behind him in his show, were singing around the piano with Elvis when the phone rang. Sonny West answered it and said to Joe Mescale, a member of the quartet, "It's your wife. . . ."

She was calling from their motel room and told Joe that a neighbor back home in Franklin, Tennessee, had called to say their house was burglarized. Joe's wife sounded extremely upset, so he said he'd go back to the motel immediately; then he told Sonny, "Don't say anything to E. . . ."

Joe exited the suite and Sonny went right to Elvis to give him a full report. Whereupon, Elvis strode swiftly to the door, threw it open and called out to Joe, who was waiting for the elevator: "Mescale, goddammit, come back here!"

Elvis's orders continued to bark through the suite as Joe meekly returned. "Sonny, call the airport and get the plane warmed up! Red, get my guns! We're goin' home, we gone find that sonabitch! Tonight!" He turned to Linda Thompson, a girl he had with him, and shouted, "Darlin', get your coat. We're goin' on a posse!"

People were jumping all over the room, making arrangements, collecting a small arsenal of rifles and .38s. Only his date, who wasn't used to Elvis's sense of police drama, stood still. Elvis suddenly looked at her and said, "DARLIN', GODDAMMIT, GET YOUR COAT!" She got her coat and like a bunch of angry cowboys they rode over to the Bali Hai Motel in a pack of white Cadillacs.

All the way Elvis kept up a running monologue about the burglary. "Gotta tell your wife, Joe, that everythin' goin'a be all right, probably just some kid broke in, took the TV for dope. . . ."

Joe finally uttered some resistance to the idea of going. "It's not necessary, I appreciate your concern, E, but the police can handle it, and besides, we have a show tomorrow. . . ."

Elvis was determined. "We gone get that sonabitch, Joe, we gone get him!"

The three limousines rolled into the motel parking lot and Elvis, wearing a white leather coat with a mink collar and cuffs and a big floppy "Superfly" hat, a thin cigar clenched in his teeth, followed Joe up to his room.

Joe's wife was stunned. She was wearing only a nightgown and her hair was in curlers. Elvis hugged her and told her, "Now don't you worry, I'm gone replace everything that's been taken; I'll replace it with better than what you had. . . ." Then he went to the telephone and began a marathon series of calls, telling his producer, Felton Jarvis, who lived in Nashville a few miles from the Mescale house, to get over there to supervise; calling the local police; calling the FBI.

"Okay," he said finally at six o'clock in the morning, seeming to have tired of the game, "that's it! Let's go back to the hotel."

Elvis didn't say a word about the incident again and no one said anything to him. "It was just something he did to have some fun," Joe says today. "He wanted some excitement. He was organizing a posse. The little boy wanted to have a good time. Yet he really cared and this was the way he showed it."

It was also that he was growing bored again. The first few engagements in Las Vegas were challenging, but now they were predictable. This didn't go unnoticed. "Uninspired Elvis Delights Vegas" is the way the *Hollywood Reporter* described the month. "As performances go," the critic wrote, "Elvis Presley's show at the Las Vegas Hilton is sloppy, hurriedly rehearsed, uneven, mundanely lit, poorly amplified, occasionally monotonous, often silly, and haphazardly coordinated. Elvis looked drawn, tired, and noticeably heavier—weight-wise, not musically—than in his last Vegas appearance. He wasn't in his strongest voice, his costume of studded white slacks and vest with black satin high collar and scarf was not his sexiest or most flattering. And do you know what? The packed to over-capacity audience . . . positively couldn't have cared less about any pros, cons or comparisons. They absolutely loved, honored, and obeyed his every whim with screams, shrieks, whistles and dashes to the stage apron whenever Elvis decided to wander downstage to kiss, touch, or wipe his brow amidst the adoring throng."

Elvis never saw this review—such things usually were kept away from him—and two months later he took the same show on the road again. Fourteen shows in twelve days, zigzagging all over the East and Midwest, starting in Minneapolis, going to Cleveland, Louisville, Philadelphia, Baltimore and Boston, then heading west and south to Cincinnati, Houston, Dallas, Tuscaloosa, Kansas City, and Salt Lake City. In each venue he played to sold-out auditoriums—never outdoors; Elvis knew he could draw larger crowds in stadiums, but hated the acoustics. Again tickets sold for as much as $10 apiece. Total take for the tour, his first in a year, was close to one-and-a-half million dollars.

With so much time to plan it, this tour ran more smoothly than the first two in 1970. A year before, only the orchestra leader, Joe Guercio, and two of the horn players went along and pickup bands were assembled in each city and quickly rehearsed for what was in large part a spontaneous show. It didn't work well. Elvis was not comfortable and he let the Colonel know that he wanted familiar faces in the orchestra, so in 1971 the pickup band concept—a popular one with many touring singers—was dropped and now Joe Guercio began taking not two but twelve musicians. With Elvis's six friends in the rhythm section, eight backup singers, the comedian who was in his show, half a dozen in his personal entourage, the sound men and people who drove the trucks of equipment from city to city, the Colonel and *his* entourage (including people from RCA), there now were nearly fifty in the group. The logistics were impressive. The number of plane tickets, bus seats, and hotel rooms handled each day—not to mention the number of tickets sold—made it clear that behind the scenes were at least another hundred, perhaps several thousand or more individuals who kept the machine running.

In each city there were bus and limousine drivers, ushers, souvenir salesmen, food concessionaires, box office representatives, telephone answerers, auditorium staff members. In Minneapolis a small company paid its bills with the money earned from the production of Elvis Presley pennants. How many secretaries and executives at RCA earned salaries directly linked to success of *their* Number One boy? How many lawyers and accountants and booking agents (and *their* secretaries!)? How many fan magazine writers and editors and sneaky photographers trying to get a picture of little Lisa Marie? How many people *were* there tied into Elvis's career, dependent on his continuing success?

It cost Elvis money to keep this industry going.

There were agent's and manager's commissions—35 percent off the top of all earnings went there—and other sums were paid to the concert promoters, the picture-book publishers, and the makers of scarves and teddy bears. The huge six-figure daily grosses dwindled rapidly. It was abundantly clear to anyone keeping track that being a giant star was costly. With taxes on top of expenses, it was a good month when Elvis managed to keep one dollar out of every ten he earned.

There were other problems too.

The first was brewing in August, in Las Vegas, when the Imperials, part of Elvis's backup chorus, decided they wanted more money and a solo spot in the show. They believed that musically they were at least as good as the Sweet Inspirations who opened the show and when Joe Mescale, who also served as the quartet's manager, admitted he'd asked for too little money in the beginning, the other three insisted he confront the Colonel instantly. Nervously, Joe approached the hulking Colonel, who was sitting at the roulette table. Standing next to him, protectively, was Tom Diskin, the Colonel's number one lieutenant and whipping boy.

"Uh, Tom," said Joe, "I'd like to talk to the Colonel for a minute. It's important."

Diskin waited until the play was finished on the table and said, "Colonel, Joe Mescale wants to talk to you."

The Colonel didn't even look around. He said, "Tell Mr. Mescale I'm busy."

"Tom," said Joe, "the Colonel has to understand that we need more money, or at least he has to pay for our motel rooms, or our outfits. We're just not making enough to cover it. We're staying in crappy motels and . . ."

The Colonel interrupted, but still refused to turn around. "Tell Mr. Mescale," he said to his assistant, "that he's not gonna get it, he's wastin' his and my time."

Diskin turned to Joe and said, "The Colonel says you're not gonna get it and there's no way you can change the deal in the middle of an engagement."

"Well, we can't live with it."

Diskin relayed that message: "Joe says he can't live with it, Colonel."

And so it went for a full 15 minutes. Both the Colonel and Joe talked through Tom Diskin; neither one ever made direct contact with the other, although they stood within arm's reach. Finally, Joe walked dejectedly away.

The Colonel may have handled the confrontation brusquely, even rudely, but he felt somewhat justified in turning Joe away, believing that Elvis had been more than generous. The Imperials also had been working with Jimmy Dean and, in fact, for part of the Vegas engagement Elvis had agreed to let them sing for Dean in Arizona, then flew them to Vegas in time to make his second show. Their pay wasn't cut during this period and Elvis paid for the plane tickets.

Soon after that Joe went to Elvis and told him the Imperials wouldn't be going with him on the fall tour. Jimmy Dean had offered them the same money and a chance to open the concerts, as well as a feature spot on a television show. Elvis was hurt.

"You gone with that *cowboy?*" he said. "That *sausage-maker!* You're not gone have any fun with him."

He then asked Joe who he'd recommend to take his place. Joe suggested the Oak Ridge Boys or J. D. Sumner's Stamps. J. D. was the godfather of the gospel field. Elvis had worshiped him as a child and so it was the Stamps who went on the road with him.

Worse than changing four backup singers was what came to a head in November, the same month Elvis finished his tour—a widely publicized paternity suit. Over the years Elvis was the subject of more than a dozen such suits, but this one was the first to reach the courts and the press covered each tiny development as if the future of Western civilization depended on it. For more than a month Rona Barrett made it a lead item in her network television reports and lawyers argued on newspaper front pages—as well as in court —about whose blood test meant what.

Eventually the girl's case was dismissed for a lack of believable evidence, but the repercussions of the suit were significant, because the party scene she described was accurate and never really denied. Worse, the details of the Vegas evening now were a matter of public record, printed in publications and broadcast by radio and television stations.

Priscilla and the other wives had had their suspicions about what went on. Elvis's prodigious appetite for sex was well known and only a fool would have been surprised to learn that many of the guys in his entourage helped themselves to the overflow. Still, as one insider said, "Priscilla and the other wives didn't like having their noses rubbed in it. They started asking questions. Some insisted on going on the next tour. And when they were told it wasn't practical, which it really wasn't, that only made it worse. What it all came down to was that when the shit hit the newspapers, it also hit the fan."

Of course it had been building for a long time. For years Priscilla and Elvis had been drifting slowly, subtly apart. Back at Graceland following the December tour, they tried to pretend nothing was wrong and it seemed in most ways to be a typical Presley Christmas and New Year's.

For the whole month of December, the big house and winding drive were outlined with thousands of tiny blue lights, a large tree went up in the living room, and Elvis settled into his habit of renting a movie theater for the after-midnight screenings that he held for himself and friends. The movies he saw reflected his fascination with police and violence and included some that were among his all-time favorites—James Bond's *Diamonds Are Forever*, the bloody Sam Peckinpah western *Straw Dogs*, and Clint Eastwood's portrayal of a macho San Francisco cop in *Dirty Harry*.

For little Lisa Marie and others, Elvis and Priscilla usually erected a compatible facade. She accompanied him to the movies and they exchanged expensive gifts. (When she refused a new car, he gave her ten new thousand-dollar bills.) And they hosted a party a few days before Christmas at Graceland. Ironically, it was at that party that it became clear to everyone that the seams of the marriage were pulling apart. It was as if Priscilla had decided to drop the front.

All night long, Priscilla virtually ignored Elvis as she chatted amiably and somewhat smugly with some of the wives present, hinting at an affair that Elvis still didn't suspect. "This," Priscilla told the girls, "was the year that I came out." Puzzled by her behavior, Elvis slumped into depression and even began to drink, something he ordinarily never did.

Suddenly, smoke began filling the room. Vernon and Jerry Schilling traced it to a wall and knocked a hole in the plaster with a sledgehammer, snipping the wiring that had heated up. Elvis watched them dejectedly and grumbled, "That's the funniest thing I've seen all night."

Priscilla left for California with Lisa Marie the following day, to be away from Elvis and near her new man. The story would be kept from Elvis for another two weeks and Elvis, in all innocence, still suspected nothing. He merely thought she was tired of his lifestyle, was fed up with all the boys in his life, and weary of all the girls.

December, 1971–
February, 1972

At midnight one night soon after Priscilla left, Elvis told Charlie Hodge to turn on the lights in the well house behind Graceland and set up some targets. Another of Elvis's hands was sent upstairs to Elvis's bedroom to collect an assortment of rifles and handguns. He returned with such a load of weaponry that he bent over backward as he walked. Meanwhile, Charlie had erected a man-sized target against the well-house door. Elvis picked one of the army-issue automatic rifles—illegal for a private citizen to own—and said, "Charlie, put up a row of clay ducks. See if I can get 'em with one burst."

First, they warmed up with some of the handguns and rifles. Finally, Elvis put the machine–gun–like Browning automatic rifle under one arm and, like John Wayne spraying an enemy pillbox, he fired forty or fifty rounds into the well house, sending bits of clay and wood flying in all directions, and setting the old well house aflame.

Elvis doubled over laughing as his father rushed to smother the flames with his jacket. "Oh, daddy," Elvis finally said, still laughing, "let it burn. It's only money."

As usual when Elvis and his boys began banging away in the middle of the night, Graceland was visited by the police. By now, of course, the guns had been put away and when asked about all the noise, Elvis and his pals denied hearing anything, or said, "Musta been a truck backfirin'." The policemen knew better, but never followed through, choosing to tell Elvis to keep it down as they left with smiles on their faces. After all, they'd got to meet the King. And a king can get away with anything.

New Year's Eve he decided to stage another, slightly quieter but possibly more dangerous war. He and eleven of his friends pulled on heavy gloves and jackets and football helmets and went into the yard, where they chose up sides and Elvis distributed over a thousand dollars' worth of roman candles, firecrackers, and cherry bombs. No one was hurt, but when the play ended, the air stank with the smell of scorched wool and cotton and melting polyester, and everyone's clothes were gaping with blackened holes.

The diversion was short-lived, the mood shattered when early in the New Year Priscilla returned from Los Angeles to share her secret: She was in love with someone else. Elvis was crushed. It would've been bad enough if she'd fallen for a total stranger, but the man, Mike Stone, was a friend! When Elvis and Priscilla had been trying to prop up their sagging partnership a year earlier, it was decided that she would begin taking karate lessons, to give them another common interest. The instructor Elvis selected was Ed Parker, one of his own teachers, and Ed passed her along to Stone, who was, like Ed, part-Hawaiian. He was also an international champion, then running a karate school in a Los Angeles suburb and separated from his wife.

Soon after they met, Priscilla's brown Mercedes was often to be seen parked behind the Sherman Oaks studio and she became one of Mike's most attentive students. After a while Mike and Priscilla agreed that her presence in the big classroom seemed to upset some of the other students, so private instruction began. Priscilla began sneaking letters and small packages into the mail, giving them to the secretaries at Graceland to post. While Elvis was in Las Vegas in August, the two began going to chic Los Angeles restaurants together. It seemed as if she were determined to let Elvis know, without directly telling him. The degree of Elvis's isolation is shown by the fact that he never heard a word of it from anyone.

Priscilla didn't torture Elvis with details about her romance with Mike. She merely said she had been seeing him, liked him a lot, and wanted a separation, and then she returned to California.

Elvis's reaction ranged from hurt to fury and according to those around him, he alternately sulked and raged. His friend Ed Parker, who had introduced Mike and Priscilla and who was still on Elvis's security staff, wrote in his book *Inside Elvis*, "The biggest setback in his life was the death of his mother, but the biggest threat to his ego was the loss of his wife. Had Priscilla died, he could have coped, but to lose her to another man was a mortal blow. There is no way to forget the night he took me aside at his home in Beverly Hills and told me of his impending divorce. He poured out his soul that night, and I saw him cry for the first time.

" 'She has everything money can buy, Ed—cars, homes, an expense account. And she knows that all she has to do is ask, and I'll get her whatever she wants. I can't understand, Ed. I love that woman.' "

No matter what his personal state, another Las Vegas engagement was only a week off. Traditionally this was a time for him to—literally—get his act together. First, there was the matter of new costumes. Ironically, it was Priscilla who'd started Elvis wearing capes, starting just over two years before when she gave him the one he wore when he met Nixon. A year later, Elvis told his costume designer, Bill Belew—who was making some of Elvis's personal wardrobe by then —to make him a black brocade suit and red-lined cape. Now, in January 1972, Elvis was ready to add a flowing, full-length cape to his Vegas costume, an act that made him appear, as he stood in front of the mirror and looked at himself, more than ever like a hero from a Marvel comic book.

This was also the time for him to add new material to his showroom repertoire, requiring rehearsals. One of the new songs would fit the cape perfectly. This was a medley called "American Trilogy," three songs successfully pieced together a few months earlier by a singer named Mickey Newbury.

Although the original arrangement was little changed in Elvis's hands—only made flashier, somewhat more dramatic—"Dixie," "The Battle Hymn of the Republic," and "All My Trials"—in time it would assume the proportions of a personal anthem.

There was another new song added during this Las Vegas engagement and in its lyrics Elvis opened a small window into his carefully guarded personal life. "You Gave Me a Mountain This Time" was a ten-year-old song (written by Marty Robbins), whose second half seemed ripped from Elvis's own life.

> *My woman got tired of the hardships,*
> *Tired of the grief and the strife;*
> *So tired of workin' for nothin',*
> *Tired of bein' my wife.*
>
> *She took my one ray of sunshine,*
> *She took my pride and my joy;*
> *She took my reason for living,*
> *She took my small baby boy.*
>
> *So this time, Lord, you gave me a mountain,*
> *A mountain I may never climb;*
> *And it isn't a hill any longer,*
> *You gave me a mountain this time.*

In Vegas, Elvis's moods soared and plummeted erratically. He thought about how he'd loaned Mike money to start his own studio at the same time Priscilla was getting serious about her new relationship. He felt as if he'd been set up and he sought refuge where he often did, moving from the uppers he had taken to lose weight the last few days before opening, to the wide assortment of sleeping pills that doctors had prescribed, allegedly to combat his insomnia. Without the pills, Elvis was able to demonstrate anger that challenged Thor's thunderbolts. Under the influence of his "medication," his rage may have been insane.

His performances were affected. Some nights, when he decided to "show her" and be the biggest rock-and-roll-superhero-movie-star-sex-idol-in-the-sunny-West, he was a consummate performer. Other nights the show was not so good. Reviews by the two Los Angeles newspaper critics presented divergent views. His reaction to the reviews revealed much more.

Frank Lieberman, the chatty entertainment writer for the *Los Angeles Herald-Examiner*, made Elvis a friend when he wrote a review that included such phrases as ". . . has finally got it together . . . devastating showman; confident, compelling and in control . . . power and thrust reminiscent of the glory days . . . sensitive, emotionally assertive presence . . . creative artist and craftsman . . . electrifying, rambunctious, resourceful and perceptive . . ." Elvis was so pleased that he had Lieberman summoned and, when asked, gave the first interview that he'd given in several years.

Two days after Lieberman's review appeared, the *Los Angeles Times*'s man, Robert Hillburn, said he was disappointed. He said Elvis was no longer a leader, but a follower in singing so many songs previously recorded by others. Besides "American Trilogy," he noted Hoyt Axton's "Never Been to Spain" recorded by Three Dog Night, and Buffy Sainte-Marie's "Until It's Time for You to Go." It was, he said, an "alarming" trend. Hillburn previously had been one of Elvis's favorites and was granted several brief audiences in the past. Never again. Now Hillburn was on the Presley shit list.

Priscilla moved out of the Los Angeles house on February 23, 1972, the same day Elvis closed at the Hilton.

February, 1972–
May, 1972

Elvis had only a little time free following the Vegas
engagement before reporting to MGM in Culver City
for what would be his final film, another documentary,
originally titled *Sold Out*, ultimately called *Elvis on
Tour*. The filmmakers suggested by the studio, Bob
Abel and Pierre Adidge, had met the Colonel and then
Elvis backstage after one of the February shows at the
Hilton.

 Abel was a young intellectual who'd worked on
David Wolper's prizewinning film about Bobby Kennedy, and with Adidge he'd just made a documentary
about a Joe Cocker tour, *Mad Dogs and Englishmen*.
"At that time," he says today, "music was where it
was really at. To me, it was the great artistic statement of our time. With the other great artistic statement of its time, film—what an incredible marriage. I
felt like Alan Lomax out there recording Woodie Guth-
rie. I was recording for posterity this great phenomenon. *Woodstock* had just hit and everybody was
suddenly aware that it was an incredibly artistic, social
revolution going on and I'd always wanted to trace its
roots and I'd always wanted to make a film on Elvis.
Then, again, I think it was partly ego. Because I saw
all the film that'd been made, all the records that'd
been made, and it was all pretty shoddy. I couldn't

believe this crap that was turned out by various studios. I think Don Siegel did a good job with *Flaming Star* and there were some things about *King Creole* and *Jailhouse Rock* that I liked, but for the most part it was utter drivel. So when Pierre and I went backstage, we didn't know what to say."

At first there was small talk. Elvis was charming—a relaxed and congenial host amid a welter of suspicious yet anxious-to-please employees who remained pretty much in the background. Finally Elvis said, "The Colonel told me you're gonna make a film. . . ."

"Possibly so," Abel said. *"Hopefully* so. If the mood and atmosphere are right, if the conditions are right, I have the desire, but not the commitment."

Elvis looked puzzled. "What d'you mean?"

"Well, I'm a documentary filmmaker and I'm really interested in the man who makes the music, not just in recording the music, although I'd like to get your real music on film, too, because I haven't been too impressed by the music you've put on film so far. If we can develop an interest in you, it might be an interesting film to make . . ."

Elvis interrupted: "Do you like my music?"

Abel said he did, delivering a monologue that focused on Elvis's music in the 1950s. He once took a long train ride with Willie Mae "Big Mama" Thornton, he said, and talked with her about how hard it was for blacks to get certain songs played back then and about how this guy Elvis Presley came and stole their music. He talked about the two top songwriters of the period, Jerry Leiber and Mike Stoller, who'd written many of Elvis's early hits ("Jailhouse Rock," "Love Me," "Hound Dog," etc.). Abel said that during the 1950s, "I really wanted to take a punch at you."

Elvis rocked back in his chair and laughed. "A lot of people did take punches at me. . . ."

"It's true," Abel said. "I admired you on the one hand, and yet on the other hand I was trying too hard to get a girl to kiss me or to let me get my hand under her sweater, when I knew that any girl would have pulled her pants down for Elvis Presley. I hated you for that. Because you had total access to their pants and I couldn't even get access to their lips."

Now Elvis practically fell off his chair with laughter. "That's . . . that's . . . that's the funniest fuckin' thing I've ever heard."

"I didn't like the first documentary," Abel says today. "Denis Sanders did a hatchet job on Elvis, quite frankly. There's a part of me that's a missionary and I think the world deserved a better image of Elvis than cross-cutting him with a guy who's cutting up the meat eating dinner. When the Beatles met Elvis, there was this incredible silence across the room. Then John Lennon came forward and said, 'Until there was you, there was no one.' And that's how I felt. I told Elvis that everybody had photographed and filmed Mount Rushmore and the Washington Monument, but no one had done him yet. I told him there was no lovely, permanent record that we could refer back to in a positive way. I said I thought it was about time someone did something, since we were all getting along in years.

"I liked him," Abel says, "I really did. There was an ingenuous quality about him. There was a brightness and an awareness, and a vulnerability and a sensitivity about him that I really liked. I said, 'Look, if we make a film, we'll have to get access to old pictures, we'd want to talk about your childhood.' Later that was a problem, but at the time he said he'd talk to the Colonel, and we left."

A week later Abel and Adidge were told they probably, but not definitely, had the assignment—the Colonel played his game this way—and while Abel organized crews and equipment in Los Angeles, Adidge, the more gregarious of the two, went on a 72-hour jet tour with Parker to look at the auditoriums Elvis would play in April, to see which ones were best for filming.

Before going on the road with Elvis, they then filmed in MGM's Culver City recording studio, where on March 27, 28, and 29 Elvis and his show band rehearsed and joked around for the cameras. Although Elvis had used these musicians in live recording in Las Vegas, this was the first time he'd taken all of them into the studio together.

Elvis and his musicians recorded seven songs in the three days and less than a week later left for Buffalo, New York. Abel and Adidge had picked four cities in the South for major filming and Abel went along to Buffalo to familiarize himself with Elvis's repertoire and stage movements.

"He came out on stage, in total blackness. The orchestra went into 'Thus Spake Zarathustra.' I'm sure he hadn't read Nietzsche or understood his concepts, or knew about [Richard] Strauss and the Third Reich, but it was the perfect piece of music for him. So, there was total darkness, then this blinding flash of light. I'm not talking about the super trooper—the big spotlight—but the 15,000 flashbulbs from the Instamatics going off simultaneously.

"I saw a woman run down the aisle at full speed and launch herself like a SAM missile, like an Evel Kneivel motorcycle. . . . From four rows back she just took a leap and sailed through the air and landed with a splat, skidding across the stage the way you'd see a seal or a walrus at Marineland. Elvis saw her coming and sidestepped her and she slid right into the drums. I knew then that that was the kind of stuff we had to put into the movie."

Buffalo was still thawing after a bitter winter, and from there Elvis and the fifty or sixty persons in his entourage went to Detroit and Dayton, then dove into the South, where they knew the weather would be warmer, and also the audiences. There were two shows —afternoon and evening—in Knoxville, another two in Hampton Roads, individual concerts in Richmond,

Roanoke Indianapolis, Charlotte, and Greensboro. Double concerts followed those in Macon and Jacksonville; then there were evening shows in Little Rock and San Antonio. The tour closed in Albuquerque. Nineteen shows in fifteen days, in huge arenas and coliseums. Again all the shows were sold out, leaving Elvis with grosses of about $100,000 for each show.

"I took a 3/4-inch Sony Portapack with me when I previewed the show in Buffalo to videotape the concert so we could study the music and study all his moves," Abel says, "so that when we went in to shoot we'd know the entire choreography of the show. It was mandatory that any cameraman who was to work for us had to watch the tape I'd made to know all the moves. We knew that by the time we got to San Antonio and the music started it'd be so loud we couldn't maintain communication with any of the cameramen."

Incredibly, even after they began filming in Hampton Roads April 9 they didn't have a final go-ahead from the Colonel, so they took no chances and went out of their way to please. They rehearsed the camera moves during the matinee and filmed that night, then Abel rushed the film to Hollywood where he had it developed, meeting the Colonel the following day in Charlotte to show it to him, without sound, on a 16-mm projector in the local auditorium. At the time, Abel thought his beard might have made the Colonel wary.

"Hollywood guys with beards were suspect," he says. "It wasn't that long after *Easy Rider*. The Colonel said he'd watched us and he'd gotten reports about us and he was confident we were doing a superb job. He said he'd misjudged us and we could shoot anything we wanted up on the stage and he didn't want to impede us and we had his blessings."

"I feel honored," Abel told the Colonel. "There is one thing we need. We need more access. We have to get closer to Elvis."

The Colonel looked at Abel for a minute and said, "If you deliver, I'll deliver."

The Colonel talked for the next fifteen minutes. It seemed a rambling sort of monologue, but there wasn't a thing casual about it. The messages came through loud and clear.

"He went into a long rap about how many people had fucked over Elvis in the past and he was the only one who'd looked after his image and how careful he'd had to be. He told a story about how, when he was in the carnival, he charged people to get into the show and then collected again on the way out when he sold donkey rides through the area outside the exit, an area strewn with fresh elephant dung. He told us, 'Don't ever try to put something over on me, you'll be up to your ears in elephant shit.' He told that story in the middle of his halftime pep talk. It was like he was the coach and we had just joined the Elvis team. He said we'd proven ourselves."

"Now," the Colonel barked, ending the monologue, "I want you to go out there and make the best Elvis Presley movie anybody ever made!"

So saying, he lifted his cane and slammed it down on the auditorium floor near his chair. Abel and Adidge got up and left, to begin planning the next day's filming.

Abel was a worrier with a tendency to overshoot. "Hampton Roads was fabulous, the best we ever got. Everything worked and what we filmed that first night was most of what we used in the film. The night he wore the powder-blue jumpsuit. It was a magic night. We wanted something more. A good concert doesn't make a good film. Throughout, I experienced a general despondency about not having enough."

As a consequence, Abel and Adidge and their pack of cameramen followed Elvis virtually everywhere, once he exited his hotel rooms—backstage, into his dressing rooms, into the limousines after the shows, and then into his chartered jet. The mayor of Roanoke presented him with a key to the city, shaped like a guitar; Elvis, dressed immaculately in one of his dark blue, high-collared suits, accepted the honor most graciously. In this and in every other public and semi-public situation, Abel says, Elvis revealed little more than his politeness and a good-natured, macho camaraderie with those in his personal entourage. Once he was unfailingly kind to an aggressive, obnoxious fan, refusing, as Abel put it, to "spoil that person's moment." Another time, when Adidge got into a limousine with a small tape recorder stuck into his pocket, he asked Elvis about the night before and Elvis, slumped in his seat, wearing the dark glasses he wore all the time now, mumbled, "Sheeeeet, last night I had my face buried in a beaver." Joe and Sonny and Red laughed loudly in response.

"I heard the same jokes and small talk over and over," says Bob Abel, "and I'd been there only four or five weeks. After every show, you knew what was going to be said in the limousine. He'd be sweating, a towel around his neck, and breathing hard, very nervous. In Jacksonville, I remember he'd cut his finger when a girl from the audience had rushed the stage and grabbed for a ring. The boys fussed over the cut. Elvis didn't care about that. He wanted to know, 'How'd it go?' 'Good show, boss!' they said back to him. And then I caught a moment, I think. He said the people had started coming at him as he left, the security wasn't good enough. He felt he hadn't given a good performance. The guys started talking and Elvis tuned them out and started gazing out the window. It was just a sliver of film out of maybe 100,000 feet of film that we shot, about fifty hours in all, and it was that unguarded moment that I was looking for. He got a faraway look in his eyes. They were going over a bridge. He'd done this hundreds and hundreds and hundreds of times and I wondered what it was like when he was seventeen. When I got back to Hollywood I asked James Burton to do a funky, slowed-down version of 'Don't Be Cruel' for the soundtrack. I grease-penciled the position of Elvis's face on the movieola and sifted through hundreds of old pictures we'd collected until I found the shot that matched, from when he was seventeen. He was on a train, looking out of the window. And I did a match dissolve. The point I wanted to make was that this man had been doing this for seventeen or eighteen years. What loneliness he must've felt!"

Each day the film was flown to Los Angeles for processing, so that a day after the tour was complete, editing could begin. At the same time, a research staff was collecting more photographs from the 1950s, along with early television film, from Steve Allen, Jackie Gléason, and Ed Sullivan, while still others began cutting out all the romantic scenes from Elvis's movies to create a montage of Elvis kissing his leading ladies. Initially, Elvis and the Colonel opposed the use of old pictures. Elvis had worked to remove the anti-establishment stance of his past and this wasn't an image he wished to project, even as part of a historical retrospective. Finally, Jerry Schilling, who'd gone to work for Abel and Adidge as an assistant film editor, went to Elvis and asked him to reconsider. Jerry caught him alone at home, brushing his teeth, and after Jerry made his appeal, Elvis relented.

Another time Jerry went to Elvis, this time with Joe Esposito present, to ask Elvis to let Adidge and Abel do an interview. "What they want to do, Elvis, is get your thoughts about performing and rehearsing and stuff and then use your voice over the pictures and some of the film." Elvis didn't like interviews and it was against the Colonel's policy. Again he relented, however, and the first week of May he and Red, Sonny, Joe, and Charlie Hodge entered a small dressing room at MGM where Pierre and Bob were waiting with a cassette tape recorder.

Afterward, transcripts of the two-hour interview were

guarded like high-level war plans and Adidge was quoted in *Rolling Stone* as saying Jerry Schilling learned more about his boss that afternoon than he had in seven years. Stan Brossette, who worked as Elvis's publicist on many of his MGM movies, said much the same thing. A year after Elvis's death the transcript was still being talked about in whispers and when finally a copy was produced, it was handed over with the strongest plea to keep the source unknown.

One wonders why. Though it may be the longest and most helpful interview Elvis ever gave, there were no big surprises and only a little new information. He remembered singing when he was only two years old, he said, and he reminisced about the talent shows he entered as a youngster, remembering that one of the songs he sang was Teresa Brewer's "Till I Waltz Again with You." Asked about his musical influences, he ignored the most obvious blues and country sounds and named, instead, Mario Lanza.

Slowly, haltingly, and simply, with only a few of the usual self-deprecating jokes that punctuated his press conferences, Elvis took his rapt listeners through his life. He said he was kicked off the high school football team because of his sideburns and honestly didn't know why the girls screamed the first time he shook his legs. He said he was driving a truck and waiting for his girlfriend to finish high school so they could get married when he got the call from Sun Records, in 1954.

At this point, Jerry Schilling asked, "What did your dad say about a guy who played a guitar . . . ?"

Elvis smiled. "My daddy had seen a lot of people who played guitars and stuff and didn't work, so he said, 'You should make up your mind—either about being an electrician or playing a guitar. I never saw a guitar player that was worth a damn.' "

Elvis talked about the army years when, he said, he finally was treated "normally," although he had to resist some pressure to perform, and he talked about how the movies that followed were so uninspiring they sometimes made him physically ill. He was glad, he said, to be performing in front of audiences again.

"A funny thing happened to me about a year ago," Elvis said. "Joe was showing me how to get up on stage and it was at intermission and the lights were still on and I looked out and saw the crowd of people and I got weak in the knees, you know, all of a sudden it just scared me, 'cause I'm used to going out when the lights are down. So I've never gotten over what they call stage fright. I go through it every show."

Never was anything controversial said. Even the questions were friendly, almost patronizing. The good-guy image held, the modesty seemed real, unshakable.

February, 1972–
June, 1972

Life wasn't all smooth. Elvis may have given a relaxed and reflective interview and between sellout concerts occasionally he may have found himself face-down between someone's thighs—as he so bluntly phrased it for Pierre Adidge—but in between all of that, he remained depressed about the formal and final split with Priscilla.

"For six months after Priscilla left, he wouldn't allow our wives or girlfriends around," says T. G. Sheppard, the country singer then working as a promotion man for RCA. "I was going by my real name, Bill Browder, then. I went to work for RCA in Memphis; I was their promotion manager and if you're a promotion man and you have an artist in your area, you're there to assist that artist with anything he may need as far as business is concerned. Far as RCA was concerned, if Elvis wanted anything, I had to pick up the phone and call RCA. And if Elvis wanted me to go somewhere with him and I'd say, 'I can't, I have to go to work tomorrow,' he'd say, 'Hey, wait a minute, I *am* RCA!' If he said go, I'd go. Over the years, we got close. I remember, after Priscilla moved out, we'd get calls from Charlie Hodge to tell us that Elvis was wanting some company up to the house, at Graceland. Because I was married to Diana and I knew Elvis liked her and all,

I'd ask Charlie, 'Do we bring'the wives?' And Charlie always said, 'No, no women.' "

According to Becky Yancey, then a secretary at Graceland, "He tried to be cheerful during those days and occasionally he stopped in the office to talk. Now and then he warned us to watch out, because he was a swinging bachelor again. But he didn't fool us. He was terribly hurt. . . ."

T. G. Sheppard agrees: "I saw so many hours of sadness and hurt and bewilderment, as to life in general, as to maybe what was happening to him. When the marriage failed, it was such a damaging blow. Here's a man who was brought up in a southern, Christian environment, where marriage was labeled forever. It was very special. You got married, you had kids and you grew old together. Divorce didn't happen. Marriage was very sacred. I think when that failed, it was a turning point in his life. Things seemed to change. It never was the same. The health problems came, the problems that didn't seem to appear before. Seemed like life became more difficult. It didn't flow like it did before.

"After a while, he began to let the girlfriends and wives come back. He talked about his marriage a lot to my wife and myself. He'd say, 'I don't want you two to ever split up.' And his voice would crack sometimes. I could see he was hurtin'. And this wasn't just after she moved out, it was years later too, after I'd started singing. He'd say, 'Bill, you don't know what's in store for you. . . .' "

"What do you mean, Elvis?"

"You gone be successful and it's gone be tough on your marriage. Always remember, if you leave your home and walk away from that door and that woman is smiling, it can make your day or your night real easy. But if you walk away and she's unhappy, it can make it very miserable. So always take that extra few minutes to leave your home in order. Take the time with your wife. Don't take her for granted."

T. G. says today, "He always preached to my wife and me the importance of staying together and working things out, never divorcin' because of the music industry. He would turn to Diana and say, 'Try to understand what he'll be goin' through. Stay with him, because he's gonna need you.' Then he would always slide over into religion or go in another direction. You could see he was gettin' so deep into it, he'd have to shrug it off and go in another direction. And we had this conversation often."

T. G. was not alone. Others agreed with his assessment. "After he and 'Cilla split up, he lost control," says Dee Presley, his stepmother from soon after his army days until she and Vernon separated in 1974. Almost to a man, Elvis's hired hands now say the same thing. "It was as if he took the third strike," says one. "His twin brother died at birth—that was strike one. Then his mama died—that was strike two. Number three was Priscilla divorcin' him."

The songs he sang showed the same melancholy. One he had included on the tour—the first featured in the documentary, in fact—was one that would be released as a single. "Separate Ways" was written by his close friend and bodyguard, Red West, and it probably seemed the most autobiographical of his career (although written before the split-up).

Songs like this and "You Gave Me a Mountain This Time" and others that followed in the next year or so represented a significant departure for Elvis. In the past, very little of the personal side of Elvis showed through in the material he selected for performance and recording. In the 1950s they were, with rare exception, predictably macho ("Baby, Let's Play House," "Hound Dog," "Treat Me Nice") or reflected what then was called teenaged lovesickness ("Dont Be Cruel," "Love Me Tender," "Wear My Ring Around Your Neck"). Then in the 1960s they became as bland as the movies most of them were recorded for.

Now in the 1970s, following his separation from Priscilla, Elvis was taking an inward look, so once again the texture and tone of his songs took a turn. There were critics who said Elvis never really showed his soul except in his gospel songs. That may have been true in the early years. In the final years, Elvis was hurting and he didn't seem to care who knew it.

This didn't go unnoticed by the Colonel. While touring, he and Elvis saw each other daily, even if only for a few minutes at the airport and then again just before beginning the evening show. (The Colonel then flew on to the next city to begin advance work for the following day's concert.) Between tours, they communicated less frequently and usually by telephone. Sometimes they talked directly, other times it was through the Colonel's lieutenant, Tom Diskin, and Elvis's man Friday, Joe Esposito. In this way, the news that another one of Elvis's records had been certified a million-seller sometimes reached Elvis after it first had been passed from the Colonel to Diskin and finally to Esposito.

This didn't mean the Colonel didn't know what was going on. If he didn't get it directly from Elvis, or Joe Esposito, or Vernon, there was always someone else. "I kept him up on a lot of things," says Ed Hookstratton, Elvis's attorney in Beverly Hills, who handled almost all of his personal matters, including the patrimony suit in 1970 and then the divorce. "I made regular reports."

Sometimes it seemed as if the Colonel were anticipating the command, predicting his boy's needs, and preparing for them. He may not have spent much actual time with Elvis, but the Colonel believed he knew him well. He saw the way Elvis got bored—and then fat—first in the movies and then in Las Vegas, so he conjured up new challenges to keep Elvis excited, exciting, and slim.

It had almost worked for the *On Tour* film. Elvis ate voluminously and compulsively in the weeks after Vegas, then crash-dieted to look good for the MGM cameras. This was a pattern that had started many years earlier, in Hollywood, when he worried about how he looked on the movie screen. "He was overweight and pale on the tour," says Bob Abel. "We lighted him carefully. We used a lot of flesh tones. We used reds and ambers and golds and things like that to try to give him better color. We used camera angles and lighting tricks that would make him look better. He'd taken off a little bit of weight, but he was paunchy and he looked bloated. So we tried as much as we could."

The Colonel had another challenge planned: the most prestigious hall of all in a city Elvis had never played in his life, Madison Square Garden in New York, the first stop on the spring (1972) tour. If Elvis said stage fright was part of every concert on the road, the series of four shows the Colonel scheduled in two days in Manhattan had him downright scared. This was where all the journalists and critics and editorial writers who'd attacked him in the 1950s worked. Friends say Elvis was certain they'd tear him apart again.

"He really wanted to be accepted by everybody," says Jerry Schilling, who was on the tour. "It stemmed back to the early days when he wasn't. He always tried to make up for that, he tried to set that right."

He needn't have worried. New York was waiting for him not with animosity, but affection. In 1972 a nostalgia craze was forming. The media were developing and exploiting an interest in 1950s' American kitsch, and many thought Elvis was a prime subject.

Elvis sweated and worried and dieted and exercised and took a big handful of diet pills every day for nearly a week before opening the tour June 9, so he looked pretty good. Not great—he still was overweight, his eyes were heavily lidded and there were bags underneath. Still, his mood was light and the press conference was as smooth—and bland—as grits. Elvis was the master of the Nothing Rock and Roll Press Conference, saying nothing, doing nothing, grabbing headlines anyway. It was a style he had perfected in the 1950s, a style the Beatles used later for *their* meetings with the press: cotton candy "news."

Elvis, why have you waited so long to come to New York?

"Well sir, we had trouble finding a good building. And once we found one, we had to wait our turn."

Mr. Presley, why have you outlasted all your competition?

"I take a lot of vitamin E. No, actually, honey, I suppose I've just been very fortunate."

Elvis, are you satisfied with your image?

"Well sir, it's very hard to live up to an image."

You seem to have less grease in your hair these days.

"Yes sir, I've stopped using that greasy kid stuff."

Elvis, we're told that deep down you're really very shy and humble.

"What do you mean shy?" Elvis said, grinning widely and standing up to pull back the folds of his powder-blue jacket to reveal his $10,000 gold belt buckle, a gift from the Las Vegas Hilton. It was a moment of braggadocio that captured his boyishness perfectly, and Bob Abel decided to use the scene in the *On Tour* documentary for just that reason.

Pretty soon after that the Colonel jumped onto the stage and said, "I'd like to live up to my reputation of being a nice guy. This is it, folks."

With that, Elvis and his father, who had sat next to him through the affair, were whisked away.

The first show was the most difficult—because it was the first, also because it was the first time that an audience turned against Elvis's friend, comedian Jackie Kahane.

"To begin with, his material was no good," said columnist Chris Chase in the *New York Times* a week later. "And when the audience began to turn on him, he whined. The rhythmic clapping began in the middle of one of his lousier jokes, and at first the comic didn't understand, or acted as though he didn't understand. 'Whatza matter? You can't hear?' he cried, and grabbed another microphone.

"Ah, but we could hear; that was the trouble. He tried to settle the crowd down. 'All right, friends, I'm gonna be here a few minutes . . .' But the catcalls and boos were building, along with shouts of 'We want Elvis!' and the comic shared his self-pity with the audience. 'You are 20,000, I am one . . . that's pretty rough odds.' Nobody cared. They howled until he gave up. 'You win,' he said, quitting the stage."

Backstage, when Elvis was told what had happened, he was furious. "Fuck 'em!" he barked. "Just plain fuck 'em! If they can't be polite, I'm not gonna sing for 'em."

Elvis was pacing nervously. His bodyguards were upset, running in several directions, seeking the Colonel. Finally the Colonel appeared and calmed Elvis down.

"At 9:15, Elvis appeared, *materialized,* in a white suit of lights, shining with golden appliqués, the shirt front slashed to show his chest," the *Times* reviewer wrote. "Around his shoulders was a cape lined in cloth of gold, its collar faced with scarlet. It was anything you wanted to call it, gaudy, vulgar, magnificent. . . ."

This—from the *New York Times,* mind you—was typical. "A stone gas," said *Billboard*'s writer. "Elvis has nothing really to do with time. To our everlasting love and envy, he has transcended the exasperating constrictions of time and place." "Pure entertainment," said *Cashbox,* the other music business weekly; while *Variety,* the "bible" of show business, said, "Presley is now a highly polished, perfectly timed, spectacularly successful show business machine. He performed about 20 numbers with supreme confidence in routines which were better constructed and choreographed than the terping of most Broadway musicals."

The Lively Arts writer for *New York* magazine went

farther out on the same limb: "The performance he gave us was a spectacular triumph of insight into the mind of our mindless era. No demagogue of fact or legend has ever seen more keenly into the blackest depths of his followers, or grasped them in so many ways. He knows what ails and uplifts us, he rubs each of our dirtiest little secrets until it shines brightly in the dark, hollow arena of our souls."

One wonders what Elvis could have thought if he had read such analysis. Chances are, he didn't see it. As such stuff was being written in New York, Elvis was back on the road moving from the Garden into the humid, summer gray Midwest, with shows in Fort Wayne, Evansville, Milwaukee, Chicago, Fort Worth, Wichita, and Tulsa.

In RCA's offices in New York and Los Angeles, meanwhile, dozens were readying the release of an album that Elvis didn't even know about. The decision to record some of the Garden shows was made less than a week earlier. "I don't know why Elvis wasn't told," says Joan Deary of RCA. "Maybe they thought it would make him nervous."

Like many others on the Presley team, Joan had been around for a long, long time. In 1954, she was secretary to RCA's Steve Sholes, the brilliant record producer and talent scout who authorized payment of $35,000, then an astronomical sum, to buy Elvis from Sun Records. In 1972, she was an assistant to Harry Jenkins, the RCA vice-president "in charge of Elvis Presley." That meant the Colonel was one of Harry's primary friends and associates. It also meant that Joan Deary was part of the RCA Presley fire squad.

"We recorded two of the shows," Joan says. "The first was a dry run. The second was what we put out. We recorded on Saturday and Sunday. You never knew with Elvis what order anything was coming in. It was spontaneous. You'd have a list of songs that he thought he would use, a list he prepared for each show and sent down a few minutes before he went on——Charlie Hodge would bring the list to the guys in the band and the orchestra.

"We started mixing on Monday and decided to produce the record without any 'bands' or silent space between the songs. We knew that would make the disc jockeys mad, because they couldn't cue up to the beginning of any song, but we didn't have a choice. We'd have had to drop the level and we wanted to keep it up for the excitement. A week later we mixed another version for the radio stations, banding it.

"On Monday night we approved the lacquers and they were shipped to the plants so we could begin pressing records on Tuesday. We were in the stores on Wednesday. We went from actual concert onto the street in under three days. I don't think anyone's topped that yet. Everybody just dropped whatever else they were doing and we just sailed."

For the four New York shows, Elvis grossed $730,000 and the album sold the by-now predictable million-plus copies at six dollars apiece. Elvis got to keep about a third of the concert money and a sixth of the record take. That eventually came to about $1.2 million for six hours of singing.

1971–1972

The Colonel had set up a month-on, month-off schedule in 1972—Vegas in February, tours in April and June, back to Nevada in August, the final tour of the year in November. It was a schedule designed to get the most from Elvis, without taxing him. Even so, Elvis usually played as hard as he worked.

Following the April tour, for instance, he took a bunch of his boys and went to Hawaii to watch a karate demonstration, and a few days before the Fourth of July he took some of the same guys over the Tennessee-Mississippi border to buy $500 worth of firecrackers and roman candles for a reenactment of his New Year's backyard shootout.

"He liked to watch movies," says T. G. Sheppard, "and he'd watch the same ones over and over again. Sometimes he stopped the film and had 'em run it back to a particular scene and watch that scene all over again. Sometimes we watched the same scene five or six times in a row."

"Other times," says Diana Sheppard, "he'd run a movie thirty minutes and if he didn't like it, he'd turn it off and you might like it, it didn't matter, that was it. You were left hanging."

"There were lots of movies I never got to see the end of," says T. G. "And sometimes people'd fall asleep. After all, it was the middle of the night, maybe even getting on to breakfast time. Diana'd fall asleep. And George Klein would too, but he'd snore and get caught. Others would do the same and Elvis would get on 'em. He'd say, 'Who's asleep? Who's sleeping? Charlie! Find out who's sleeping and wake that sucker up!' "

In assembling a picture of The King at play, the images loom big and bright, like the garish rings and buckles he wore. Lowell Hays, a Memphis jeweler who sold Elvis nearly a million dollars' worth of "sparklers" (as Elvis called them), remembers when they first met. It was two in the morning, Lowell says, and Elvis was wearing a full-length ranch mink coat and kneeling in the mud behind Graceland, banging away with a .45 caliber pistol at a target pinned to the side of his father's office.

Elvis *liked* guns, really liked them. Living on Audubon Drive in Memphis back in 1956 after his first records hit and before he bought Graceland, Elvis broke a thousand pop bottles with an air rifle. In Hollywood some years later, whiling away time between movies, he and his hired hands fired at flashbulbs floating in the swimming pool; they not only exploded, they flared into light, making this a popular nighttime stunt. Nowadays, Elvis always carried a derringer in his boot, or in the pocket of his robe, and liked nothing better than to shoot out the front of television sets when he didn't like the programming; Robert Goulet was shot more than once—Elvis *hated* Goulet.

Personal paranoia explained part of his fascination with guns. In an era of growing terrorist violence, airplane skyjacking, and political assassination, much of the Third World and all of the modern West was becoming paranoiac. Everywhere one looked there were plots and threats and conspiracies. Elvis had experienced his share of them.

More than that though, for Elvis, guns were toys. When he became an excellent shot, it wasn't because he was in training, but because he enjoyed shooting guns and insisted upon being good at anything he enjoyed.

Thus he drove motorcycles and automobiles well, and got so he could stand up in the front car of the roller coaster and go the full ride without holding on. He may have held the unofficial world's record for the number of cheeseburgers consumed at one sitting. When he got into pills, and religions, he knew all there was to know about them, too.

Elvis was the ultimate expert. He bought (and gave away) more cars and took more drugs and hired more bodyguards and sang more songs and entertained more girls and collected more awards (and badges) than anyone.

"He was really into the police," says John O'Grady, the private detective who still works occasionally for Elvis's attorney. "He'd watch stories on TV about police officers being injured or killed and he'd give me money to take to them. One time he called up Kelly Lang, the newsgirl at NBC in Burbank, when she reported on one of these stories, and he had her take money to the policeman's wife.

"When he wanted to know about something, he'd go to experts. I explained the penal codes over and over, until he understood them. He really liked the idea of being a police officer. I think he could have been happy at that, except for one thing. I remember him asking me once what kind of salary a policeman made. I told him what I made as a sergeant in Hollywood. He laughed. He said, 'Christ, that wouldn't pay my water bill.' "

During his days as a movie star in Hollywood, it was one movie after another—often as many as three in a year—and now the bursts of personal appearances were coming at the same or greater frequency. And as was true in the Hollywood period, when each movie had its soundtrack album, now the engagements in Las Vegas and Madison Square Garden and on the road in the South were being recorded for "live" release. As before, these on-the-road and in-performance recordings did well in the marketplace. Individually the albums and singles rarely appeared in the top ten of the bestseller charts, but many sold a million anyway, because once Elvis released an album, no matter how shallow or repetitious the material, it stayed in the record stores for longer than most others. Elvis had what is called, in the retail business, a "long shelf life." Go into a record store today and you will be able to buy more of Elvis's records than any other artist in the history of recording. Even many of the worst movie soundtracks are still selling well enough to make all that display and warehouse space profitable.

As ever, he was prolific, too. Where most artists are generally pleased to release two albums and two singles a year, Elvis and RCA managed to release more than double that. This was true throughout his career. Once in the 1950s, the Colonel had convinced RCA to release seven singles simultaneously, a stunt he repeated more than once in the 1970s. It seemed impossible to saturate the market.

And so it was now, in Elvis's eighteenth year as a recording star. New records appeared with the predictability and frequency of holidays—usually with the same kind of hoopla and noise.

In 1971 there were seven album releases, one of them a four-record set. A year earlier RCA had repackaged fifty of Elvis's best-known songs, calling it *Elvis: Worldwide 50 Gold Award Hits, Volume I*. The boxed set—it came with a picture book—rose to the number 45 position on *Billboard* magazine's "Hot LP" chart and remained on best-selling charts for almost six months. So, in 1971 RCA marketed another four-record package of old songs, the flip sides of the previously rereleased million-selling hits. This was *Elvis: The*

Other Sides, Worldwide 50 Gold Award Hits, Volume II, and it, too, sold well, despite its $20 price tag.

The other albums released in 1971 offered more substance. The first was *Elvis Country,* drawing its repertoire of songs mostly from the 1950s and 1960s country charts, hits by Billy Walker ("Funny How Time Slips Away"), Stonewall Jackson ("I Washed My Hands in Muddy Water"). Patsy Cline ("Faded Love"), Jack Greene ("There Goes My Everything"), and Eddy Arnold ("I Really Don't Want to Know" and "Make the World Go Away").

Paying visual tribute to his country roots, the album cover showed a picture of Elvis at the age of two, the perfect 1930s southern urchin, wearing a lopsided hat and grin. Inside was the rest of the period piece, the same corduroy bib overalls and soft brown eyes, now with his parents next to him. His mother, Gladys, a young, attractive sewing-machine operator who took in the wash on weekends in a tiny shotgun-style house on the wrong side of the tracks, stared into the camera as if in a trance, her expression as lifeless as her print dress. Her husband, Elvis's father, Vernon, matching her hypnotized stare, wore a blue workshirt and a worn fedora pushed back on his head. On both sides of the album sleeve were the words—in quotes—"I'm 10,000 Years Old." This was a song Elvis had recorded and asked to have cut into bits and pieces and inserted between all the other tracks on the album. It contributed nothing artistically to the album, but Elvis wanted the people to know where he felt he was sometimes. Many of Elvis's friends say this is the way he often felt, that this is the way Elvis chose to share that feeling with others.

The other albums released in 1971 were a disparate and generally undistinguished lot, including *The Wonderful World of Christmas,* comprised of the holiday songs recorded earlier in the year, and four collections of nine or ten songs apiece, stitched together from the recent and distant past. Three of these—*You'll Never Walk Alone, C'mon Everybody,* and *I Got Lucky*—were released on the budget Camden label, a subsidiary of RCA. The final—seventh—was called *Love Letters from Elvis* and was the only one offering new material, and with the exception of one or two cuts (such as "Got My Mojo Working") it, too, left much to be desired. It didn't matter. They all went onto the best-selling album charts.

Three of the five albums released in 1972 were little better, seemed held together with the weakest mucilage and defying ordinary reasoning. Released on Camden, for example, was something called *Burning Love and Hits from His Movies, Volume 2.* The title of the album said it all. "Burning Love" was Elvis's first gold record in more than two years and his best rock and roll performance in probably ten. Most artists would have included this song—it went to the number 2 spot in the late summer of 1972—on an album of recent material. Not Elvis. If you wanted "Burning Love" on an album, you had to buy it as part of a hodgepodge of forgettable songs like "Guadalajara" and "Santa Lucia." These performances were turkeys like "When the Saints Go Marching In" and "Old MacDonald," which were included in *Elvis Sings Hits from His Movies, Volume 1,* released by Camden the same year. One wondered why the Colonel, who orchestrated these albums, did it. Was the answer to that question in the sales report? Both albums hit the bestseller charts. The one with "Burning Love" went up to number 22 and remained on the list for six months. Perhaps this is the only way Colonel Parker could've slipped so many turkeys back onto the marketplace and not only get away with it, but make money on it, too.

One could ask many questions. The "greatest movie hit" idea was valid and with more than thirty musicals behind him, Elvis had a lot of good material to draw from. One wondered, then, why the dogs were dragged out of the closet instead of songs like "Love Me Tender," "Hard-Headed Woman" (from *King Creole*), "Blue Hawaii," and "Jailhouse Rock"? With very little effort an excellent package of recycled songs could've been created. Why, then, these duds?

At the time, John Wasserman pointed a finger of accusation at the Colonel in his column in the *San Francisco Chronicle:* "On the back cover of the album *(Elvis Now)* is 'Elvis—Now—Now,' which is almost the trademark of Colonel Tom Parker, his manager. Remember '50 Girls 50' at the vaudeville shows? Well, that's where the good Colonel's head is still at. He was a carny barker once, and a good one. He is still a carny barker but Presley is not the bearded lady, I sincerely hope."

One does not argue esthetics with an accountant, however. At RCA it was noticed that the albums all sold well. That meant they were successful albums. And that's what the recording business was, in 1972, all about.

Elvis never objected. He may have been handed a lot of bad material over the years, but he had final say about which songs he recorded, while the Colonel took care of packaging and marketing. That was their agreement.

Lest all this make Elvis's early 1970s album production sound dismal, or worse, keep in mind that there were highs to match the lows. "Burning Love" *was* an exciting single release, sung somewhat in the Vegas/ Tom Jones style—Elvis liked Jones—and worthy of the sales success it got. A gospel album, named for the song "He Touched Me," took many of its arrangements from previously recorded albums by the Imperials and was recorded when that quartet backed him up in performance; it went on to win a Grammy Award—Elvis's first, and only—for best gospel album of the year. And an hour of Elvis live from Madison Square Garden was another natural for the Colonel's excitation machine, and Elvis's performance came across well on the record as well as in concert.

"This is a damn fine record, friend, and you're going to like it whether you like it or not," said Bob Palmer in *Rolling Stone*. "There's Wagnerian bombast, plenty of your favorite songs, some jukebox music and some Las Vegas lounge music. There's even some old fashioned rock 'n' roll. And most of all there's lots of Elvis, doing what he does best, strutting his stuff before his adoring fans." Elvis had come through superstardom, Palmer said, "without forgetting what it means to rock, that's the important thing. Now I personally feel that he could save a lot of money and tighten up his act by firing his orchestra and making do with a couple of tympanists and the Memphis Horns, and if he just did stuff like 'Polk Salad Annie' and 'That's All Right' and forgot about Las Vegas for a while, I'd like that too. But there's lots of people rocking and rolling to Elvis who wouldn't be caught dead at a Faces or a Stones concert, people who don't know the difference between Sun Records and Sun Ra, but who will be more than happy to tell you what they like. And what *they* like is remembering sock hops and looking forward to that big Vegas vacation. So everybody gets enough of what they want to get what they need."

Another top critic, Bob Christgau, writing in Long Island's leading newspaper, *Newsday*, was inspired by the same Manhattan concerts and made much the same point. Elvis didn't do it alone in Madison Square Garden, ". . . he was working in concert with all of my brothers and sisters in the audience. Of course, under most circumstances those people wouldn't have felt like my brothers and sisters at all. Some of them had probably threatened to beat me up in high school, and I would certainly never attend a reunion with them. So Elvis's genius was—he enticed me into communion with people whose values were very unlike my own."

How many other entertainers could do that?

Like any performer. Elvis wanted to know what others thought of him but after being criticized so severely and universally in the 1950s, he generally stopped reading newspapers and popular magazines. Nor did he subscribe to any publications, except for hot rod and karate magazines He watched television, of course, but the only times that medium regarded him was for causing another crowd of ladies in beehive hairdos to scream and wet their pants, or for giving away another Cadillac, not for the way he sang.

On top of that the bad reviews that began to come in 1972 the hired hands kept away from their boss as best they could while many of the good ones, like Palmer's and Christgau's were so intellectual they really didn't know what to make of them. The result was Elvis saw mostly the stories reviewing his presence, his image, rather than his performance.

For Elvis in the 1970s, critical feedback was almost nonexistent.

In a way, it was as if Elvis were in quarantine, as if he were the modern equivalent of literature's "man in the iron mask." a sort of opposite bookend to another famous Las Vegas recluse. Howard Hughes. The time spent locked away in a heavily guarded penthouse suite, the whispered stories of his appetite for sex and drugs and guns the eccentric generosity, all this came together to give Elvis a mythic persona almost equal to that of Hughes. In fact, his persona was perhaps stronger. By going on the road and singing in Las Vegas and Lake Tahoe Elvis gave his public a peek, leaving them wanting more It was almost magical; now you see it, now you don't Hughes, on the other hand, never gave his curious public anything but rumor.

It was inevitable that forces would be put into motion for Elvis and Howard Hughes to meet, and it was Elvis who started the big ball rolling. On a whim one day, after thinking about it off and on for a year or so, he asked one of his boys to call Hughes at the Desert Inn and request a meeting. (The meeting never advanced any further than Elvis's man talking to Howard's man.)

In August 1972, Elvis returned to Las Vegas. Each night before he did his noisy dinner show, Elvis met with the Colonel, who told him if there'd be any celebrities in the audience and then passed along the day's news. On August 4, for example, the day Elvis opened, the Record Industry Association of America announced that retail sales of Elvis's Madison Square Garden album had passed the million-dollar mark. Elvis was presented with a gold record. Pictures were taken.

On another night the news passed along to Elvis was not festive. This was on August 18, halfway through the engagement, when he was told that earlier that day his attorney in Beverly Hills, Ed Hookstratton, had appeared in Santa Monica divorce court. The lawsuit filed was typical for the time; the male (Elvis) was doing the suing, claiming "irreconcilable differences," a standard California catch-all of the time, and Priscilla got custody of Lisa, who was then four years old. When the Colonel passed along this news, alone with Elvis in his dressing room—having dismissed the bodyguards —Elvis merely nodded.

On still another night, the news was cause for celebration. This was just before closing, when Elvis was given a copy of a press release that would be issued by RCA the following day, September 4. In just over 200 words, RCA was announcing what represented the fruition of a year-long dream of the Colonel's, a milestone in entertainment, and what would later come to be regarded as Elvis's most memorable performance. This was "the Aloha satellite show," an hour-long concert to be televised in Honolulu in January and broadcast by Globcom's satellite around the world.

As usual, the Colonel was leaving nothing out. The way he planned it, and described it to Elvis backstage, the show would be televised at 1 A.M. local Hawaiian time to allow the live performance to be viewed in prime time in Australia. Japan, Korea, New Zealand, the Philippines, Thailand and South Vietnam. The following night the show would be shown in twenty-eight European countries via a Eurovision simulcast, and NBC-TV would show the concert in the United States still later. Ultimately, this concert would be seen by an estimated one-and-a-half billion people.

That wasn't all. Within days of the concert, RCA expected to release a two-record album simultaneously throughout the world.

Elvis finished reading the press release and handed it back to the Colonel. This time he smiled.

September, 1972–
January, 1973

Obviously, the Colonel and others had been at work for some time, booking the 8,500-seat Honolulu International Center, getting NBC-TV's agreement to pay much of the production cost in exchange for the right to broadcast the concert twice, getting RCA to provide further backing and agree to release the two-record set practically overnight.

As the Colonel and his staff supervised the setting of details for the show, and incidentally began planning a November tour, Elvis's health and habits went downhill again. Years later, three of his bodyguards would write a book that emphasized the darker side, *Elvis: What Happened?* The singer's separation from Priscilla and the subsequent divorce action, they said, resulted in a "yo-yo" pattern of behavior.

"Man, we were going through tough times," said Sonny West. "Elvis's diet was going mad. He would eat whole gigantic cakes all by himself. He would get mad at us after he ate the stuff, and if we hid it from him he would get mad again."

Elvis's diet had never been good. That is, at best he preferred the simple things—meat and potatoes, and never anything fancy. Occasionally, Jerry Schilling's devotion to "health foods" would rub off on Elvis, or Elvis would go on a yogurt kick. But generally he ate sweets and starch—hamburgers by the stack, ice cream by the half gallon. bacon a pound at a time, a dozen deviled eggs, bags and bags of potato chips.

"When Elvis was troubled." Ed Parker wrote in his book, *Inside Elvis,* "all of his resolve would fly out of the window. Without consciously realizing what he was doing he would consume cheeseburgers, french fries, pizzas, ice cream. popsicles by the box, banana and peanut butter sandwiches. Pepsi-Cola and a stomach-wrenching assortment of junk foods. It was as though he were trying to comfort the spirit within by stroking it with food."

As Elvis's bodyweight increased, as his moods swung wildly, in Los Angeles the Presley machine ground feverishly on. The Colonel received weekly reports from Memphis, when Joe Esposito called. By now, he'd learned to read between Joe's lines, as Joe always said Elvis was fine, "No problems. Colonel. . . ." The Colonel, and others at RCA and in the Colonel's office, knew what that meant. They also knew that Elvis always rose to a challenge and if an audience of more than a billion wasn't a challenge, what was?

In offices at RCA. artwork was being readied for the album and time was being reserved at the pressing plant; initial reports indicated that orders for the record would go well past the one-million album mark. Across town, in the Colonel's circus of offices at MGM, his staff was hammering out final details of the tour schedule that would climax in Honolulu November 18, when Elvis would hold a press conference personally announcing details of the satellite show The Colonel also was on the phone daily to NBC-TV in New York, talking to Bob Sarnoff, the network president, about who would produce and direct the show.

"Now, Bob," the Colonel would say, "mah boy deserves the very best in the business, not just the best at NBC. . . ."

The one suggested by Sarnoff was Marty Pasetta, a

Californian then in his late forties whose forte was the entertainment special. An independent who didn't work for any network, he had a forceful personality and a proven ability to juggle many complicated details simultaneously, a claim backed up by his directing the Emmy, Grammy, and Oscar shows for television. He also had produced and directed five Don Ho specials in Hawaii, so he knew the islands fairly well.

"The way I got it," Marty says now, "Elvis had liked the first NBC show, the one he did in 1968, but he wasn't knocked out by all the production. He wanted the pure sense of a concert. NBC called me and I went to look at Elvis in performance in Long Beach. I expected to see a gyrating person moving all over the stage. He was far from that. He was staged, quiet. In fact, I was wondering how I was going to make an hour-and-a-half show sustain without anybody else on it with what I saw. I went back to discuss it with NBC and they said, 'You're on your own—discuss it with the Colonel.' "

Elvis had lost some weight for the tour, but not much. His face and torso were still bloated, his movement on stage sluggish, as Pasetta noted. The performances also were, for Elvis, short—lasting just under an hour in Oakland, for example, which is longer than most top-name performers were staying on stage, but represented considerably less than what Elvis gave his audiences when he felt and looked better.

The tour was one of Elvis's easiest, with short flights to Tucson, El Paso, and Oakland, and after that, leisurely drives from his Los Angeles home to the big auditoriums in nearby San Bernardino and Long Beach. The tour group then took a full day to travel to Hawaii and settle into—and throughout—the thirtieth floor of the Hilton Hawaiian Village on the sands at Waikiki. The press conference, Elvis's fourth in a dozen years, was held in one of the hotel ballrooms the day after his second Honolulu concert.

Elvis sat behind a mass of microphones, wearing a black corduroy suit and white shirt, silver-trimmed sunglasses, and a coral and turquoise necklace. He seemed rested, agreeable, at ease, and in control.

"Uhhh . . . we'd like to . . . that is, we'd like to announce that it's our great pleasure," he began "to do the satellite show as a benefit for the Kui Lee Cancer Fund. . . ."

Elvis never faced a more receptive press. In Hawaii, Elvis was practically worshipped, for the island state owed him much. In 1961 he had given a benefit performance—his last before retiring from the stage to make movies—for a memorial to the USS *Arizona*, the battleship sunk in Pearl Harbor in 1941; the money he raised made the memorial possible. He also had made two films about Hawaii, *Blue Hawaii* and *Paradise, Hawaiian Style*, which had done much to foster tourism and promote Hawaiian music. So popular was he that a third performance was scheduled to accommodate ticket demand; considering the limited population of the state, this was highly flattering. And now to have selected the Kui Lee Cancer Fund . . . well, no one could have picked a better cause. Kui Lee was a revered Hawaiian singer and composer who'd died of cancer in 1966, when he was only thirty-four. In all three of his concert performances Elvis sang Kui Lee's best-known song, "I'll Remember You."

Seated near Elvis was Rocco Laginestra, the president of RCA. He told everyone that because the January satellite show was being broadcast, admission couldn't be charged. However, he said, there was nothing to stop anyone from making a contribution to the Kui Lee Cancer Fund on the way in. "Our goal is $25,000," he said, "and Elvis wants to put in the first thousand. He's already written his check. . . ."

After this the questions were so mild as to cause wonder about the reporters' credentials. (In fact, many were representing their high school newspapers—and the Colonel honored them all.)

"What about marriage in the future?"

"Uh . . . I haven't thought about it. I have a little girl, four years old. It's hard to put the two, marriage and the career, together."

"Are you a religious person, Elvis?"

"It's played a major role in my life, gospel music. I like it. We often go into our suite and sing all night."

"How do you account for your success after seventeen years?"

Elvis laughed: "A lot of praying, sir."

Once again Elvis had pulled it off, appearing somewhat jowly, but otherwise untouched by time, still the southern gentleman, still generous, still boyishly innocent and ebullient.

After seeing Elvis in the Long Beach Arena, Marty Pasetta took a few sketches of stage design to the Colonel and said he wanted to build some excitement into the show. "I wanted to put a ramp in, I wanted to lower the stage, I wanted to get closer to the fans and the people, I wanted to generate excitement, so they could get to him," Pasetta says. "And the Colonel said no, no, no to everything. Finally he said, 'Well, you take it up with Elvis.' I said, 'Okay, I'll take my shot and go.' "

Elvis was vacationing in Las Vegas in October when Pasetta first met him. He went upstairs to Elvis's suite alone and Elvis was flanked by Sonny and Red and one other. As the producer sat down, the three took out silver-plated pistols and laid them down on the table. Pasetta was visibly shaken, but plunged ahead: "I saw your show in Long Beach and I didn't think it was that exciting . . ."

The three bodyguards sat forward in their chairs and Elvis just stared at Pasetta.

". . . but," Pasetta continued, literally sweating now, "I've got a lot of ideas about how to make it an exceptionally exciting television show. . . ."

Elvis was amused by the producer's forwardness, and he began to laugh. They spent the next four hours talking and when Pasetta left, it was with Elvis's arm draped casually over his shoulder.

"Y'know," Elvis said, "this is the first time I've ever sat with a producer for longer than a half hour. Normally they come in and talk to me and they're out."

Says Pasetta today, "I felt I had to be honest in front or it wouldn't work. He understood what I was going for. I said, 'You're overweight, you've got to lose weight. . . .'"

Elvis went home to Memphis after that and started "taking care of business," a phrase that was his motto and that was hanging around the necks of so many of his friends and associates. These gold pendants carried the symbol of a lightning bolt and the letters TCB, which meant do it right and do it now.

Elvis was genuinely excited by the satellite challenge and once he was back behind the Graceland gates he began to exercise and diet like a man possessed. He increased the frequency of his karate workouts, often with Kang Rhee, his karate instructor since early in 1970. "Master Rhee," as Elvis unfailingly addressed him, was one of those recurring figures in Elvis's life to whom he turned for spiritual sustenance.

An immigrant from Korea, the fortyish instructor spoke in the uncertain manner of those still learning a new language, but his meaning was always clear. "My school in Memphis basically about self-refine, self-reform, and self-respect. Not trying to raise champion, but help the weak and to build confidence, to make better human beings. I'm teaching here as an art, in the traditional manner. Anybody can fit this training. Some institutes, they emphasize power, breaking concrete blocks. Very, very few people can do this kind of power. Seems to me karate has to be, as long as they respect themselves, as long as they get better, that's what we try to do."

With Rhee around, it seemed Elvis read more in his well-thumbed Bible and other inspirational books—Chairo's *Book of Numbers*, Kahlil Gibran's *The Prophet*, Linda Goodman's *Sun Signs*, various texts obtained from the Self Realization Fellowship. Journalist Frank Lieberman recalls an incident in Elvis's hotel suite during the same period, when Frank was there with his fiancée, Karen.

"It was loaded with people, and we watched. All the guys were there with girls they'd picked up. Elvis knew they weren't there to be with the guys, but were using the guys to get to him. It was so damned awkward. Elvis disappeared after a while into the bedroom with a bunch of the girls. Karen and I were talking outside with Elvis's date and Karen was confused. Elvis's date said, 'Elvis is only reading the Bible to them.' We snuck up to the door and watched, and that's what he was doing. So many times I saw that happen."

It worked. As Elvis turned his thoughts toward his spirit, he also cleansed and tuned his body. He helped the process along with diet pills, but he also consumed large quantities of protein drink to make the number of karate and racquetball workouts reasonable. He drank only mineral water and began swallowing vitamin pills by the handful.

"He was fat and he had a lot of problems with his stomach, which just quit working," Sonny reflected in his book. "His body wasn't working. The pills were doing all the work, and yet when that television special came up, he dropped down to 165 pounds, thin as a rake and more handsome than ten movie stars."

Quickly, the pieces came together. Usually a new costume was designed only for Las Vegas, but Elvis wanted something special for Hawaii, so he asked Bill Belew to make an all-white outfit with a huge eagle on the front of the jumpsuit and back of the full-length cape.

In Los Angeles, meanwhile, "We love Elvis" was being translated into the languages of countries where the concert was to be shown and the album sold; for this, RCA actually hired the Berlitz firm, while Marty Pasetta had the same phrases reproduced in neon and began designing a stage set that was so big it would cover 3,500 seats in the Honolulu auditorium.

Back in Memphis, although it was the first Christmas since Priscilla moved out, Elvis was feeling good. His daughter Lisa was present and would be visiting her daddy for two weeks. He also had Linda Thompson with him. In fact, Elvis and Linda had been inseparable for several months now.

They had met through their mutual friend Bill Browder, in August, six months after Priscilla left, when Elvis began dating again. While an undergraduate at Memphis State University, majoring in theater and English, she had held a few small beauty titles, then went to the Miss USA pageant as Miss Tennessee. She had finished four years at Memphis State, but still was twelve hours short of her degree and undecided about what to do when she met Elvis. Would it be Hollywood, where she wanted to act, or New York, where she thought she could model, or someplace else, as an airline stewardess? She says it was "my Prince Charming who decided for me."

From the start they were inseparable, and although there were many others who came and went quickly, Linda was the most important woman in Elvis's life for the next four-and-a-half years, until only a few months before he died. They had much in common, including a strong religious streak and a love of gospel music. As a youngster growing up in Memphis she sang in her Southern Baptist church choir and as a contestant in the Miss USA contest, she was laughed at for reading her Bible daily.

Linda remembers their first date vividly. She took a girlfriend, Miss Rhode Island, for protection, "in case it got too wild and too Hollywood," and left her car parked illegally near the Memphian Theater entrance, "in case we had to make a quick getaway." After that it was pretty ordinary, she says, in a way that reveals her sense of humor, one of the things that Elvis liked best in her. "He came and sat next to me and started getting a little friendly—you know, the old yawn and stretch of the arm behind the seat."

Linda would do practically anything to get him to laugh. That first Christmas together, Elvis was entertaining a bunch of his guys and their wives and girlfriends at Graceland, when he told Linda to go upstairs and put on her crown and Miss Tennessee banner.

"He was trying to show me off," she says. "He had bought me a full-length mink coat and had had one of his big diamond rings made over into a ring for me. He was happy to have a new love in his life. I was kind of embarrassed about it. He didn't know that, so I went up and put on an evening gown and put my banner on and then my crown, and I blacked out my two front teeth with mascara. Then I descended the stairs as if I were really into it, my beauty queen role, keeping my mouth shut. When I got to the bottom step, I smiled and said, 'Is this what you have in mind, darling?' "

Elvis's laughter rocked the room. One of the things Elvis's hired hands worried about in the final years was his mood. "How's his mood today?" they'd nervously ask each other. Linda did her best for the next four years to keep it cheerful.

January 1973 began with final fittings for his jewel-encrusted white costume and the shipment of tons of equipment from Los Angeles to Honolulu. Several days ahead of Elvis's departure, Pasetta and his crew flew over to begin filming big waves, misty mountain ridges, flowered trees, Diamond Head, and coconut palms—footage that would be edited into the satellite show to expand it to ninety minutes for telecast on the Mainland. At the same time, RCA's Rocky Laginestra decided that the album would be recorded and released in quadrophonic sound, the process that recorded sound for four speakers, rather than stereo's two. Finally, on the tenth, two days after quietly celebrating his thirty-eighth birthday with Linda at Graceland, Elvis flew to the islands.

There were problems right away, one of them caused by Elvis, when he gave the belt to his costume to actor Jack Lord, star of television's long-running "Hawaii Five-O." Bill Belew was called in a panic in Los Angeles and told to make another, fast. "But we've used the last of the rubies," he cried. "We'll have to get more from Europe. . . ."

A second problem involved Elvis when he saw the stage for the first time, with individual risers, or platforms, for the members of his backup band, scattered widely.

"I'm sorry, sir," he told Pasetta, "but I like to have my boys with me. Isn't there some way we can keep everybody together?"

Pasetta crumbled before such manners and the risers were taken away. The rehearsals went without a hitch. The musicians and singers, who had arrived a few days before Elvis, were given books when they arrived, giving them their schedules for the next eight days, through the videotaping on the fifteenth.

"We rehearsed at the Honolulu International Center for seven evenings—singers one night, us the next," says John Wilkinson, Elvis's rhythm guitarist. "We had our days clear. We'd check with Tom Diskin and then lie around on the beach or go shopping, rent motorcycles and ride around the island, we rented paddle boats, we went on the Hilton luau cruise. Some of the guys brought their wives and girlfriends. It was a vacation, it really was."

For the Honolulu media, it was a field day, and now that Elvis remained in one place for longer than it took to sleep for a while and then do a concert, he began to see some of the stories. All were filled with praise. And on the thirteenth, the mayor of Honolulu declared an "Elvis Presley Day."

Elvis enjoyed himself. His rehearsals were held secretly in the Hilton Hawaiian Dome, a geodesic dome on his hotel's front lawn; he wore some of his most outrageous outfits, including a long mink coat and white "Superfly" fedora, telling everyone that he was "in disguise." When he wanted to go shopping, one of his boys made the call for him and the store was opened at two o'clock in the morning. When Pasetta filmed his "arrival" at the Hilton's helicopter pad, more than a thousand fans were there. "It's just like the old days," Elvis said. Linda was at his side through it all and, after losing so much weight, he looked the way he liked to look: "Thin as a rake and handsomer than ten movie stars," as Sonny had put it.

Nearly 10,000 persons were squeezed into the big auditorium for the dress rehearsal Friday night. On Saturday the audience size was more restricted and to accommodate those who were turned away, the Colonel arranged to have a virtual circus of entertainment outside—robots and clowns and high school bands.

Suddenly there were technical problems. Pasetta and the engineer from Hollywood present to record the album, Wally Heider, had brought so much electrical equipment with them, they ran out of power and two hours before going on the air they picked up a hum from the lighting system. "We thought we'd lose the album and had to go scrounging to the navy to borrow thick lead sheets to baffle the hum," Pasetta recalls. "They came in, sirens blaring from Pearl Harbor, and we got them in place just minutes before we started broadcasting."

They also discovered a ten-minute error in the timing of the show. "We had it all timed out exactly in rehearsals," Pasetta says. "We'd whittled down the timings on Friday apparently." When told about needing more material, Elvis merely nodded and sent Charlie Hodge out with the titles of three more songs for the orchestra. When your show was generally as loose as Elvis's was, with the repertoire often shifting mid-song, last-minute changes meant nothing.

From the moment he walked on-stage, wrapped in Richard Strauss and illuminated by thousands of Instamatics and hundreds of spotlights, Elvis was in total control, giving the viewer the appearance of looseness while adhering to a precise schedule.

After that, Elvis sang twenty-three songs, a wide assortment that swept up some of his distant past ("Love Me," "Blue Suede Shoes," "Long Tall Sally") and mixed it dexterously with the more recent ("American Trilogy," "You Gave Me a Mountain," "Suspicious Minds"), as well as a song that Frank Sinatra had more or less made his own, "My Way." Conforming to patterns long established now, Elvis leaned down into the audience so fans could kiss him and encircle his neck with hugs and leis. Behind him "We love Elvis" blinked and flashed in a dozen languages. The backup band provided a thunderous beat, the audience a constant roar.

As he finished his traditional closing song, "I Can't Help Falling in Love with You," striking a dramatic pose, legs stretched apart, head bowed, one fist thrown up and out, Charlie picked up his jeweled cape and, as Elvis slowly stood, draped it gently on his shoulders. Elvis stood with his head bowed for a moment and then took the cape and sailed it into the audience like a Frisbee.

Then, throwing up his hand in the Hawaiian, thumbs-up "shaka" sign—thumb and little finger extended simultaneously—he strode back into the off-stage darkness, leaped into a limousine, and was whooshed back to his hotel.

"Great show, boss, great show," the guys seated around him in the Rolls Royce said.

Linda snuggled into his side and purred, "Personally I was hoping you'd rip your pants."

The show went "on the air" by satellite at 12:30 in the morning Sunday. At that moment it was 7:30 P.M.

Saturday in Tokyo and the show was the climax of a Japan-wide "Elvis Presley Week." The singer's popularity in that country was made clear when the station broadcasting the relayed program announced the next day that Elvis had broken all Japanese television records, capturing an astonishing 98 percent share of the audience.

The two shows also raised $85,000 for the Kui Lee Cancer Fund, $60,000 more than the goal set in November. In part, this was because of the Colonel's pressuring prominent figures, such as Jack Lord, to contribute $1,000 apiece to watch the show . . . while many children got in for a penny.

If Elvis was good for charity, he was better for business. According to Marty Pasetta, production of the satellite show cost $2.5 million. It was, he said at the time, "the most expensive entertainment special ever done." Elvis, of course, got a million of that, a figure far greater than any other performer had received for just two hours in concert. The rest was spread over a large area, providing work for hundreds of individuals.

Elvis took a half dozen of these with him as he left Hawaii, flying to Los Angeles and then to Las Vegas for a few days, and then on home to Graceland, partying all the way.

February, 1973–
April, 1973

In the late winter of 1972–73 and on into the following spring it seemed that Elvis could do no wrong, that he was, clearly, the man with the Midas touch. In every medium—in film, television, and recording—he broke records and received prestigious awards.

The first accolades came following the release of the Adidge-Abel documentary, *Elvis: On Tour*. Originally released to coincide with the fall tour, it remained in scattered locations for several months. According to Bob Abel, the film cost only $600,000 to make—not counting Elvis's million-dollar fee—and MGM got that negative cost back in the first three days in the theaters.

The reviews, on the other hand, were not so generous, were what Abel calls, sadly, "lukewarm." *Rolling Stone* exulted: "At last—the first Elvis Presley Movie!" But others cast the thing aside as if it were merely another in a series of Elvis Presley promotional pieces. Abel and most who worked on the film were surprised when it was nominated for a Golden Globe award and astonished when it won.

Elvis was in Las Vegas, following the hugely satisfying satellite show, when the Golden Globe awards banquet was held in the Hollywood Palladium. Elvis was between his 8:15 and midnight shows when the ceremony was broadcast, and he watched it on his bathroom television. A few of the guys were nearby, relaxing elsewhere in the hotel suite, when they suddenly heard Elvis yell.

"My God! Sonofabitch, we won!"

With that, Elvis came running out of the bathroom, pulling up his pants.

"We won," he said, looking around at the others, who had risen and started for the bathroom when they heard his shout. "We won the Golden Globe!"

It was also while in Vegas that Elvis was given two more gold records, for the four-record *Elvis: Worldwide 50 Gold Award Hits, Volume 1*—a first of its kind, recycling earlier gold for newer gold—released two years before, and for *Elvis: Aloha from Hawaii,* available for less than a month.

In Las Vegas, of course, both shows sold out every night for a month.

Then, on April 4, NBC-TV broadcast the ninety-minute version of the Aloha satellite show, claiming, the following day, a 57 percent share of the audience, swamping the popular "All in the Family" and all other competition. The *Daily News* called the show "most impressive," the *Los Angeles Times*, "stunning . . . one of those rare television moments." Executives at NBC began talking about three more specials and Marty Pasetta decided that the first of these would have Elvis dropped into the Ginza in Tokyo by helicopter, the second would be in London, the third in Moscow.

As sweet as things were, they quickly turned sour. Even while in Las Vegas Elvis had begun to put weight back on again, as boredom returned and depression followed.

First there was an incident onstage at the Hilton when, according to Gene Dessel, the hotel's head of security, ". . . this guy next to the stage was trying to shake Elvis's hand all night and for some reason Elvis avoided him. He walked back to the band area where Charlie Hodge was at and got a drink of water. A girl ran up and before she could get to him, a bodyguard ran out. Elvis gave her a kiss and sent her back to the audience. The guy saw that and with Elvis's back to the audience, he jumped onstage and started running toward Elvis. So Red West comes running off the side of the stage and grabs the guy and takes him offstage. Another friend of his sitting at the table gets up on stage to see where his buddy went. Well, Elvis thought they were coming after him. J.D. Sumner went to defend Elvis and Elvis stiff-armed the guy and he went flying back onto his table. They started cussin' Elvis out and Elvis started cussin' back at them. And the band kept playing. Elvis's dad and the bodyguards are holding Elvis. One of my guys was in front of Elvis and I was next to him. Then somebody else from that table tries to get onstage. My guy and I, we threw him offstage. My guards took him out along with the other guy who was knocked down. The insults went on for like a minute, minute-and-a-half. but it seemed like an hour. Elvis was so excited afterwards up in his room he didn't even know he had hit the guy."

It was also while he was appearing in Las Vegas that Priscilla hit him with a blockbuster that turned Elvis into a raging, shouting. vindictive man. She never said she exactly went along with the idea, but when she said her boyfriend, Mike Stone. thought it would be a good idea if Elvis didn't see Lisa Marie for a while, Elvis started screaming. Priscilla had tried to word the notion tactfully, referring to Elvis's "demanding career" rather than making direct charges about his use of pills. This, according to Priscilla's friends. had become a major concern and she actually feared for Lisa Marie when Elvis was so often experiencing the effects of what he called "medication." Elvis reacted to the idea violently. He decided he wanted Mike Stone killed.

Ed Parker, the karate instructor still on the scene as a paid bodyguard during the Vegas engagement, recalled in his book that Elvis made such threats repeatedly. Red and Sonny West devoted an entire chapter in their book to an evening when Elvis walked back and forth in his suite and said, almost as a mantra, "Mike Stone must die, he must die. You will do it for me, you must, he has no right to live." During that awful night, the Wests said, Elvis actually pulled an M-16 army rifle out of the closet and pushed it into Sonny's hands and said, "The sonofabitch must go!"

Linda was the first to act. She suggested calling Elias Ghanem, the Lebanese-born physician who was building a reputation in Las Vegas for helping singers cope with "Las Vegas throat," a loss of voice caused by the hot, dry air. Elvis liked Elias, in time would give him expensive cars, over the years gave him tens if not hundreds of thousands of dollars, too. Whenever Elvis was in town, he was on twenty-four-hour call. He came and gave Elvis a sedative.

Red recalls that the rage continued for several days, with Elvis insisting that if Red refused to kill Stone, he must hire someone else to do the job. Red says he actually talked to someone who said he would do it for $10,000, and nervously told him, "I'll call you back." Then when he went to Elvis with his report, Elvis said, "Aw, hell, just let's leave it for now. Maybe it's a bit heavy. Just let's leave it off for now."

Red went to his friend Bob Conrad, the actor, and shared the incident. Conrad said he'd seen that same sort of reaction to amphetamines in others and told Red to humor his boss. This, essentially, is what Red and the others did for the following several years. However, they did make one significant attempt to dissuade Elvis from taking so much of his prescribed "medication." All had tried very casually to discourage his use of pills over the years, but always Elvis had ended up snubbing them, or cutting them out of the inner circle they all worked so hard to stay within. This time, Red and Jerry and Lamar Fike went to Kang Rhee. They knew

Elvis respected the diminutive karate instructor and
thought he would listen if he warned him.

"They ask me to tell him not to take any pills," Kang
recalls. "Stop him take pill. At the same time, Elvis ask
me to give him my certificate for sixth degree black belt
in karate. I said, 'Let me think about it.' I ask Red and
Sonny and the others come to my room. I was stay
with Elvis in his house in Beverly Hills. I ask them,
'What should I do?' They said, 'As long as he wants
it . . .' Ed Parker already give sixth degree to him and
in the morning he expect the same from me."

The scene the next morning described by Kang and
the others is a study in tension. Conversation between
the bodyguards was minimal and forced, Elvis was nowhere in sight, remaining upstairs in his room because,
according to Kang, "He afraid I say no when he comes
down."

Finally Elvis appeared.

"When Elvis start to study with me in Memphis,"
Kang says, "I give everybody titles real quickly. Red
West always walk behind Elvis, so I call him the Dra-
gon. Sonny was always in front, so he is the Eagle. Joe
Esposito is the Lion. Jerry Schilling is the Cougar. Elvis
I call the Tiger. So when he come down that morning, I
told him, 'You are the Tiger already and if you are going to be king of the jungle you have to lick yourself
well, like a cat licking his wound.'

"I say, 'You should not depend on any pill or medicine to get well, you have to get well yourself.' I think
he understood. And then I presented the sixth degree
black belt.

"Everybody standing around say, 'You know, Elvis,
Master Rhee is right. . . .' "

The feeling remained tense, but some of the tension
disappeared as Elvis took the advice without reacting
angrily.

That night, Elvis took Kang Rhee aside and showed

him his badge from the U.S. Nacrotics Bureau and said the Beatles were the ones who took drugs, not him.

A few weeks later there was another incident with another bodyguard, a blow-up over the use of Elvis's name to promote a karate competition in San Francisco. This was the California State Karate Championship, probably the biggest karate tournament held anywhere in the Western world. One of the organizers was Ed Parker.

Elvis's interest in the martial arts was strengthening during this period, despite, or perhaps because of, the decline in his physical appearance and condition. The new television series in which David Carradine played a kung-fu master was one of Elvis's favorites. In performance, he continued to feature many moves from karate in his choreography and, after the shows, he still held classes or staged demonstrations in his hotel suites. So when Parker's big tournament was coming up, he invited Elvis, who accepted with glee.

Elvis organized the event as if he and friends were going on a safari. He had one of the boys charter a plane. He had others make calls for limousines and hotel rooms in San Francisco. He decided, carefully, what clothes he would take and supervised the packing. He bought Linda a new outfit. He invited Kang Rhee and had him flown into Los Angeles from Memphis. He decided who was, and was not, to go with him: Linda and Joe Esposito and Charlie Hodge, of course, and Geegee and Patsy Gamble, Jerry Schilling . . .

All went well, spirits were high. Though overweight, Elvis joked on the short flight up from Los Angeles, and sat back into the seat of the limousine, puffing on an expensive cigar. Then, on the way to the hotel, the mood changed. As they passed the auditorium, Jerry Schilling noticed that in big letters on the marquee it said, "Elvis Presley—In Person." He called it to Elvis's attention. Elvis jammed his cigar into the limousine ashtray and cursed.

"Those fuckers are doing it again! Goddammit, Ed Parker knows better than that! Jerry, when we get to the hotel, you get your ass over there and you get my name offa that signboard, you hear! Charlie, you go with Jerry! Joe, you call the Colonel and then get us a plane to Los Angeles! Linda, I'm sorry, goddammit, we're going home. The fuckers . . ."

As the limousine fell into a horrible silence, Elvis retrieved his mashed cigar and stuck it in his mouth. No one moved.

"Goddammit," Elvis said, looking very foolish, "isn't anybody going to light my cigar!"

The Colonel was so mad you could hear him all over the hotel room through the telephone. Elvis stood listening impassively. There was a clause in Elvis's contract that forbade his appearing publicly anywhere within 500 miles of Lake Tahoe within six weeks of one of the singer's appearances there and Elvis opened in Tahoe in three.

Ed Parker blamed the local promoters, said they put Elvis's name on the marquee before he arrived and now the union people had gone home, so no one could touch it. Jerry and Charlie made it clear how unhappy Elvis was. Ed and one of his instructors took the letters down, violating union rules, and then hurried to the hotel to apologize.

Elvis wasn't ready to listen. "Okay," he said finally, "we're going." And with that, he led the troupe out of the rooms and down the elevator, through the hotel lobby, into the limousines and back to the airport.

"We spent an hour at the airport," says Kang Rhee, "waiting for the airplane to be ready. Elvis was still mad, he couldn't control himself. I told him to give Ed a chance, I asked him to accept Ed's apology. He felt Ed was using him."

Says Jerry Schilling, "It was a long time before we ever saw Ed again."

April, 1973–
June, 1973

There was a short West Coast tour the last week of April, a dozen shows in nine days, in Phoenix, Anaheim, Fresno, San Diego, Portland, Seattle, and Denver. Five days after that, on May 5, Elvis was back in Lake Tahoe, thirty pounds overweight and looking tired. Then, on the sixteenth, four days short of his scheduled closing date, Elvis canceled all remaining performances and went home to California to rest. The announced explanation varied somewhat, from "throat congestion" to "pneumonia." While the reports of ill health weren't lies, the truth encompassed much more than was said. What was bothering Elvis more than anything else was an accelerated use, or abuse, of drugs and the announcement of cancellation due to sickness was merely part of an ongoing cover-up.

If Elvis's habitual and aggravated use of prescribed medicines was effectively kept secret from his public, it was well known to those around him, and a growing source of worry. Already, Elvis's lawyer, Ed Hookstratton, had put private detective John O'Grady back on the job. This time Elvis didn't know. What O'Grady and another detective named Jack Kelly were hired to do was make a full-scale investigation into the sources of Elvis's drugs.

"His asking for our investigation was an obvious attempt to save Presley's life," O'Grady said much later. "Hookstratton hired us to investigate the doctors to see if we could scare them off."

For six weeks O'Grady and Kelly nosed around, confirming that not only were doctors prescribing depressants, painkillers, and amphetamines directly to their patient, but they also were writing prescriptions for several of his employees, who then would pass the medicine along to their boss. Often, they found, the prescriptions were telephoned in by the doctors, then delivered to Elvis's homes and hotel rooms. Three doctors and one dentist were named by the detectives and, although the information was turned over to federal and state drug authorities, no immediate action was taken. Nor did any of the doctors concerned back off when confronted by O'Grady.

There were more problems for Elvis in May, when Priscilla hired a new attorney, Arthur Toll, who filed a petition on the twenty-ninth in Los Angeles Superior Court charging that his client was a victim of "intrinsic fraud" during the divorce settlement negotiations. Elvis, Toll said, had failed to make a full disclosure of his assets. California law gave her the right to half of Elvis's "community property"—bank accounts, houses, cars, business, the works—but, the attorney said, Priscilla was tricked into accepting a $100,000 property settlement, $1,000 a month alimony, and $500 a month for child support.

The picture she painted in her complaint wasn't pretty. She had lived with the Presley family from age fourteen, she said, and during that time had come to trust Elvis, his father, and their lawyers. She had, in fact, permitted Elvis's attorney, Ed Hookstratton, to select her first attorney, and then took Hookstratton's advice to tell that attorney that she had been fully informed about Elvis's finances. She did as she was told and when Elvis filed the original divorce complaint, she didn't contest it.

Now, nine months later, she said she wanted more money. Much more money. And to back up her claim she listed monthly expenses for herself and Lisa amounting to $14,900. This sum included, among other items, $400 for the telephone, $2,500 for clothing (and $300 to keep it clean), $1,000 for transportation (plus $500 for car expenses), $1,000 for food and household supplies, and $1,500 for "incidentals." Priscilla further said that although she had no idea how much Elvis was worth, his monthly income was "in excess of $200,000." Describing herself as a "housewife," she said she had no income of her own.

The renegotiated settlement would drag on for the next several months, delaying the divorce and causing great strain on Elvis's relationship with Priscilla. The image projected publicly was that everything was friendly, and during this period it was not, although Elvis told friends repeatedly that Priscilla could have anything she wanted. The lawyers, apparently, had negotiated with Elvis's "best interest" in mind, but without Elvis's full knowledge of what they were doing.

In the end, Priscilla improved her position enormously. Now she was to get $4,200 a month alimony for one year, $4,000 a month for the support and education of Lisa Marie until she became of age or married, half of the proceeds from the sale of their Los Angeles home (which Elvis then put on the block for $500,000), and 5 percent of the stock in Elvis Presley Music, Inc. and White Haven Music, Inc., two of his song publishing companies. Elvis also agreed to give Priscilla $750,000 in cash and another $720,000—payable at $6,000 a month—to discharge any further claims on community property. And . . . picked up the $75,000 legal bill.

There was one other change in the settlement: whereas before Priscilla had full custody of Lisa Marie, now the couple shared "joint legal custody," although she continued to live with her mother. Priscilla additionally agreed that Lisa Marie could visit her father whenever it was convenient and always during the Christmas holidays.

One of the reasons she felt she needed more money, Priscilla told Elvis, was that she wanted to go to work —to open a Beverly Hills boutique with a new friend, designer Olivia Bis. The shop on Little Santa Monica Boulevard would be called *Bis and Beau*—for Priscilla's maiden name Beaulieu—and cater to young, rich Beverly Hills. That, Priscilla said, was why she wanted so much money for her wardrobe. She thought it was important to dress well in order to convince others to do the same.

Elvis nodded his approval as Priscilla talked. He'd watched her change much over the years. An innocent teenager when she moved in with him, she'd become a mature woman with, really, very little help from him. He'd given her an unlimited checking account and a purseful of credit cards, paid for her lessons in karate —including Mike Stone's—and paid for her finishing and modeling school. Over the years an army sergeant's daughter had become a polished and graceful woman. Elvis had given 'Cilla a hard time, too—with a house full of loud, grab-assing bodyguards, a head full of pills, and a record of sexual infidelity. Yet, he loved her still —if not as a husband and lover, at least as a respected friend, and as one whose love he wished returned. For years after the separation and subsequent divorce, he gave her cars and fur coats and expensive jewelry. More than one friend remembers that whenever Priscilla visited Graceland, Elvis always shaved and dressed nicely and put on lots of cologne.

Elvis had gone through some changes, too. Following a long period of bitterness, rejection, and rage, he had literally gotten down on his knees and prayed to God and then scribbled out something he called "The Promise." In this, Elvis asked God to help him not do anything to hurt Priscilla, Mike, or Lisa Marie.

Besides that, Elvis didn't feel he had lost anything in

the renegotiated settlement; he believed he had gained. Money meant little to Elvis and Lisa Marie meant everything. Having the threat of not seeing her removed —legally—allowed Elvis to relax around Priscilla, to switch from legal adversary to supportive friend. When it came close to the time her new boutique opened, for example, he called Frank Lieberman, the Los Angeles nightclub writer he'd befriended a couple of years earlier, now publicity director for the Tropicana in Las Vegas.

"He called me," Frank remembers, "and he wanted me to help however I could. He knew I knew people in the media, that sort of thing. I helped with who to invite to the opening, wrote some of her press releases. Elvis asked if she ever needed help, would I help? I said yes."

There was a two-week tour of the South and East in June—five shows in Atlanta, four more in Uniondale, New York, others in Pittsburgh, Cincinnati, St. Louis, Mobile, Nashville, and Oklahoma City, sixteen performances in thirteen days.

By now the Presley tour machine was finely tuned. The way the Colonel found it worked best was to arrive in a city in three waves. The first was led by the Colonel himself, with his staff and at least one of Elvis's representatives. This was the advance team, arriving in a city the night before a scheduled concert, to supervise last-minute details and prepare for Elvis's arrival later the same night.

"Security was the first thing," says Jerry Schilling, who often went ahead with the Colonel when he wasn't working in Hollywood's film studios. "We'd check out the hotel and figure which entrance he could use to get to the room without using the lobby, avoiding the kitchen and employees if possible. Second priority was that his rooms be quiet and with adequate space to have all his personal people around. We'd take all the rooms on the floor, so we could have our security outside the elevator. That way no one could get on the floor except those people we knew. All doors to the floor, even to the fire escape, would be bolted or tied with bedsheets or barred with broomsticks. Room service would be told to deliver food to the elevator or to the door, but never go into Elvis's room. That was to avoid the inevitable staring and dumb questions.

"Then we prepared Elvis's room. That meant blacking out all the windows of Elvis's bedroom with aluminum foil. Elvis was a nocturnal person and this was to keep out the light so he could sleep the next day. It meant checking the air conditioning, to make sure it worked, because Elvis liked it cold. Cold and dark. Then we'd go down the list of people on that particular tour and assign rooms. The room assignments would be typed up by one of the Colonel's men, in an office we'd set up in one of the rooms."

The Colonel would then return to the airport in time to meet Elvis's plane, to hand out room assignment lists and room keys. Elvis and those in his immediate party would get into a waiting limousine and be taken directly to the hotel.

"Occasionally there'd be problems," Schilling says. "Sometimes we couldn't get an entire floor in the hotel and it'd be overrun with people, so that when Elvis came in, people'd be hanging out of the doorways. When Elvis came in at two in the morning, he didn't look his best and he didn't want to be seen by a lot of people. He was adamant about that. And the next day he didn't want to be seen on the way to a show. He wanted to be seen on the stage and that's it."

Elvis would come in the second wave, right after the concert. In the early tours, he went to a hotel after a show and flew on to the next city the following day, along with everyone else. But Elvis suffered a kind of insomnia common among entertainers; after completing an energetic performance, and experiencing the high degree of excitement that goes with it, he was "wired," as so many put it, and needed time to "come down" or relax.

"So," says Jerry, "rather than him stay up half the night and have to get up the next morning and fly to the next city, we found through experience to use that energy flying to the next city right away. This way you couldn't have people up to the dressing room after a show. Elvis wasn't real crazy about that scene anyway. So when somebody announced in the auditorium that Elvis had already left the building, it was true. He was on his way to the airport."

The next morning. as Elvis slept, the Colonel and his advance team continued to work their way down their checklist, seeing that the sound system had arrived, making a dry run with the driver of Elvis's limousine from the hotel to the auditorium and planning alternate routes, visiting local radio stations, picking up a cashier's check for the box-office receipts, leaving behind a cloud of cigar smoke and a sprinkling of what he called Super Souvenir Elvis Presley Pitcha Books— brochures produced by RCA that would, incredibly, be sold for five dollars apiece at the concert, although each was clearly marked, "Photo album—For record promotion only."

"Elvis told me himself to be sure that you got a copy of this," the Colonel said to everyone. "He wanted you to have it at absolutely no cost, as a gift."

In the afternoon the third wave would arrive by chartered jet. "It was a big plane. an Electra 99, a four-engine workhorse." says guitarist John Wilkinson. "We took the seats out of the first class cabin and used that for cargo, all the sound equipment that didn't go on trucks, all the instruments. the luggage, a lot of the Colonel's promotional material, the pennants and posters he sold at the show. The rest of the plane was for the band, the Vegas orchestra, the singers, eight or ten roadies, the sound guys, the light crew, I guess maybe thirty-five or forty all told.

"There'd be buses waiting for us at the airport to take us to the hotel. And a luggage truck. When we checked out of a hotel, we just put our luggage outside our room an hour before we had to get on the bus and the luggage handlers took care of it. They also took care of it in the next city. All we had to do was walk off the plane and get on the bus again. We were given our room keys and the luggage would be delivered to our door within an hour. It was the smoothest operation I ever experienced, before or since."

That night, just before Elvis went onstage, the Colonel nodded his hello and passed along any information he felt that Elvis should have, then left immediately for the airport, and the process began again.

"Thin as a rake and more handsome than ten movie stars." Elvis at press conference following his Las Vegas opening at the International Hotel in August 1969—his first public stage appearance in nine years. (Courtesy: Wide World Photos)

Above: In the Oval Room with the President, December 1970. From left: Richard Nixon, Sonny West, Jerry Schilling, and The Boss. (White House Photo; Courtesy Jerry Schilling) Below: The larger-than-life-sized statue of The King, outside the showroom of the Las Vegas Hilton Hotel. (Courtesy: Las Vegas Hilton Hotel)

Memphis Sheriff Roy Nixon (behind Elvis, under wreath) poses with his deputies at Christmas in 1971. Standing left to right: Billy Smith, Bill Morris, Lamar Fike, Jerry Schilling, Nixon, Vernon Presley, Charlie Hodge, Sonny West, George Klein, Marty Lacker; kneeling to Elvis's right, Dr. George Nichopoulos; kneeling to Elvis's left, Red West. (Courtesy: Jerry Schilling)

Left: Elvis on tour in 1972, in his famous jewel-encrusted costume. (Courtesy: Metro-Goldwyn-Mayer, Inc.) Above: Elvis with his Memphis karate instructor, Kang Rhee. (Courtesy: Kang Rhee Institute, Inc.)

Elvis, Priscilla, and The Cake at the champagne breakfast following their Las Vegas wedding in 1967. (Courtesy: Wide World Photos)

Six years later: leaving the divorce court in Santa Monica, California, in 1973. (Courtesy: Wide World Photos)

Above: One of Elvis's girlfriends, Linda Thompson, with Foxhugh, a Maltese that Elvis gave her in 1973. (Courtesy: Linda Thompson) Right: A bloated Elvis walking with girlfriend Linda Thompson backstage, on tour in 1975. (Courtesy: Linda Thompson)

Another girlfriend: Ginger Alden. This was taken while on the beach in Kailua, Hawaii, in March of 1977. (Courtesy: Ginger Alden)

Above: Sign directing tourists to the Graceland estate. (Courtesy: Jerry Hopkins, 1979) Below: Graffiti on the stone wall outside Graceland. (Courtesy: Jerry Hopkins, 1979)

The gravesite by the Graceland home's meditation pool.
The inscription is by Elvis's father, Vernon Presley.
(Courtesy: WKNO-TV 10, Memphis)

One of many Memphis stores (a number of which are on land actually owned by Elvis) selling Elvis Presley souvenirs—this one is across the street from Graceland. (Courtesy: Jerry Hopkins, 1979)

July, 1973–
December, 1973

After the tour, Elvis went home to Memphis where, on July 21, he was to begin a week of recording. It'd been sixteen months since Elvis had been in a studio, and that was only to record half a dozen songs at MGM, included in the *On Tour* documentary. A number of live albums had been released in recent months, and RCA was anxious for new material.

In many ways this session was reminiscent of an earlier Memphis session in 1969 at the American Studios. It was there that Elvis cut thirty-six songs in six days, three of them million-sellers, including "Suspicious Minds." Although he didn't use the same studio—this time going to Stax—there were many similarities. Both American and Stax were located in funky black Memphis neighborhoods and both were known for the number of hits produced within. At American, when Elvis walked in, the studio was producing hits by the Box Tops, Neil Diamond, Dionne Warwick, Joe Tex, Wilson Pickett, Joe Simon, and Merilee Rush. Stax was known as home base for many other top performers, including the late Otis Redding, Booker T and the MGs, and Sam and Dave, predominantly rhythm and blues acts. When Felton Jarvis put the studio band together, he also used some of the same musicians from the American sessions, including bassist Tommy Cogbill, guitarist Reggie Young, and organist Bobby Wood.

Elvis arrived five hours late, his ballooning body wrapped in a long black cape over a white suit, his "Superfly" hat pulled down over his eyes.

"I thought I'd dress for the part," he cracked.

The session that followed set the scene for those that followed. It was terrible. The studio was crowded with singers and musicians and hangers-on, much like the sessions two years earlier in Nashville, and Elvis didn't seem overly excited about recording. Nor was he any more prepared than he often was, hearing the songs for the first time after entering.

It was, to many around him, astonishing. Elvis had been recording for twenty years and still he didn't prepare his material beforehand, still he waited for his publishing representatives to show up with a stack of demonstration discs. This wasn't the way he always did it, but for Elvis to be doing it at all in 1973 was puzzling. This seemed an acceptable way to produce movie soundtrack albums, where songs were forced into creaking scripts to fit specific dramatic situations. But for the production of albums in the seventies? When Elvis's man from New York began playing demo after demo, waiting for Elvis to find one that he liked, the musicians in the studio looked at each other and shook their heads.

"The first night there were two drummers," says Jerry Carrigan, who was one of them. "Me and Al Jackson, who was the black drummer who usually worked at Stax. Elvis finally heard a song he wanted to record, called 'Three Corn Patches.' I guess maybe he just gave up and said he'd do it because he'd already broken several of the demos, just twisted them and broke them in his hands. You talk about pieces of junk, that was junk. It was so corny, Al Jackson listens to the song and looks at me and says, 'Shit, I cain't play that, I'se raised on chitlins . . . *you* do the song.' I said, 'Not me, man, I'm gonna watch you.' And he did it.

"Now, Al drank and he drank when he worked. They told him he couldn't drink, Elvis didn't like it. He told them, 'I been working here for years and I drink in the studio.' And with that he turned back to that big rolling bar of his and poured himself another milkshake cup of Tanqueray gin. He did not return the next night."

That's the way it went for four days. The musicians arrived at seven, and Elvis entered wearing his big white hat about five hours late, flanked by his good-natured, but doting and protective entourage.

"The second night," Carrigan recalls, "Felton Jarvis called some of us into the control room and said, 'Now, look, don't you guys yawn. It brings him down. If you feel like yawning, go outside and splash your face off or get a breath of fresh air, but don't yawn. It brings him down, okay?' They called Tommy Cogbill down because he was laying down on the floor, worn out and tired from playing bass all night. He was still playing, but laying down. They said, 'Don't you be layin' down on the floor and playin'. Set up in a chair, or stand up. No layin' down.' "

On the first day Elvis recorded three songs. On the second day, another three. On the third day, only two. Then three again on the fourth day, a final three on the fifth. The sixth and seventh days he never showed up and the musicians sat there, waiting. Finally they were told that Elvis was sick and they went home.

"He was just visibly miserable," says Carrigan. "And he did something I never saw him do before. He wore the same clothes two days in a row. Normally, his valet would bring clothes and he'd change during the course of the evening."

Elvis was in a slump. He had his daughter Lisa Marie with him, and Linda, when he went to some of those recording sessions, and he had them with him at home. But it didn't seem to help. Carrigan noticed it, saying, "He was down, man—just down, down, down. Super down." Says the organist, Bobby Wood: "Elvis just didn't seem to care."

However depressed the scene at the time, the material produced during the sessions included several songs that either went on to be hits or, at the least, critically successful. One was "I've Got a Thing About You Baby," a song originally recorded by Billy Lee Riley using some of the same musicians that Elvis had in the studio with him. Elvis also followed the original arrangement, merely changing the guitar lead to an organ lead. This same approach to recording—putting his own distinctive voice on top of someone else's proven arrangement—previously had produced a hit in "Suspicious Minds" (a copy of Mark James's original version) and Elvis and Felton hoped this song could duplicate that earlier success. It didn't do nearly so well, but was a hit the following winter.

Thus Elvis's declining health and increasing dependence on drugs didn't seem to affect his career. No matter how low he got, he remained at the top in his field, able through sheer willpower, mixed with momentum, to continue his string of record hits and crisscross the country every year—when other top acts such as the Rolling Stones and Bob Dylan toured every three years or less frequently.

No doubt about it, Elvis was still some sort of superhero, able to fill buildings, bridge gaps, and capture the most unlikely audience. For example, the Colonel took an ad in the *Wall Street Journal* listing the dates and cities of his June tour and then, just above the signature "ELVIS and the Colonel" he said, "This advertising is not intended to sell tickets—only to let our friends know where we are."

One wondered: Which friends of Elvis's and the Colonel's read the *Wall Street Journal?* Was the Colonel bragging again? Or merely doing his job—building the Presley image of respectability?

The Colonel's weird and wonderful touch was apparent at every turn in Presley's career. The same month the ad ran he was hawking tacky promotional brochures for five dollars to the fans who'd already paid ten for a ticket to one of Elvis's shows, selling pennants and posters and leftover styrofoam skimmers from Las Vegas like peanuts at a baseball game. It was behavior composed of arrogance or innocence, good fun or sheer con, and the Colonel never let you know which, and that mystery pulled you even closer to the flame.

At the same time, the Colonel went on making his fabulous deals. Elvis's contract had run out at the Las Vegas Hilton and in the past several months the Colonel and Elvis had been courted both subtly and strongly to leave the Hilton for another hotel.

Says Henri Lewin, the Hilton vice-president who negotiated the Presley contracts, "The Aladdin offered him anything. He didn't even talk to them. They just opened their big showroom. He never came to me and said, 'I have an offer from the Aladdin, will you pay me more?' I know that they called him. The MGM Grand had good reason, because Kirk Kerkorian (the president of MGM) was very close with him. I said to the Colonel, 'I want to know one thing—when the MGM opens do I have to fight with you or do you stay with me?' He said, 'Henri, I will give you an opportunity in two months from now to make a deal with me, which will go over the opening date of the MGM Grand. If you make that deal, I don't go to MGM. If you don't make that deal, I might go anyplace.' The man never gave us an exclusive. He could have played another three days, four days, five days, or ten weeks at any hotel in the world, or in Las Vegas, but verbally he says, 'I don't do that.' I said, 'That's good enough, you don't have to put it on paper.' "

Eventually it *was* put on paper, of course, and during the last week of July the Colonel and Lewin agreed that Elvis would appear at the Hilton two times a year for the next two years. Elvis was also given the option of working the hotel only two weeks at a time instead of four. And he was to be paid $150,000 a week—more than any other Las Vegas performer—as well as get his room and "incidentals" picked up. Sometimes these "incidentals" added more than $25,000 to his cost. The hotel never, ever complained.

"He was just as important to Vegas as he was to the hotel," says Bruce Banke, the Hilton's publicity executive. "It was like bringing in a major convention. Everybody reaped the benefits. His August 1973 engagement was his last full month in Vegas. He was doing two shows a day for twenty-eight days. That's 100,000 people a month. We've never seen anything like it and probably never will again."

If the fans remained loyal, the critics did not. "It's Elvis at his most indifferent, uninterested, and unappealing," said *The Hollywood Reporter*. "He's not just a little out of shape, not just a bit chubbier than usual, the Living Legend is fat and ludicrously aping his former self. . . . Since his return to live performing, Elvis has apparently lost interest. . . . It is a tragedy, disheartening and absolutely depressing to see Elvis in such diminishing stature. . . ."

After closing September 3, Elvis zigzagged around the country with Linda and his hired hands, flying to Memphis and then to Los Angeles and finally to his home in Palm Springs, as if looking for a comfortable roost. He bought cars in Memphis, jewelry in Beverly Hills, and ammunition for his guns in Palm Springs. He watched movies late at night on television wherever midnight caught him. Linda made him goodies—popcorn balls held together with caramel—and shoved them into his mouth like a mama bird feeding her young. He went through the motions of practicing his karate, but the efforts were little more than self-parody.

"Then to make matters worse," one close friend confides, "Elvis broke his wrist, so he had his arm in a sling.

He tried, man; oh, he tried. But have you ever seen a one-armed man, greatly overweight, thrashing around in a karate suit, huffin' and puffin'? It was sad, man, very, very sad."

Despite all this, Elvis attempted to record in Palm Springs, using equipment taken right to his door by RCA. Working with his guitarist, James Burton, he struggled through two songs and then hung it up.

Two weeks later, on October 9, Elvis appeared in Santa Monica Superior Court with Priscilla in private session with Judge Laurence J. Rittenband, who granted Elvis's petition for divorce. They emerged from the judge's chambers arm-in-arm, kissed for the collected photographers, and then parted. They had been married for just under six-and-a-half years.

Then, only six days after that, Elvis checked himself into Baptist Memorial Hospital in Memphis for what the press was told was "recurring pneumonia."

"It's common knowledge now that Elvis had a number of chronic type medical problems," says Maurice Elliott, the hospital vice-president who got the job of talking to the press when Elvis entered the giant medical facility, "but whenever he came in they'd say all they wanted said was that Elvis was in for rest, or had the flu. Now, I didn't want to lie, but I felt our first responsibility was to the patient, so we told the press basically what the doctor and Joe [Esposito] told me, even though I was aware it wasn't totally the truth. We didn't lie, but we didn't tell the total facts of the case. And that made it difficult."

The truth was, Elvis *did* have trouble breathing and congestion that bordered on pneumonia. These problems had caused him to cancel his Lake Tahoe engagement early in May. And he *did* need rest; recent events had conspired to exhaust him, psychologically as well as physically. The boredom in Las Vegas, the aborted recording session in Palm Springs, the divorce hearing in Santa Monica had created uncommon pressure. However, the real problem or problems he was experiencing were not caused by that pressure, but by how he attempted to relieve it. No one was saying so aloud at the time, but Elvis checked into the hospital October 15 to dry out. This was confirmed two years after Elvis's death, when Dr. Nick testified at a Tennessee Board of Medical Examiners hearing to determine whether or not he was guilty of prescribing drugs to Elvis illegally.

"I thought he was probably addicted to Demerol [a painkiller] at the time of his first hospitalization," the doctor said. "We tried to detoxify him from everything he was taking."

This was Elvis's first prolonged visit to a hospital, the only time he had been in one except to have a broken finger put in a cast—the result of a touch football game—and to attend the birth of Lisa Marie. Elvis didn't like hospitals particularly, so everything was done to make it as much like home—or, more accurately, another hotel room—as possible.

"We put tinfoil on the windows first thing," says Maurice Elliott, "to keep the sunlight out and allow him to stay to his nocturnal habits. It affected normal hospital routines a little bit, but with 1,900 beds in the hospital, we have at least 250 special diets a day and special requests like Elvis's weren't too much of a problem. The problem was that Elvis had no spokesman. It would have been nice if Joe or Dr. Nick would release the information, but they didn't."

The result was that, when anyone wanted information, they called the hospital and as soon as word got out that Elvis was in a sixteenth floor suite of rooms, all hell broke loose. Newsmen from all over the world began calling, at all hours of the day and night, by telephone and in person. Get-well cards arrived by the tens of thousands, filling up the small hospital mailroom and piling ceiling-high in the hallways. There were enough flowers for almost every patient in the entire building.

The hospital did what it could. A private telephone line was installed, so that calls couldn't be made direct to Elvis's rooms, as was the case in all other rooms. Hospital guards were assigned twenty-four-hour duty outside Elvis's rooms and given a list of those who were permitted to come and go. The switchboard was told what to say to the hundreds of daily callers. Fans were ejected from the hallways. When some on the hospital staff added to the problem by trying to visit or sneak a look, a policy decision had to be made about personnel.

"At first it was exciting, it was kinda fun having a celebrity in the hospital," Elliott says, "but after that it really wore on you, it just wore you out dealing with the press. As long as he was there, I wasn't able to do anything else."

To assure the star's comfort, hospital rules were waived to allow Linda Thompson to move into the room with Elvis, where she remained for more than two weeks. "I had a cot in there right next to his bed," Linda says, "and at night he lowered his bed to the height of the cot. Finally they brought in a hospital bed for me. Then they started treating me like a patient. I never got out of my nightgown. The nurses came and said, 'And how are our patients today?' I tried to go downstairs and look at the magazine rack. I was going stir crazy, so I got dressed and Elvis said, 'What're you doing?' I said, 'I'm going downstairs to look at the magazines.' He said, 'Oh, no, honey. If I can't have my clothes on, you can't.' He made me put my gown back on and get back into bed. He was just like a little kid and I was his little buddy. Whatever he had to go through I had to go through."

Elvis remained in the hospital for eighteen days, checking himself out on November 1. During that time, he got rest and ate almost normally—although on his orders, his boys smuggled in bags of cheeseburgers and fried potatoes. He was also visited daily by Dr. Nick, who continued to keep an eye on Elvis's medication.

Then the night he went home, he got stoned again.

Elvis spent most of the final months of 1973 in Memphis, where in November he watched a rerun of the NBC-TV "Aloha from Hawaii" satellite show and from December tenth through the sixteenth went again into the Stax recording studio for RCA. Although this session was considerably more satisfying than the one in July—eighteen songs in seven days—in no way did it represent Elvis at his most productive. Or happiest. Still overweight and depressed about the year behind him, many of the songs seemed as autobiographical—and sad—as anything he ever recorded.

Some of the material reflected his general mood, such as in Larry Gatlin's composition, "Help Me," where Elvis literally dropped to his knees in the studio to sing the song.

Others were more specific, as in "Take Good Care of Her," where he seemed to be singing to Priscilla's new escort, Mike Stone. Perhaps the saddest of all—and ultimately most prophetic—was the mournful "Goodtime Charlie's Got the Blues."

Three of these songs would be released as singles in the next year and all would be included on his albums. There were up-tempo songs as well—including Chuck Berry's rocker, "Promised Land"—but it was the mournful ballads that set the tone and remained most memorable.

Christmas Eve 1973 was not the happiest of times. Again three stockings were hung on the staircase with Linda's name replacing Priscilla's. The usual bounty of gifts were exchanged. But many of Elvis's presents were still under the tree unopened a week later.

New Year's Eve was quiet, too, as Elvis held another party at Graceland rather than rent a nightclub, and pared the guest list to about thirty of his closest friends.

There was champagne, but no food until someone went out and bought chips and dip at Pancho's, a Mexican fast-food takeout place not far away. Elvis and Linda didn't come downstairs to join the party until after eleven.

Elvis finally appeared, freshly shaved and cologned, wearing an all-black fringed "Superfly" outfit, a knee-length coat and a wide-brimmed, floppy hat. Linda looked as if she had spent a lot of time making up and was wearing a silver lamé pants suit with a transparent top. They made one circuit of the room, greeting everyone cordially, then went back upstairs. Total time they were at the party was under fifteen minutes.

In their wake they left a disgruntled and deflated party. "I flew eighteen hundred miles for this?" Joe Esposito grumbled. "This is the greatest party on earth," said Lamar Fike. "Fun! This is really great."

At midnight, the men started playing cards and the women gathered in front of Elvis's closed-circuit television and waved Happy New Year to him. He had a monitor in his bedroom, but no one knew if he was watching.

January, 1974–
March, 1974

Elvis may've been suffering emotionally, and it's undeniable that the negative reviews and comments were accumulating. Yet, the image prevailed; the momentum seemed unstoppable. In the winter of 1973–74, The King's legendary shaky legs may have turned rubbery, and critical arrows were beginning to pierce his flesh, but there was no toppling him, no denying his ongoing monarchy. In fact, in January 1974, RCA executed a master stroke that put their moneymaker on top for many years to come without his doing a thing.

This came in the release of a well-researched and elaborately packaged single record album called *Elvis— A Legendary Performer, Volume 1*. "It was my idea," says Joan Deary, the person at RCA responsible for much of the nuts-and-bolts work of assembling Elvis's records, "and when I took it to Rocco [Laginestra], I thought its appeal was to the Elvis collector. And it went gold. It sold better than a lot of his regular albums." Eventually the series went to Volume 3 and all sold enormously, prompting RCA to use the same packaging approach to other of its artists.

The timing was perfect. In 1974, nostalgia for the 1950s was reaching a crest. This was the year Henry Winkler became an overnight star as television's Fonz; *Grease* was a smash on Broadway; and *American*

Graffiti won an Academy Award. In Elvis's first *Legendary* album, Joan capsuled the same decade, presenting a series of musical milestones in Elvis's career: his first single ("That's All Right, Mama"), his first million-seller ("Heartbreak Hotel"), his biggest-selling record ("Don't Be Cruel"), his first gospel hit ("Peace in the Valley") and his biggest-selling movie record ("Can't Help Falling in Love" from *Blue Hawaii*). She also dropped in excerpts from a 1958 interview and several previously unreleased cuts, including some material Elvis recorded when he was still with Sun Records. With this came a slickly produced book of historic photographs (Elvis with the Dorsey Brothers, Elvis singing to a hound dog on the Steve Allen television show, Elvis with Ed Sullivan, etc.), newspaper clippings, material from RCA's files showing recording dates, and other session information.

The album served Elvis in several ways. Besides giving him product that he didn't have to go into a studio to record, and giving his fans a well-produced nostalgia trip, it also gave the reviewers and rock pundits another Elvis "event" to use as a springboard for one of their by now predictable retrospective glances. For example, Jim Miller wrote in *Rolling Stone*, "Elvis Presley remains the quintessential American pop star; gaudy, garish, compromised in his middle age by commercial considerations, yet gifted with an enormous talent and a charismatic appeal beyond mere nostalgia. Presley remains a true American artist—one of the greatest in American popular music, a singer of native brilliance and a performer of magnetic dimensions."

Greil Marcus went Miller even one better in *Oui:* "If Elvis's genius is as simple as inborn talent, its result has been as complex as the U.S.A. His goal (if the idea that a hillbilly thinks is still a bit strange, you can call it his instinct) has been to make music that touches, takes, and personalizes virtually every positive side of the American soul; a completely innocent and mature delight in sex; a love of roots and a respect for the past; a rejection of roots and a demand for novelty; the liberating arrogance and sense of self-worth that grows out of the most commonplace understanding of what 'democracy' and 'equality' are all about (no man is better than me); the humility, piety, and self-deprecating humor that spring from the same source (I am not better than no man); a burning desire to get rich, to have fun; a natural affection for big cars and flashy clothes, the symbols of status that deliver pleasure both as symbols and on their own terms. There are a lot of contradictions there; Elvis, after all, has become one of those symbols himself. Perhaps that is why one of his earliest critics pronounced him 'morally insane.' "

The critics also loved the album itself. "Listening to *Legendary Performer* is almost like discovering Elvis for the first time," said Ed Ward in *Phonograph* magazine. "What," asked San Francisco's *City* magazine, "another Elvis reissue? Well, yes and, as it happens, it's one of the best ever." "RCA has at last recognized that some of Elvis's buyers are not just fans—or blind consumers ready to buy anything with the name on the package—but *collectors,* interested in the performer's social, historical and musical contributions," said the writer in the Los Angeles *Free Press.* And as for Greil Marcus, he believed that *"Legendary Performer* does justice not only to Elvis's talent but, dare I say it, to his vision."

By mid-January, Elvis was—using his phrase—gearing up for Las Vegas again, this time with less than the usual apprehension. This was because now Elvis would perform only one show a night during the week, instead of two—two on Fridays and Saturdays—for only two weeks instead of four. Thus, Elvis was cutting his commitment from fifty-five or sixty shows to half the number, without a cut in pay.

In the week or two before leaving Memphis, Elvis remained closeted with friends. Still practicing karate and dieting—that is, taking more than the usual number of amphetamines—he began to lose weight. New costumes were designed and fitted—the first without a cape and the first non-jumpsuit in years and, as the last days before he had to fly to Nevada approached, he began to sing more. Among those singing with him were three young men that Elvis had put on his personal payroll the previous summer, in time to record with him in Palm Springs.

"Hey, daddy," Elvis told his father when he hired them, "you never gonna guess what I bought me this time."

It was a game Elvis and Vernon played.

"What?" Vernon asked. "What in goddamn hell you buy? Is it another car? Is it . . ."

"Daddy, you're never gonna guess. I got me my own group."

"Your own what?"

"My own group, daddy. I got me three singers and a piano player and I'm calling them Voice."

"Elvis, what in goddamn hell you need three more singers for? You already got nine. . . ."

"Daddy, I don't want to talk about it. . . ." Elvis said.

Of course they went on the payroll, and Vernon began writing out $10,000 or more a month in checks to the three young singers and a piano player.

"Anything he wanted he got, right?" says Tony Brown, the pianist, who later replaced Glenn D. Hardin in the backup band. "He allus wanted to be in a gospel group and there were a bunch of singers who were out of work—Donny Sumner, who was J.D. Sumner's stepson; Sherrill Neilson, who used to be with the Statesmen and the Imperials, and was one of the greatest Irish tenor gospel singers in the world; and Tim Batey, a bass player who could sing, who played in the Stamps.

"Elvis let Donny arrange songs on the albums and cut two or three of his songs. Elvis catered to Donny. He offered to buy him a house outside Chicago. Elvis was always calling Donny to talk to, because J.D. allus treated Donny like a lamebrain, like he was dumb and stuff. I remember the night when Elvis told Donny, 'Pick out the land and pick an architect and build you a house.' He came and told me and I said, 'Donnnnn-eeeeee, God, do it!' And he said, 'I couldn't do it.' There were others who would've got right on the phone and called about the house. Donny just blew it off.

"Elvis was in awe of Sherrill's talent, but he didn't treat him as nice as Donny. He got featured a lot, got a lot of solos in Elvis's shows. He sang 'Softly, I'll Leave You' and 'Killing Me Softly' and Elvis sang a duet with him, 'Spanish Eyes.'

"Tim Batey was the weird one of us. He looked like a white black man—tall and lanky—and he could play anything. He was a rock and roller, really, and the Stamps had a school in Dallas and he took a job playing bass for the group because it was a job. Tim was good at karate. He was into all the books Elvis was into, he's the one turned me onto Elvis bein' heavy.

"He was into karate, Elvis, and it was into his head to teach us. Used to be every day at six we'd be at the house to take karate. Elvis bought us outfits. We studied with Dave Hebler, who was one of Elvis's bodyguards. Then we'd get into settin' around and seein' your aura and like that. He really was a heavy person. He had a stack a' books all times. He was into numerology, psychogenetics, all those kind of things. He'd take everybody in the group and get you in a room and read from one of the books and make you feel important. He told us what our number was—he was an 'eight' because he was born January 8—and then go on for an hour about what that meant.

"We were paid $10,000 a month for the group, plus all expenses. We had a Master Charge. We flew first class. Everywhere we went, everything was covered. We got bonuses—allus big bonuses. He gave us a $34,000 camper. After a while, some people started to get really pissed-off at us because they thought we were taking advantage of Elvis. But it was Elvis's idea all along. He *wanted* us there. He wanted us to come runnin' whenever he wanted, and that's what we did. When we weren't touring with him, we'd be off months at a time and we could count on ten days out of every month we'd get a phone call. Joe Esposito would call and say Elvis wants you to come to Palm Springs, so we'd go to Palm Springs from Nashville and check into the hotel until Elvis woke up and called. Some nights it'd be all hymns. Some nights it'd be all rock and roll. Some nights it'd be nothing. Sometimes we'd fly out to Palm Springs and check into the hotel and they'd call from the house and say, 'Elvis just went to L.A., go to L.A.' We had rent-a-cars, so we'd drive to L.A., we'd get there and check into a hotel, they'd call, say Elvis was in a bad mood, go back to Nashville. So we'd go back home. We never knew."

There's a long-standing tradition in the American South in which getting drunk and/or stoned and chasing women and shooting off pistols and racing cars around for the sheer hell of it are normal, everyday male activities, generally accepted with a resigned or amused shrug by much of southern society. In the show business part of this society they called this "roarin' with the billies [hillbillies]." In country music, tradition practically dictated that as soon as you got a little money, you went out and spent it on cars, clothes, rings, and women, all flashy. Many in rock and roll adhered to the same self-indulgent philosophy.

Elvis was a product of this culture and when you traveled with Elvis, you were roarin' with the Number One Billy. It was just the way Tony Brown described it. Even when the weekly paycheck wasn't so large— the boys in the "Mafia" still rarely got more than $250 a week, for example—the fringe benefits were appreciable. All expenses were paid, everybody had a Master Charge card and, besides that, for the male employees (and most were male), the women were plentiful and available. And it was exciting. You never knew what Elvis would do next.

In Las Vegas in February 1974 there was an incident that had everyone talking for weeks. That was when Elvis fired his .22 caliber Savage at a light switch in his hotel suite and the bullet pierced the wall behind it, ripping through the bathroom and missing Linda Thompson by only a few inches. Some of the bodyguards who were present later recalled in their book, *Elvis: What Happened?*, that when Linda came panicking out of the bathroom seconds later, Elvis merely grinned and said, "Hey, now, hon, just don't get excited."

And what about the time he started banging away at the chandelier? All the guys froze when that happened, relaxing finally when a dumbfounded Elvis said to them, "What'sa matter? We're in the penthouse. Nobody gonna get hit long as you shoot straight up." He then shot at the chandelier some more.

"It was somethin' to do," nearly all of the boys say. "You ever spent a month in a hotel room?"

After closing in Vegas, Elvis took his family of fifty dependents on the road again on March 1 and in the next twenty-two days performed twenty-five times in fourteen southern cities. It was a strange tour, crisscrossing eight states, and entering and leaving Monroe, Memphis, Murfreesboro, and Richmond two times apiece, while visiting Tulsa, Houston, Auburn, Montgomery, Charlotte, Roanoke, Hampton, Greensboro, and Knoxville once apiece.

Two of the shows were held in Houston's Astrodome, Sunday, March 3. There he did matinee and evening performances to a total of nearly 90,000—the headline act for the annual Houston Livestock Show and Rodeo. Each show opened with the orchestra members, the backup band, the Sweet Inspirations, J.D. Sumner and the Stamps, Jackie Kahane, and Voice being towed

aboard a portable bandstand to the middle of the
Astroturf field. There they waited in place as the chuck-
wagon races were run around them, which just about
freaked out the Sweet Inspirations. Then Elvis appeared
in a jeep that circled the field twice, before depositing
him by the stage to perform his fifty-minute Vegas set.

In Monroe his shows were attended by the mayor
and the governor of Louisiana and the fans nearly tore
the motel apart. In Auburn, when he offhandedly tossed
one of his scarves to a lady in the front row, she hugged
the memento to her bosom and raced frantically across
the coliseum, screaming. Elvis arrived in Montgomery
on the sixth of March, midway through "Elvis Presley
Week" in Alabama, proclaimed thus by Governor
George Wallace, who sat with his wife through Elvis's
show. In Memphis, more shows were added until there
were five in all, and RCA rushed mobile recording
equipment to the Mid-South Coliseum to record an
album, *Elvis Recorded Live on Stage in Memphis*.

All shows were sold out. Each grossed at least
$100,000. Some went as high as four times that. The
Instamatics flashed and women of all ages threw themselves at him, night after night after night. A lot of the
time he laughed at the bizarre attention he attracted.
Other times he shook his head. "They sure are weird,
man," he'd say as he left the stage. "They gotta be. That
can't be normal, behavin' like that."

May, 1974–
September, 1974

In May, Elvis was on the road again, performed four
shows in California, then went into Lake Tahoe for two
performances a day for eleven days. In two important
ways, this was not the standard Nevada engagement. For
this one, the High Sierra Theatre in Del Webb's Sahara
Tahoe did away with dinner and presented "Elvis in
Concert." This allowed the hotel to cut its expenses and
give Elvis a larger slice of the box office. Tickets sold for
$17, which included two drinks, taxes, and gratuities.
Turning the dinner show into a cocktail show also
allowed the hotel to move in smaller tables, thereby
seating more customers.

More striking than the increased income was an incident that occurred one night outside Elvis's room. A
few months later a land developer from Grass Valley,
California, filed a $6 million lawsuit against Elvis as a
result of that incident, also naming the Sahara Tahoe
and Del Webb International Hotels. The developer,
Edward L. Ashley, said in his district court suit that on
May 20 he paid one of Elvis's hired hands $60 to be
admitted to a party in Elvis's suite following the second
show. When he knocked on the door and there was no
response, he said, he threw some breaker switches he
found on the wall in the hallway, turning off all the
lights in the area. That, he said, was when Red West

and one of Elvis's stepbrothers, David Stanley, and a former police sergeant from Palm Springs, Dick Grob, came rushing into the hallway.

"Who the fuck turned out the lights!"

"Who're you?"

"Hold this dude, David; let's get some answers."

More men were pouring out of the room, followed by Elvis himself. Someone found the breaker box and turned the lights back on. According to Ashley, Stanley and Grob and two others held his arms while Red West and two others beat him up severely. "All of which occurred," he said, "in the immediate presence of defendant, Elvis Presley, who refused plaintiff's request to stop the beating and did in fact participate in said beating.

"As a result of the aforesaid unprovoked and malicious assault and battery, plaintiff suffered severe and painful injuries, the full extent of which are not presently known, but which include severe laceration of his lips, loosened teeth, severe lacerations on the inside of plaintiff's left cheek, possible fractured jaw and severe contusions and swelling on the left side of plaintiff's face, injury to plaintiff's left ear, brain concussion, severe wrenching and torn ligaments in plaintiff's left shoulder, severe swelling due to a blow to plaintiff's throat just below his jaw, and severe bruising and straining of both of plaintiff's knees and both of plaintiff's ankles, causing swelling and severe pain therein."

Experiencing humiliation and physical pain, as well as ongoing medical expenses, Ashley wanted $250,000 for general damages and, because the beating was "intentional and malicious," an additional $5 million in punitive damages. And that was just the part dealing with the bodyguards. From Elvis he asked an additional $250,000 and from the hotel, even more. Ashley said the hotel and its owners shared responsibility for the attack because there was a known pattern of physical violence involving Red and Grob and the rest, and they were allowed to stay in the hotel anyway, a threat to the hotel's guests. From the hotel, Ashley was asking general damages of $110,000 and another million dollars in punitive damages. Altogether it came to $6,610,000.

The complaint read like a classic celebrity lawsuit. Exorbitant sums were being asked for what appeared to be minor injuries and innocent parties—in this case the hotel management and owners—were being dragged in because it was believed that they had money, too. Although later the suit was amended to remove the hotel from the complaint, unfortunately for Elvis, there was more than a little truth to the man's account of the assault. And he was correct when he pointed out a pattern of hard hitting security enforcement by some of Elvis's friends.

This didn't bother Elvis at first. Even the FBI had verified the severity of some of the threats made against him, so wasn't stiff security necessary? Sure, there'd been a couple of incidents of possible overreaction, such as the time those guys rushed onstage and even Elvis got involved. But wasn't it better to be safe than sorry? What was the old saw about survival? Shoot first and ask questions later. Hell, Elvis thought, nobody was getting shot . . . and if the people hadn't been in the wrong place, they wouldn't have got themselves hurt.

Even so, this was not an issue that would go away. For another several years it would be a time bomb that never stopped ticking.

Elvis was being attacked, too—critically. "It was a plump and sluggish Elvis Presley who gave a cookie-cutter concert at the Forum Saturday night," the critic in the *Long Beach Independent* wrote. Said a headline in the *San Francisco Sunday Examiner & Chronicle* of his Tahoe engagement: "The Pelvis Slows Down in a Show of Hokum & Ennui."

Otherwise, it was business as usual. Elvis went home

to Memphis for two weeks and then embarked on a sixteen-city tour that began in Texas, zigzagged all over the deep South and Midwest and East, reaching as far as Rhode Island, closing in Salt Lake City, Utah. Everywhere he went, the Colonel was a step ahead of him, arranging the complicated logistics and choreographing the carnival environment in which Elvis always played.

The mustachioed salesman left over from the Colonel's past, Al Dvorn, got up on the stage before every show and during the intermission before Elvis came out and sold the Super Souvenirs.

"This is your last chance to get the gen-u-wine Elvis Presley pitcha books, only five dollars while they last, also getcher official Elvis Presley pennant, only two dollars in a wide choice of colors; you will notice that Elvis will be wearing the same outfit tonight that he wears on the poster which is also available and suitable for framing for five dollars . . ."

The spiel went on and on as salesmen moved through the auditorium and 12,000 to 20,000 seats filled up.

The Colonel's cause was abetted by the daily press, the newspaper writers and editors in every city Elvis played, who welcomed him as if he were the circus or the Freedom Train, an event to be reported in fine and exuberant detail. Some excerpts from the adoring press:

A 21-year-old, nine-months pregnant lady was one of the unlikely things that happened at Elvis' sellout at Tarrant County Convention Center. Shrieking that she had to touch her idol, she charged the stage during Elvis' closing "Dixie" medley. "Let me go! Let me up there! I love him!" she screamed as a security guard manfully, if delicately, restrained her. Later she confessed she didn't know what came over her.

—Fort Worth

The Presley show arrived from Amarillo, Texas. After landing in four separate private jets, they took over 67 rooms on the top floor of the downtown Ramada Inn. The top floor is guarded and barricaded by the police, the manager said.

—Des Moines

ELVIS SHAKES, CROWD SCREAMS

—Providence

The Big E, as in electrodynamic, turned St. John Arena inside out Tuesday night and just about all of the 14,000 cash customers quaked and quivered from the supercharge. Yes, it was Elvis Presley with his mystical, mythical magic touch. . . .

—Columbus

SHRIEKING ADMIRERS ATTEST THAT ELVIS STILL IS KING OF ROCK

—Philadelphia

THEY CAN'T STOP LOVIN' ELVIS; HE STILL GETS THEM ALL SHOOK UP

—Louisville

For some 45 minutes, with flashbulbs popping like fireflies in the darkened auditorium, while strobe lights flashed with machine-gun rapidity, while graying grandmothers and halter-topped teenyboppers stood side-by-side and screamed out their ever-lovin' lungs, Elvis Presley took everyone on a trip through time and space, a journey from reality to yesterday, to fantasyland and back home again.

—Baton Rouge

They loved every second, every twitch, every eye-
lash of this shinning, spangled god. . . .

—Omaha

They came in Montereys and LTDs, in Gran Torinos
and camper vans (making a weekend of it several hundred miles from home), wearing shined shoes and summer suits, new dresses and wigs just back from the
hairdresser. And the smell in the auditorium was not of
marijuana smoke—as at other rock concerts—but of
perfume, hair spray, and after-shave. Some paid ticket
scalpers as much as $150 for a front-row seat. Many
who paid only $7.50 for a seat on the last row paid an-
other $9 for Elvis Opera Glasses.

The money came pouring in, and Elvis kept right on
spending it.

One of the ways Elvis chose to spend his earnings in
the summer of 1974 was in the production of his own
film. This, like the hiring of his own group, Voice, was
to cause friction within the Presley camp.

Jerry Schilling remembers, "Elvis'd go to the Memphian Theater and maybe see three karate films in a
row, from the best, of which there were only a few, to
the worst. Sometimes we'd sit through the WORST
films! And he loved them. They were very basic. He
could relax when he watched these films. There weren't
any problems he had to deal with. Finally, after watching so many, he thought he could do his own."

Elvis had talked about doing such a film—either a
documentary or an action adventure film—several years
earlier, and made a tentative start several times, after
talking it over with his various karate instructors. One
who played a significant role was Ed Parker.

In his book, *Inside Elvis,* Parker remembered that at
first Elvis wanted an adventure film in which he might
play the villain . . . and never play the guitar or sing.
"I want to be," Jerry remembers Elvis saying, "the bad-
dest motherfucker there is." Elvis called the Colonel

with his idea, Ed said, and then hired a Lear jet to take them to the Colonel's home in Palm Springs. There the Colonel reportedly gave his tentative approval and said he would call around to see which major movie studios might be interested.

About the same time, Elvis called in one of Jerry Schilling's old fraternity brothers from Arkansas State, Rick Husky. Elvis first met Rick soon after he'd been discharged from the army and, in a little-known ceremony, was initiated into the fraternity as an honorary member. Through Jerry they'd stayed in touch and now Rick was a successful television writer and producer for such shows as "Mod Squad," "The Rookies," and "Charlie's Angels."

There was no animosity in the meeting that took place soon after, but no one remembers it as being particularly positive or productive.

"Elvis was not a meeting type of guy," says Jerry, "so Ed [Parker] did most of the talking for him. The talk was mostly centered on action. Rick said that can be done; but karate films are over basically; they'd had their day. Rick felt Elvis could be a fantastic dramatic actor with the right script. I went out with Rick afterward and he felt down, thought he was too abstract, and didn't get his point across. Ed kept thinking about visual scenes, violent scenes, and Rick was talking more on the creative level and the meeting never really got together."

Husky recalls it much the same way. He went to Elvis's sumptuous Bel Air home, where he discovered that ". . . my ideas differed from theirs. Elvis and Ed Parker talked karate shtick, they got up and demonstrated. I said, 'Great, but you need a story.' Elvis said, 'That's why you're here.' That was when I told him about his potential as an actor. I compared him to Frank Sinatra and said I'd bet he'd get an Academy Award nomination right off the bat. His response was he didn't want to talk about acting and Oscars, he wanted to do an action film.

"I couldn't get the discussion back to acting and drama. Ed kept saying, 'What Elvis means is . . .' I also felt he had to do the best karate film ever done because karate films were on the way out. I asked to write a treatment for the film and Elvis said okay."

In the sixty-page movie story that Rick wrote, Elvis was to play a retired CIA agent running a karate school. He had a friend who was murdered by drug dealers. (Naturally, they'd made it look like an overdose.) And Elvis, like the retired gunfighter in the Old West, went out to seek revenge. Rick brought it to Jerry, who took it and put it on Elvis's bedroom desk. So far, Elvis's investment in the film was minimal. In the months to come it would swell.

In the meantime, Elvis continued to write checks—or caused his father to write them—to buy extravagant gifts for his friends. One such incident occurred shortly after Elvis reopened for two more weeks August 19 at the Las Vegas Hilton Hotel.

"I was still working as an assistant film editor for Paramount," says Jerry Schilling, "and I went to Vegas on Friday night after work and brought Elvis up to date on the karate film. We talked to about 3 A.M., then I said I was going to my hotel room. Elvis asked me to stick around. I said, 'Okay, I'll be downstairs [in the casino].' Thirty or forty minutes later Charlie Hodge came, found me, and said Elvis wanted to see me.

"I went back up. It was just Elvis and Linda and me. He said, 'I want you to have a home.' I said, 'I don't know how to handle this, Elvis.' He said, 'You been looking at a house and I don't want the banks to mess you up.' "

Jerry had been house-hunting, but his salary at Paramount wasn't high enough to satisfy the customary bank demands to buy the house he wanted in the Hollywood hills. As it happened, the present owner was Jerry's

friend Rick Husky, and with Jerry in the room, Elvis—
at 3 A.M.—called Rick and woke him up.

Elvis was sitting on his bed, wearing a karate jacket
and pants, his pistol on the table nearby, a cigar gone
dead in the ashtray. Linda sat proudly at his side, hug-
ging a pillow. Jerry sat about fifteen feet away in a
chair.

"Hello, Rick," Elvis said, "did I wake you up?"

Rick shook himself and said it was all right.

"I wanna ask you some questions, do you mind?"

"No . . ."

"Look, is it a good house? Are you asking a fair
price? Is it really right for Jerry? Tell me the truth.
We're talking about a good friend, your good friend and
mine."

Rick gulped and said yes to every question.

"We talked about the loan situation," Rick says.
Jerry had the down payment and needed $35,000 more
in his account to get the bank loan. Elvis said, "I don't
want those bankers screwing around with Jerry and I've
got my checkbook out here and I'm writing a check for
the house, is that all right with you?"

"Yes, of course."

"Well," said Elvis, "how soon can you get out?"

"Jesus, Elvis, can I stay the rest of the night?"

Of course this situation led to more friction. Jerry
wasn't even on Elvis's payroll at the time and when
those who were heard about it, they wanted houses, too,
and began jockeying for position, dropping hints. Elvis
liked keeping his boys on their toes—stirred up—and
he ignored them all.

Two other things about this engagement in Las Vegas
made it remarkable. One was a visit backstage by Barbra Streisand and her live-in boyfriend, a hairdresser
named Jon Peters. Jerry Schilling, Joe Esposito, and
Rick Husky were with Elvis in his dressing room when
they entered. Following the cordial introductions and a

few minutes of small talk, Barbra asked, "Is there any place we can talk privately?"

Elvis nodded and excused himself, then led them into the dressing room behind the backstage reception area. There, Barbra told Elvis that she and Jon were going to do a remake of the classic film *A Star Is Born*. She said she wanted him to be her co-star.

Although Rick Husky subsequently told Joe and Jerry and Elvis and several others on the team that the part and story were "fantastic," it never happened. While Elvis worried quietly about how well he could handle the competition of a big co-star like Streisand—used to playing opposite unknown starlets as he was—negotiations broke down between Jon Peters and the Colonel. Peters, who was to be the film's producer, wouldn't meet the Colonel's salary demands.

More memorable and less interesting was the boredom that Elvis felt. Even though the Nevada engagement had been pared to about a third of what it had been previously, Elvis quickly tired of the hotel room/dressing room/showroom routine. He reacted by taking more sleeping pills to sleep longer, then needed more amphetamines to stay on his feet and be alert onstage. Consequently, his onstage monologues grew longer and more discursive. From a tape recording of a typical performance:

"The other night there was a minister in town to raise money for a new Evangelical church. He had an all-night telethon and J. D. Sumner and the Stamps went over and sang. The minister asked J.D. if maybe I would come by, and J.D. replied, 'If he does, I'll jump in the pool.' Later I called and told the minister that because of my contract I can't appear in Las Vegas outside of the Hilton. But I told him I'd donate $2,500 if J.D. and the Stamps did jump into the pool. And they did. I told the minister I'd give another $1,000 if he'd jump in the pool. They had to throw him in!

"When I was a child I always wanted to be in a

gospel quartet. When I was sixteen I went to the Ellis Auditorium in Memphis to an all-night gospel session. I went alone because none of the other kids my age liked that kind of music. J.D. Sumner was then a member of the Blackwood Brothers Quartet. I never dreamed that some day I'd be on the same stage with him. I've known this man all the time since I was sixteen years old. He's been singing on stage for thirty-one years. He's the lowest bass singer in the world—goes down four keys off the piano keyboard. Now, I found these guys [pointing to the right] working in an upholstery shop in Nashville, Tennessee. I knew some of them years back. They'd formed a group and were working in the daytime and singing at night. I think they're fantastic! I brought them to Las Vegas with the act, and I call them Voice.

"I couldn't have a better audience if I stood outside and paid everyone $20 each to come in and listen. You're outtasight! You see him—that's Charlton Heston, ladies and gentlemen. He's made some dillies, hasn't he? *Ben Hur, The Ten Commandments*—I'll never forget that in my life. When he comes off that mountain, from Mount Sinai with those white tablets, and all that white hair. I'd like to talk to him sometime to find out what state of mind he had to get himself into to play that part. Can you imagine that? He had just talked to God, and came down the mountainside with those tablets under his arms and that white hair. I'd like to ask him how he got to thinkin' that part. Phew—it's tougher than a nickel stovepipe.

"See that ring? I wore this ring on the 'Aloha' special. It's not just one big diamond at all. The center stone is eleven-and-a-half carats, and there are several diamonds surrounding it. It was a Christmas present to myself. I was looking for gifts for my father, my grandmother, and my daughter, and when the jeweler came—this just accidentally fell from his case. I was really suckered into buying it. It's the biggest diamond I've ever seen—I just thought I deserved it.

"You know I've never liked the way this showroom's looked—the interior decorating. It's too wide for a performer. I had this ramp made so I could come out a little closer to the audience. Put a spotlight onto the statues on that wall. Okay. That's nice. I don't know what it is, but that's nice. Tom Jones was in here the other night, and he's from Wales. I asked Tom who it was, and he said it was King Edward. King George, sorry, excuse me your majesty. Now take the spotlight and put it on those angels. Just look at those dudes, boy! Big fat angels. Put the spotlight onto this wall over here. You will notice a slight difference. Those of the Caucasian race. That's what it is, isn't it? Caucasian? It was on my army draft card. I thought it meant 'circumcised'! Anyway, the other night, I came down here at about 4:30 in the morning with a couple of friends who work for me—Jerry Schilling and Red West. Red is a second degree black belt in karate—he's got a school in Memphis, and I'm very proud of him. Red wrote 'Separate Ways' and 'Why Can't Everyday Be Like Christmas' and 'If You Talk in Your Sleep.' Anyway, he climbed the fence where they keep the supplies, the paint and so forth, he climbed the fence, as high as this curtain; he went down and got a little can of black paint. He put it in his belt, came back, climbed over, and we went over there and stacked up two tables. I got up with the paint and brush, and I was Michelangelo, or the guy that painted the ceiling in the Vatican—the Sistine Chapel. I painted that statue—it took thirty minutes to do. The hotel hasn't said a word. I just thought I'd share it with you.

"I have been involved in the art of karate for some time—most people don't know to what extent. It's become to me like a way of life. I started doing it some sixteen years ago as a hobby, not as self-defense. It started in 1959 when I was in the army; I study and learn every day for two to three, even six hours. It's helped me in self-control, body discipline, mind discipline, in my stage work, diet, and breathing techniques. It involves yoga. It involves meditation. Kung Fu and karate are two different things. Kung Fu is slower—like sand blowing in your face. Karate is quicker—karate gets on with it. There's a lot to do. It's not just breaking boards. The word *karate, kara* means open, and *te* means hand—open hand. It's an art, not a sport. It has a much deeper meaning. It involved the Buddhist monks. They had no way of protecting themselves from robbers, so evolved a way to keep themselves from being killed or robbed. They studied different animals. They studied the tiger. The tiger fights on its back. All cats do—your house cat does. They roll into a ball, and fight on their backs and you can't get near them. My karate name is 'Tiger.' The cobra snake will approach its victim and mesmerize it, hypnotize it. The eagle is the highest flyer of all birds. He sees his prey, and comes out of the sky and gets his food in his all-powerful talons, and breaks bones and crushes its victim. They devised this over hundreds of years for humans to do it, using their hands, feet, legs, and elbows. I've never had to use it in my life in any violent way. It's not for that reason. On the contrary, it gives you self-confidence. It makes you a better citizen in your daily life. I'm sworn to a pledge never to use that which I have learned to harm, frighten, or to disable. If so I could be stripped of my belt, and turned over to the law—the authorities.

"I teach—we have a class upstairs in my suite. We do it every day at six o'clock for about an hour-and-a-half. In Los Angeles I study under Ed Parker, who teaches *kempo*. In Memphis I study under a fellow who came from Korea, Mr. Kang Rhee. Mr. Rhee teaches the *pasatu* system, which means all systems in one. You take the best ingredients from all the systems. There's no age limit in this. Half the classes around the country are children, women, and older folk. They realize that this doesn't require tremendous physical strength. One man came to my instructors' school in Los Angeles. He was a businessman in Beverly Hills and about fifty-four years old. He watched the class and told my instructors that he thought he was too old to go for his black belt. But the guy's been coming along every day in his lunch hours for two to three years, and now he's a black belt. You go through seven degrees before you get to the black-belt category. You test for each one of these. In 1960 I tested for my first degree black belt. I had to fight two guys both at once and then separately. This one guy had a smile on his face all the time. I couldn't get near him. Next morning I was so sore, I couldn't get a comb through my hair. In 1963 I got the second degree black belt. They skipped the third and made me a fourth which carries the title 'Associate Professor of the Art.' The fifth degree holds the title 'Professor of the Art.' I got that four years ago. The sixth is 'Senior Professor,' and seventh 'Associate Master.' My eighth I got a few days ago and I now hold the title 'Master of the Art.' Ninth degree would be 'Senior Master of the Art,' and tenth degree would be 'Grand Master' and there are only a few of those guys in the world. You never hear about 'em. They don't appear on no TV shows, or in no black-belt magazines because they are trained as a religious order, a devotion, a way of life. Now that I've reached eighth degree I can start my own Karate Association. We are due to start our own style of karate under the heading of the 'American Karate Institute.' We intend it to become an Americanization of the art, using numbers one, two, and three, in place of a foreign language."

And on and on and on.

These long monologues left little time for music and when Elvis did sing, often he didn't finish the song, or he walked through it as if he were bored to death. Had he no respect for his audience? Was he trying to bore them, too?

Of course not. At all times he thought he was giving the people exactly what they paid to get. And he wasn't entirely wrong; they had come to see him and that's what they were doing. He was confident about that. The strong central nervous system stimulants that he took before going on—the amphetamines and cocaine—saw to that. They also made him talkative.

His abuse of prescription drugs already had caused cancellations. Now they were radically affecting the shows he did perform.

September, 1974–
January, 1975

It was a bad time for Elvis. Everything seemed to be coming apart. First, his father and his father's wife of ten years, Dee, separated. "I'm a self-centered person," she says. "Vernon made me that way. He treated me like a child, he kept me in a cage. I was about the last to know about Priscilla and Elvis's problem. The business is something I never knew about. I started writing songs. I wanted a life of my own."

It was a familiar theme. Priscilla had felt suffocated, restricted, too. Now, as Dee was packing up and leaving Vernon's house nearby, Elvis saw his friend Linda Thompson move her things out of Graceland. Their relationship was an emotional one and there would be flare-ups off and on for years to come. Elvis was not one to remain alone, however, and when he went on the road only two weeks after closing in Las Vegas, he had a new girl on his arm, Sheila Ryan, another Memphis beauty queen, who later would marry actor James Caan.

Elvis had lost his longtime piano player, David Briggs, who was being paid $3,000 a week by Elvis, but wanted to return to the Nashville recording studios, where he knew he could earn even more.

His health plummeted as his weight ballooned. Never again would he be measured by his costume designer,

163

Bill Belew. "That stopped sometime that year, 1974," Bill says. "After that I'd make the costumes by guess and take them to Elvis and leave them for him to try on. Joe Espisito would call and say they needed letting out, so I'd go back and pick them up, then take them back, pick them up and take them back, until we got it right. It was never explained why no measurements were taken. It was just understood. You didn't ask questions. Ever!"

Just how much weight Elvis had put on, and how quickly, became apparent when he arrived at the University of Maryland in College Park on September 27, just three weeks after closing in Vegas. So great was the change, some of the boys in the band say they had trouble recognizing him.

Tony Brown, the pianist for Voice, had taken Briggs's place in the backup band and he watched Elvis arrive. "He fell out of the limousine to his knees," Tony says. "People jumped to help and he pushed them away, like, 'Don't help me!' He always did that when he fell. He walked onstage and he held onto the mike for the first thirty minutes like it was a post. Everybody was scared. It was the talk of the . . . is the tour gonna happen? Is he sick? Is it gonna be canceled?"

Guitarist John Wilkinson was standing a few feet away on the stage. "The lights go down," he recalls, "and Elvis comes up the stairs. He was all gut. He was slurring. He was so fucked up. I looked at Kathy Westmoreland. She looked at me. What happened? It was obvious he was drugged. It was obvious there was something terribly wrong with his body. It was so bad the words to the songs were barely intelligible. You couldn't hear him hardly. College Park let it be known they wouldn't have him back. We were in a state of shock. Joe Guercio said, 'He's finished. . . .' I remember crying. He could barely get through the introductions on the stage. He cut the show very short and it seemed like it went on forever."

The rest of the tour was, as Tony put it, "uphill." For three nights, in Detroit, South Bend, and St. Paul, Elvis seemed in control. His eyes were bright and the shows were energetic and musical, giving hope to those around him. Back in Detroit, he slipped again.

"I watched him in his dressing room, just draped over a chair, unable to move," says John Wilkinson. "So often I thought, 'Boss, why don't you just cancel this tour and take a year off . . . ?' I mentioned something once in a guarded moment. He patted me on the back and said, 'It'll be all right. Don't you worry about it.' "

The cities rolled by like commercials on a television set, all of them very much alike, all noisy and somewhat numbing. Dayton, Wichita, San Antonio, and Abilene. The Playboy jet that Elvis had chartered for the tour flew in, and the Playboy jet flew out. Limousines and hotel rooms and huge auditoriums became the only environments he knew. Finally, on October 10, Elvis and his entourage pulled into Lake Tahoe to make up five days for the canceled engagement in the Sahara Tahoe a year earlier.

After that, Elvis didn't work for five months.

Back in Memphis—in the final months before his fortieth birthday—it wasn't his health but finances that caused the next crisis. In all categories, costs were rising alarmingly. The paternity suit that Elvis had taken so seriously finally was dismissed after blood tests and a private detective's confidential reports made it clear that the waitress was lying, but legal fees for this and the ongoing lawsuit involving the hallway assault in Lake Tahoe topped all previous years.

Three years later that lawsuit would require Elvis's accountants in Memphis, Rhea, and Ivey, to produce a breakdown of his 1974 earnings and expenses. It was a fragmentary picture they drew, it didn't tell all the story, but even the boldest strokes were revealing. This was the first time that Elvis's finances emerged publicly.

He had earned lots, $7,273,622, in 1974—86 percent of it, $6,281,885, from Nevada and the grueling, carnivalesque one-nighters, the rest from record sales ($416,864), publishing royalties ($278,360), and movie rentals to theaters and television ($133,529). But he also spent lots—4,295,372 in what the accountants called "operating expenses" alone.

Where, and to whom, did the money go? Only tax deductible expenses were shown in the financial statement, yet these certainly are revealing enough. Colonel Parker, for instance, took as his share $1,720,067, while those on his personal payroll—an unspecified number, but probably about fifteen—split $467,599. Elvis also spent $24,300 on his wardrobe, $2,207 on cleaning and laundry, and $12,819 on telephone calls. The accountants said that they and the lawyers had earned $62,626.

On top of this, Elvis paid predictably high taxes, $1,484,867, leaving him with a net income of $1,493,384. That's not bad. Most small businesses wish they had that margin of profit. The trouble was, Elvis still managed to spend more than he made. According to the accountants' statement, he started 1974 with $2,640,355 in the bank and finished it with $1,928,746. That meant his year-end deficit was $711,609.

What *that* meant was that Elvis took in a million-and-a-half in 1974 and spent more than three . . . not on deductible expenses, but on *himself*. Jewelers and car dealers were given a lot of it, of course, and there was the matter of Jerry Schilling's house. Only the accountants knew exactly how much Linda cost; at least $250,000, according to the estimates of friends. Several rooms in Graceland were redecorated. Guns and ammunition ate up another small fortune. Television sets were blown apart and replaced. Some say the biggest expense was "medication." "Would you believe half a million dollars?" asks one insider. "It's possible, when you keep flying people to Las Vegas and Los Angeles from Memphis to pick up the prescriptions."

It didn't get any better in 1975. On January 8, Elvis celebrated his fortieth birthday and that hurt in other ways.

The press had been taking shots for several months. In October, *Pageant* magazine asked on its cover, "Elvis at 40: What's ahead for the aging star?" then warned that Elvis could be on the brink of "male menopause," raising doubts about Elvis's vanity surviving his loss of youth.

The *National Enquirer* joined the assault a month later. Again Elvis was on the cover, pictured this time in concert in a ferociously unflattering pose that gave him a hunched back, thick waist, and a visage that was a cross between Sidney Greenstreet at his most sensual and Boris Karloff at his scariest. Under the photograph were the words, "Elvis at 40—Paunchy, Depressed & Living in Fear." Most of the sources for the story were employees of motels where he stayed on his last tour through the Midwest and local police assigned to his security. The impression they left was vivid. He was afraid for his life, feared being kidnapped or assassinated, the *Enquirer* said; in Abilene, where Vernon and Lisa flew in for a sort of family reunion—Linda was back, too—Vernon was quoted as being so upset by the way Elvis looked, he had Dr. George Nichopoulos flown in from Memphis. The writers of the article also quoted a critic, in Indianapolis, who said Elvis was fat.

It wasn't much of a story, really. But many of Elvis's most avid fans read the *Enquirer* religiously and the effect was felt. Elvis's friends did their best to keep such stories away from him, but this was one that got through and Elvis was reported enraged as well.

Several other publications checked in that January to wish Elvis sardonic birthday greetings. *People* magazine also put him on the cover—by now it was clear to publishers that an Elvis cover sold magazines—and compared his "sybaritic reclusiveness" to that of Howard Hughes, his "ambivalent social consciousness" to the film character Billy Jack.

Robert Hilburn in the *Los Angeles Times* took a different, harder tack. "Elvis: Waning Legend in His Own Time?" was the title of an essay on the front page of the Sunday entertainment section that opened with the statement, "Maybe it's time for Elvis to retire."

"At 40," Hilburn—once a devoted fan—said, "his records are increasingly uneven, his choice of material sometimes ludicrous, and his concert performances often sloppy. Worst of all, there is no purpose or personal vision in his music anymore."

Hilburn went on to call Elvis's latest album, *Promised Land,* "bland and directionless." On the basis of this and other recent albums, he said, it would be difficult to convince a young music fan that Elvis was the most important figure in the birth of rock and roll. Elvis had refused to advance his music, Hilburn charged; he took the easy way, and when faced with an adoring audience that didn't seem to care what he did, or how well, came to his concerts and bought his records anyway, he put his career on "automatic pilot" and stopped growing. He weakened his standards. He *wasted* his talent.

The fans were there, to be sure. As quickly as the sea of public criticism rushed in, they sent Elvis avid confirmation of undying love.

There was a wonderful salute in *The Commercial Appeal,* Memphis's afternoon newspaper. It reported that although Elvis observed his birthday privately in "self-imposed seclusion," letters had poured in at the rate of about 600 a day for more than a week, along with hundreds of telegrams. A special "Happy Birthday Elvis" box was set up outside the Graceland gates for the wishes of the two thousand visitors who came by daily. Radio stations, the medium through which Elvis initially rose to fame, played Elvis records throughout the day, gave away birthday cakes and Elvis albums

every hour, and conducted interviews with longtime
Elvis friends and associates.

It may have helped some, but it wasn't enough. As
Ed Parker tells the story in his book, *Inside Elvis,* his
telephone rang at 5 A.M.

"Ed?"

"Yeah, Elvis."

"You could tell it was me?"

"Who else calls me at five in the morning, Elvis? And
who could mistake your voice? You sound nervous. Is
something wrong?"

There was a pause. "Ed, I'm forty years old today."

"So?"

"Yeah, well, it's getting up there. I'm no kid anymore."

"Elvis, you've got a lot of years ahead of you. Don't
you believe that?"

"Yeah . . . I . . . yeah, I do."

"Look at Sinatra. He was the teenage idol of all the
bobby-soxers. And yet his audiences continued to grow
through the years. He's more popular now than he was
then."

"Yeah! Yeah! That's right!"

Elvis wasn't convincing. He was forty years old and
it hurt.

Twenty days later Elvis was back in the hospital, this
time with, among other problems, an enlarged colon.
At least that's what the press was told. And it was true.
But it was also true that Elvis was back in the hospital
for another detoxification. This, too, would be confirmed years later by Dr. Nick. The way Nichopoulos
told the story at the time, however, merely stated that
Elvis had been sick for several days but was reluctant
to go to the hospital. He said it required several more
days of talking before he submitted to the physician's
wishes, during which time a suite was held for him on
the Baptist Hospital's eighteenth floor.

Finally, on January 28 at 5 A.M., the telephone rang

at the nurse's station. Dr. Nick said he was leaving
Graceland with Elvis and would be arriving in fifteen
minutes. Elvis was wearing navy blue pajamas and the
start of a dark beard when he entered the end-of-the-
hallway suite of rooms, with his father, Joe Esposito,
Linda Thompson, and a few of his bodyguards trailing
along behind him. Soon after that, Linda shaved Elvis
and the hospital star routine began.

The first days were uneventful, as Elvis slept long
hours in the always darkened room. When awake, he
talked with the nurses assigned to him, one of them a
recent graduate of the University of Arkansas who soon
began dating one of Elvis's hired hands, another a middle-aged woman named Marian Cocke, who later also
would write a book, *I Called Him Babe: Elvis Presley's
Nurse Remembers*.

The enlarged colon and drug detoxification were two
of several serious problems examined during his three-
week stay. Another concerned his eyes. He had been
experiencing headaches and optical pressure in recent
months; eventually this would be diagnosed as glaucoma, the third major cause of blindness in the United
States. There was no danger of Elvis losing his sight,
the doctors reported, but before he went on the road
again and exposed himself to bright lights in performance, tinted contact lenses would be made. He also
was given medication for some time and ordered to continue wearing the tinted glasses he favored.

A more serious problem—one never discussed publicly—showed itself in the results of a liver biopsy.
Later, Elvis would joke about the long needle that was
stuck into his side to extract a sample of liver tissue, but
the findings weren't at all amusing. There was severe
damage to the organ and it was clear to attending physicians that in Elvis's case that probable cause was drug
abuse.

The colon problem, Dr. Nick said, was caused by
Elvis's poor eating habits. Elvis loved fried foods and

sugar, he said, and needed a nearly complete change in his diet.

As usual, Elvis was cheerful and obedient, promising to mend his ways. Of course he did not.

It got worse before it got better during this hospital stay, when Vernon had his first heart attack and was rushed to the hospital's intensive care unit, where he remained for nearly a week. Vernon was then moved into the suite adjacent to Elvis's. Elvis was checked out of the hospital before Vernon, on February 14, but visited him often.

"Elvis would come and try to cheer him up," Jerry Schilling recalls. "It was the first time that Vernon had been in a hospital all his life. And both he and Elvis were scared to death."

"I was there the first time he went in to visit," says the hospital vice-president, Maurice Elliott. "Elvis came out crying."

There was one other incident connected to this hospital stay. Elvis wanted to put the young nurse who had begun to date Al Strada on his payroll, to accompany him to Las Vegas in March and go on tour in April and May. When she accepted his offer, he gave her a thousand dollars to buy a new wardrobe. Quitting her job at the hospital, she went home to visit her parents in Arkansas.

Several on the hospital staff, including Dr. Nick, tried to change her mind, but she was convinced. When word of her hiring reached the Colonel in California, however, the tide turned quickly. He didn't believe Elvis needed a nurse with him—certainly not one that was going with one of the bodyguards—and thought her presence would be bad for Elvis's image. The Colonel called Joe and Joe talked to Elvis, who wanted to see that the nurse kept her hospital job. Joe saw that that was done and then broke the news to the young nurse.

*　　*　　*

The Colonel's relationship with Elvis had undergone considerable stress in the previous year. They'd been partners in this multimillion-dollar enterprise for exactly twenty years by 1975, and it's doubtful that any partnership survives that long without some pulling and tugging. Still, during 1974 and on into the following year, there were recurring rumors that Elvis and the Colonel were separating.

It's true that they often disagreed—over some of the tour dates that the Colonel approved, for example, when Elvis thought the cities were too small. Another time they fought over whether or not Elvis would do a ninety-minute-long gospel show on television: the Colonel wanted it; Elvis did not. Elvis also started grumbling over an album the Colonel had released first as a joke on his own Boxcar label and then had released by RCA; this was *Having Fun with Elvis on Stage (A Talking Album Only)*, an embarrassing collection of snippets from Elvis's concert appearances—belches, burps, bad jokes, and all. More complaints were heard backstage when the Colonel suggested strongly that Elvis stop using so much karate in his act.

Their biggest fight resulted from something else that happened on the Hilton showroom stage. Elvis's favorite chef at the hotel had been fired, and he was so angry, he started badmouthing hotel management between songs. The Colonel had recently renegotiated Elvis's contract, giving the singer the same pay for less work, and after the show, he confronted Elvis outside his dressing room.

"You can't tell these people how to run their business!" the Colonel said, so angry that his jowls shook as he thumped his cane on the floor. "What right you think you got to say somethin' like that on their stage?"

Bang, bang, bang went the cane, and Elvis began shouting back. The Colonel saw an audience gathering and suddenly stopped, looking at Elvis and nodding toward the dressing room door. Silently, they went inside, where they again began to shout at each other, their words muffled by the door. A few minutes later the Colonel emerged and said, as he stalked away, still pounding his cane as he went, "All right . . . I'll call a press conference in the morning and say I'm leaving."

Elvis had to get in the final word. According to Red West, he shouted, "I'll call a press conference tonight!"

In his book *Elvis: What Happened?*, Red explained that what happened next was that the Colonel stayed up all night, figuring out how much money Elvis owed him. "I didn't see the figures," Red said, "but it was like a million due him for this and a million for that. Elvis showed Vernon the figures. Vernon was ready for the Colonel to leave, but then after looking at the figures, things seemed to quiet down."

Most of the time the relationship was a cordial one, unchanged over the years, as both remained Number One in their respective fields. In a business lubricated with snake oil, Colonel Parker seemed without peer. No one, absolutely no one, seemed to have more guts, and no one appeared to be able to pull things off with such boorish yet enviable style.

The amazing thing was that most of the stories about him were at least partly true. It was true, for example, that promoters in Britain and Australia and elsewhere made what appeared to be generous offers. The way it was reported in the press, no matter how large the sum, the Colonel always replied, "That'll be fine for me, now how much you gonna pay my boy?"

"The whole truth is," says one of the Colonel's closest associates, "Elvis didn't want to go to Europe and it didn't make any sense to go. They would've lost money. All the talk about big offers were nice publicity for the promoters, but not a one of them ever put up a certified check as a deposit, required in the business as a matter of course. The Colonel even once offered to put up a two-million-dollar bond if Elvis didn't show if the promoter (in England) would put up one-fifth of his five-million-dollar offer. The promoter wasn't heard from again. The Colonel knew that if he took the offer anyway, it'd kill Elvis in England and much of Europe for a long time, because what wasn't publicized was that the promoter wanted to get at least one TV show and at least one movie out of it besides the four concerts for his five million, which he could then turn into forty million. The Colonel said no thanks to us in the office and then called the guy's bluff."

That was when the Colonel went to the press and gave them his famous quote about the offer being fine for him, but what about "my boy."

The Colonel never gave interviews, remained as secluded as Elvis did, surrounded by a phalanx of men whose function was to preserve and perpetuate the Elvis machine and myth; this involved keeping the Colonel's image going, too, for he had to be as mysterious, and amazing, as Elvis was for the partnership to work. So it was made abundantly clear before I was taken to meet the Colonel—this more than a year following Elvis's death—that I was to ask no questions and take no notes. I had talked with the Colonel by telephone three or four times and most of these calls had been placed by him to me. He'd always been, well, kindly, projecting the image of a gruff but caring older relative.

The small suite of offices was spartan. In the room where we talked, a simple table seated six. He had the biggest, most comfortable chair and it faced a wall on which he had hung a picture of himself, growling and showing a four- or five-day growth of beard. The mood of the room was deferential, as everyone on his staff gathered for coffee and donuts, a Friday morning ritual. The Colonel began telling stories about himself. This was the way it was every Friday. Only the man in the chair to the Colonel's left changed.

"It was, oh, I guess six or seven years ago in Salt Lake [1971]," he said. "The rest of the auditorium was sold out, and we couldn't sell the last 2,000 seats for anything. Then, on the Sunday before the show, Elder Stevens died. The show was set for Wednesday. I called the radio stations and canceled all the ads. We weren't selling tickets anyway and I thought that I'd save $1,900.

"What we did"—he went on, getting to the kernel of his genius—"was that instead of taking the ads we made an announcement that we were dropping the ads until after Elder Stevens's funeral on Tuesday. Of course the radio stations gave us all the announcements free. Then, on Wednesday, the ads started again and we sold out all 2,000 seats in two hours, between ten and twelve. It had to be the Mormons who bought the tickets. Right?"

Later, on New Year's Eve in Pittsburgh in 1976, challenge presented itself again. "We were playing in a room that held 20,000," the Colonel said, "and we sold 18,900 of them. The rest were awful seats—way up in the attic, behind a post. We were selling maybe twelve or fifteen of them a day. So we pulled all our ads and put in new ones. We said, 'We still have a few seats left. They aren't very good, but it's all we've got.' When that hit the air, we sold out right away. People liked the honesty."

The Colonel worked this way for two reasons. One was that he liked to play the game. Over the years it came to be known as the Elvis Presley Game. "When the Colonel had someone important coming in," says a longtime associate, "we'd all have to get on the phone and carry on bogus conversations to make the office look busy."

There was a story that went around about the time the Colonel took a call from the man who arranged for all the White House entertainment. Because of Elvis's "close" relationship with Richard Nixon, and their mutual respect, the man said, Nixon wanted Elvis to perform in the White House. The Colonel said he thought that was a right nice invitation, he knew Elvis would be proud, and because of Elvis's "close" relationship with the President, Elvis would sing a few numbers for $25,000, and that, the Colonel said, included the orchestra: a bargain price.

The man in the White House was dumbfounded. Finally he regained his composure and said, "Why, Colonel Parker, no one ever gets paid to perform in the White House."

"Well," said the Colonel, "no one ever asks Elvis to play for free."

There was also a great need for money. Elvis made money like an Arabian prince and spent it like one. The Colonel had been doling out money for the still-limping karate film at the rate of only $10,000 at a time—not because he was a cheapskate, but because he objected to the expense. The Colonel also argued regularly with Elvis about paying the members of Voice, and he thought many of the bodyguards stayed around only for the rewards—the houses, the jewels, the cars, the drugs, the girls; he thought several could be let go. There was a cash-flow problem. It was that simple.

The Colonel wasn't the tightwad Elvis's father was. No, *he* had a real cash-flow problem, too. Over the years that Elvis had been performing in Las Vegas, while Vernon showed a fondness for the nickel slot machines, the Colonel had come to be regarded as a high-roller at the roulette wheel. Although he was a millionaire, and lived modestly, sometimes he got a little behind in his payments to the Hilton hotel.

So the Colonel learned, or invented, all the tricks.

March, 1975–
July, 1975

Elvis hadn't worked in five months when he took his gang to Las Vegas in March 1975 and although he still packed a lot of uncomfortable weight inside his jeweled white jumpsuit, his spirits were higher than they'd been at the start of a Nevada engagement in years. This was his twelfth visit and if he didn't view it with the nervous excitement of his first, at least for a change it didn't seem a boring prospect. Elvis may have been in a rut, the performances may have become more than a little routine by now, but Elvis needed them. Going face-to-face with an audience and moving it was what he was all about. A demonstration of power, a salve for wounded self-respect, it was Elvis's heaviest drug.

That and the music. Years later the leader of Iran, Ayatollah Khomeini, would ban music in his country, saying, "Music is no different from opium. If you want your country to be independent, you must turn radio and television into educational institutions and eliminate music. Music makes the brain inactive." Elvis would have disagreed. It made *his* brain active, not inactive. Of course it was like an opiate, too. Elvis really did love to sing, and he loved the sound of singing. He wasn't so insecure about his voice, as some have suggested, that he hired a chorus of backup vocalists in support. The truth was, he loved each of those singers

177

and groups, respected them, recognized talent when he heard it, and merely wanted to have it nearby for his own satisfaction—knowing at the same time that good voices made good listening for his audience, too. He especially adored good high voices and very low voices. It was for this reason above all others that he kept Kathy Westmoreland and J.D. Sumner on his permanent payroll and the songs he let them sing in his show more and more in those days were showcases for such vocal highs and lows. He also loved good harmony. Nothing pleased him more, or got him truly higher, than sitting at the piano at the end of his day in Las Vegas —about three in the morning—to sing church songs with the people who sang in his show.

The first nights in Las Vegas were good. Even the reviewers, though they noted his bulkiness, talked mostly about how good his voice was and how much fun he seemed to be having. "Fat and Sassy," was the headline on one story.

Much of his good humor took the form of self-parody, usually in the middle of "Hound Dog" or another of the 1950s songs that he was now very tired of singing. He feigned difficulty getting the left side of his upper lip into its famous curl, for example, poking it up with a finger and muttering, "When I was nineteen it worked just fine." Sometimes he pretended to be unable to get his legs to shake. These were bits of stage "business" that he used with great success for years, and they still seemed to amuse him.

This was an engagement that also was marked by changes in the hotel and in the way the audience was seated. A new $20 million tower containing 600 rooms was opened, allowing more Elvis fans than ever before to sleep under the same roof with their idol. There was a new policy in the showroom, too. Waiters no longer were required to present checks at the end of the show. Now tickets were sold. Cost of the shows was now $20 a person, up from $17.50 charged previously. That gave the customers either two drinks or a half-bottle of champagne, and included tax and tip. This was true for both shows; thus it was Elvis's first performance in Vegas that didn't have a dinner show. Drinks were easier to prepare and serve, the margin of profit was higher in alcohol (and soft drinks for the underaged fans) than it was in food, and replacing the dinner tables with smaller cocktail tables allowed the hotel management to increase the capacity of the room by 20 percent.

More money was being made on Presley product. As usual, all money from the sale of Elvis souvenir items in the hotel lobby went to a local charity, but that which was sold in the gift shops and boutiques went into Elvis's and the Colonel's pockets. Besides scarves, you could also buy pennants, picture books, and records.

The albums continued to appear with the predictability of the seasons, usually three or four a year, with the same number of singles. Those released in 1974 and 1975 showed clearly the aimless sort of career trajectory that Bob Hilburn referred to. Following the release of the inspired *Legendary Performer* album (in January 1974), there was an album (in March) called *Good Times,* a collection of songs from the autobiographical session in Memphis a year earlier ("Take Good Care of Her," "Goodtime Charlie's Got the Blues," etc.). Then there was the first of many live albums, a so-so double disc recorded during the March concerts at the Memphis Coliseum and released in June, and after that came the embarrassing "talking album."

In 1975 the same pattern of no pattern held steady. The first album, released in January, was named for his recent Top 20 hit, *Promised Land,* a rocker written by Chuck Berry. In March came a repackage of ten songs that had sold a million copies or more, called, unimaginatively, *Pure Gold*—a nice enough collection, but lacking in direction, including songs from three decades ("All Shook Up," "In the Ghetto," "It's Impossible"), with no connecting thread.

All went onto the bestseller lists, as did the four singles released in the same period.

Besides music and performing it in public, Elvis probably enjoyed spending money more than anything else, and 1975 was his year for spending it. It's unusual that a man's jeweler becomes a significant source of information in writing a biography. Again, Elvis was the exception to the rule. Elvis favored two jewelers. One had a shop in Beverly Hills that Elvis frequented the way other men frequent their neighborhood bars. The other, from Memphis, Elvis liked so much he took him on the road with him when he went touring—with the understanding that he always would have two sample cases full of trinkets for when Elvis got in the buying mood.

Sol Schwartz was a fast-talking former New Yorker with an eighth-grade education and a heart the size of the Beverly Hills Hotel. He met Elvis when the singer was making a movie with Nancy Sinatra, back in 1966. Sol's wife Betty had thrown a couple of handfuls of expensive rings and pins into her handbag and gone to Nancy's house so Nancy could pick out some gifts. Nancy bought about $7,000 worth of jewelry and Elvis, who was at the house visiting, doubled that. A few days later Elvis visited Sol's shop and soon after that offered to lend him $50,000 so he could upgrade his inventory.

"He'd be here every day, usually about four o'clock, and stand outside and hustle customers for the store," Sol says. "Everybody'd know he was in town. The fat old ladies from the department store down the street would be outside waiting for him. He used to come into the store and sit in my office with his feet up and shave himself with an electric razor. When he came in, I'd pinch him on the cheek and say, 'Hey, baby, you're gettin' fat.'

"I made Elvis a ring one day, one of Elvis's first big pieces, a coffee-colored marquise diamond ring, about five carats. It was a woman's ring in the window. His taste ran to women's jewelry. It was $18,000. He got hassled in the Hilton in Vegas two days later and one of the guards helped him. Elvis said, 'What can I do for you?' He said, 'I like your ring.' Elvis took it off and gave it to him.

"His buying habits were interesting. He used to ask me the price of everything. He'd look and ask the price, I'd put it back and then about five minutes later, before he'd leave, he'd say, 'I'll take that, that, that, that, that, that, and that.' He was like a kid in a candy store."

It was Sol's partner, Lee Ablesser, who designed the TCB neck charm that Elvis gave away to friends and people who worked for him. Sol says he sold Elvis five hundred of the chains and charms, and another five hundred charm bracelets. The "TCB" and the "Elvis bracelet," as they came to be called, cost Elvis $175 apiece.

"It was a mutual thing," says Sol. "Elvis wanted the jewelry and I wanted to sell him. And he never threw it up, like he was doing me a favor. Some of the stars, they aren't like that. Elvis musta spent half a million dollars with me, yet he didn't play the kiss-my-ass game once."

His Memphis jeweler, Lowell Hays, sold Elvis more jewelry than that, at least $800,000 worth. It was easy. After a while, Elvis not only took him on tour, he took him along on vacations, too. A soft-spoken, yet aggressive, charming university man who keeps his fraternity certificate on the wall of his office, Lowell was, by 1975, part of the regular entourage. He met Elvis through Dr. Nick.

"The first time, they called me at home and said Elvis wants to see some jewelry. They said bring it to the Memphian Theater. I said, 'What does he want?' They said he likes big, flashy things. So I came by the store and opened the vault, took out the biggest, flashiest things I had, and went to the theater. The show was already on and I found Dr. Nick and he said sit down. A few minutes later he went over to Elvis and told him I was here and Elvis got up in the middle of the movie, looked at me and motioned with his finger and took off up the aisle. I followed him to the little boys' room. He locked the door and we sat there and went through the jewelry. He had one of his bodyguards with him. He picked out Christmas gifts for several people, in the neighborhood of ten nice gifts.

"Another time they called me from Atlanta and said bring some jewelry up here, Elvis wants some. I got some jewelry together and flew to Atlanta where my instructions were to go to the top floor of the Stoffer's Hotel. He told me he wanted to buy something for the Sweet Inspirations and he did and he ended up buying several other things. I asked him, 'Can I stay with the tour?' He said sure. From then on, my name was on that list and I had a room and I could come and go as I pleased and I did. I had my room like one of the boys, I had no obligations, I had all my expenses paid for everything. Many times I joined the tour in the middle or left and went back to Memphis in the middle and then I'd pay my air fare, but otherwise it was all on Elvis. I went on every tour he had for the last three or four years. There were a lot of tours and I was on every one of them.

"I called him one time and said I'd be coming in to join the tour. I didn't take any jewelry with me. I went just to go. Elvis saw me and said, 'Bring your case, I want to buy something.' I said, 'Elvis, I didn't bring it, I didn't come on this thing to solicit you, I just wanted to be here.' He said, 'Look, I don't consider you're soliciting me. Ever' time I see you, I see diamonds. From now on, you can come on all my tours with me, but from now on, bring your jewelry with you. Don't come along as dead weight. I expect you to have jewelry with you. When I see you, I think Lowell's got his jewelry with him, I want to see what he's got. If you don't bring it with you, I'm gonna teach you a lesson some time.' "

He did, too. After Lowell and Elvis and several

others had gone to a football game in Memphis, Elvis flew them to Dallas and then to Palm Springs, where a department store opened in the middle of the night to him so he could buy everyone pajamas and toilet articles and hair dryers and a change of clothes, because they'd left Memphis on Elvis's whim and without going home to pack.

Relaxing at Elvis's Palm Springs home, Elvis told Lowell, "Bring your case."

"But, Elvis, I don't have it. We went to a football game, remember?"

Elvis glared at Lowell and said, "I told you to bring jewelry when you were around me." He then took Lowell with him as he visited a Palm Springs jeweler and spent a small fortune. Lowell never forgot again.

Such highs in Elvis's life inevitably were followed by depression. Even before he left Las Vegas in April he was slipping. His pianist, Tony Brown, remembers that the closing-night party for that engagement was one of the biggest and best, but Elvis never even appeared.

That was followed by a two-week tour of the South (including a benefit for Mississippi tornado victims) and a three-day recording session in Los Angeles. The songs he recorded during those sessions were not particularly memorable, but Elvis's reaction to the album that came from the sessions was. RCA was anxious for a May release, so rushed the tapes to New York for a quick "mix-down," returning the tapes to Los Angeles for Elvis's appraisal.

"Elvis was pissed, *really* pissed," says John Wilkinson, "because it didn't sound the same as it did when it left the studio in Hollywood. And he went into a *rage!* There was some guy from RCA in the booth when we heard the album and Elvis started saying things about RCA. He said, 'You know, if I was smart, I'd quit you sonofabitches and I'd go with White Whale (a small Hollywood record company) or somebody. I betcha I can find a job someplace. I betcha somebody'll hire me.'

He put that poor guy through some shit. We took a break after listening to the album. Red or Joe suggested a break, said we'd been working too hard. I guess they talked to him and got him calmed down. But he was mad and he had a right to be mad. After that, he said, 'By God, none of them go to New York. They go to Memphis for the re-mix and that's where it'll stay!' "

Two weeks later, at the end of May, Elvis was on the road again for another sixteen shows in twelve days, again crisscrossing the South and going as far north as Cleveland, Ohio, and Terre Haute, Indiana. The tour ended on the tenth of June and six days after that, Elvis was back in the hospital again. However, this time it was a different hospital, the Mid-South, and the press was not advised.

Later, when a few facts leaked out, Elvis's people said the two-day hospitalization was for an eye examination, which made sense, considering the recent trouble he'd had with his eyes and the seriousness of the diagnosis. In fact, his eyes did play a role in the hospitalization. The plastic surgeon Elvis saw removed bags from under them.

Elvis was familiar with cosmetic surgery. Anyone who had worked so many years in Hollywood would be; film was, after all, an industry that survived on the good features of its stars, and with the passing of time, many of those stars did whatever was possible to hold off or camouflage the aging process. Elvis, himself, had "improved on nature" when he made his first movies by having his teeth capped, and he'd dyed his light hair black for twenty years. He also paid for several small operations for friends, usually nose jobs. Now he hastily arranged plans to have some cosmetic surgery of his own.

Afterward, back at Graceland, after remaining in seclusion until the bruises around his eyes disappeared, he called one of his bodyguards into his bedroom. "Well," he said, "how do I look?"

The bodyguard said, "Good, good. Your eyes look clear, you look happy . . ."

"No," Elvis interrupted, "no . . . look here." He then lifted his hair back near his ears, revealing the stitches, explaining that he'd had a facelift.

The bodyguard just stared. He couldn't discern any change at all.

Another precipitous dive began three weeks following the operation, in early July when Elvis went back on the road. The tours were shorter now, seldom lasting more than two weeks, but they were coming more frequently; this was the third in just over two months. Elvis had been dating one of his backup singers, Kathy Westmoreland, and to that familiarity he now added some slightly risqué remarks on stage, embarrassing her. As the tour progressed, she got calls at her hotel and so asked the Colonel's man, Tom Diskin, to talk to Elvis about it. Diskin made the mistake of mentioning it to Elvis just before he walked onstage in Greensboro on July 21.

He sang a few songs and then earlier than usual he introduced some of the singers. It was apparent to everyone that he was angry. First he went over to the Sweet Inspirations, who were standing behind him, and said, "I smell catfish! You girls been eatin' catfish?"

The girls were puzzled, didn't know what Elvis meant.

"I said, 'You been eatin' catfish?'"

They got it then and one of the three singers walked off the stage. Then Elvis introduced Kathy.

"This is Kathy Westmoreland . . ." He turned to face her and curled his lip. "If you don't like the way I introduce you," he said, "get off the pot."

Hearing that, she left the stage, followed by another of the Sweet Inspirations. The odd thing was, hardly anyone noticed, outside of those on Elvis's payroll. They were swiveling their heads and necks furiously during all this, shooting signals that said, "What the hell?" Yet only ten yards away, no one was paying any attention to what Elvis was saying, or what he was causing to happen onstage. The crowd's collective attention seemed to be somewhere else instead; focused so intently as to seem mesmerized, blind to what was actually happening.

Reading the audience accurately, Elvis introduced J.D. Sumner and the Stamps as if nothing out of the ordinary had happened, then walked over to the single remaining member of the Sweet Inspirations, Myrna Smith.

"Here," he said, taking off one of his big diamond rings, "you take this, I want ya to have it."

Myrna tried to give it back. Elvis refused. Then he resumed the show. Later, he did accept the ring from Myrna.

That night after the show he felt uncomfortable. He asked Jerry Schilling and others to apologize to Kathy and the Sweet Inspirations for him. They looked away and said they didn't think the girls would accept the apology from them.

That was on the twenty-first. On the twenty-second, the tour left for Asheville, North Carolina, for three concerts. A short hop from Greensboro, departure time was at 4:30, but at two, Elvis passed the word: "We're leaving now." Everybody rushed for the bus, carrying their own luggage. Then Elvis said he was staying a little longer. He told the others to go to the airport, he'd join them later.

"On the way to the airport," says Lowell Hays, "there was an ice cream parlor. We were all kind of unhappy about his hurrying us out of the hotel for no reason and we told the driver to pull over. We got off and got us some ice cream. And who do you think passed us while we were standin' there? Elvis. He was pissed, too. We saw his face as he went by. So we jumped on the bus as fast as we could and headed for the airport. We hadn't even unloaded the luggage when he says, 'Anybody on that plane yet?'

"There were a couple and he said, 'Get 'em off!' He made everybody get off the plane and he got on and said, 'If they can't do what I tell 'em, leave 'em here!' And he took off. He left us standin' there in the middle of the runway."

In Asheville, getting into his limousine as if nothing out of the ordinary had happened, Elvis ordered the plane to return for the members of his entourage.

When the plane returned to Asheville the second time, one of Elvis's boys approached Lowell and said, "Elvis wants to see you right away."

According to Lowell, when he entered Elvis's hotel suite, he said, "I want to buy everybody something."

"He bought everything I had and he said he wanted more," Lowell recalls. "I was putting the stuff I had in envelopes and writing their names as fast as I could and I had a *lot* of jewelry with me, but we ran out. He said, 'Do you know any jewelers here in town?' I said, 'No, sir, but I can get the jewelry here from Memphis in about an hour.' He said, 'Get it here.'

"I called Memphis, made arrangements for them to get the jewelry together, jumped on a plane, flew to Memphis, picked up the jewelry, and flew right straight back. Elvis bought what I call a fortune in jewelry, practically a whole jewelry store. He gave something to everybody in the group, everybody in the band, all the backup singers, everybody who meant anything to him. I was in the dressing room when he apologized to the Sweet Inspirations. He told them it wouldn't happen again. He gave each one of them a $5,000 ring. Then he called everybody else in."

Back in Memphis, the end of July, Elvis still couldn't purge the guilt he felt, so he did what he always did in that situation—he went on another spending spree. This time he bought fourteen Cadillacs and two airplanes.

The American male's love affair with the automobile has been well examined and chronicled; it needs no amplification here. In many ways Elvis was the archetypal American male and, true to form, he had a long-standing romance with the internal combustion engine.

Unlike many other males sharing his infatuation, however, Elvis did not tinker with that engine; he merely owned it. The last ten years of his life, Elvis owned at least one hundred expensive vehicles—usually eight to ten at a time and sometimes as many as fifteen—and he bought and immediately gave away at least that many more. In ten years Elvis gave away cars—to bodyguards, maids, nurses, friends, and strangers—that cost him more than one million dollars.

A large chunk of that was spent July 27, his second day home following the embarrassing incident on tour. Late that afternoon he and some of his boys drove down to the Cadillac agency on Union Street, not far from the original Sun Records studio where Elvis had made his first records. He'd been buying Cadillacs there for twenty years, since 1967 from a white-haired, bankerish sort of man named Howard Massey.

"As a rule he'd bring the people in he was going to buy cars for," the salesman says. "He never asked you the price. And he always wanted them right away. So we'd put the hubcaps on and deliver them if there were a lot going out at once, then bring them back for servicing later. It wasn't a matter of having to sell him anything. If he saw what he wanted, he took it. Usually they'd drive the cars away themselves. He was always a perfect gentleman. He could buy as many cars here as he wanted and we never worried about payment. I doubt that I ever sold him less than three. He'd call me at home at nine, ten, eleven, one o'clock in the morning and I'd meet him here. Anything he wanted here he could get, day or night. As a matter of fact, the boss said, 'Hell, give him the front door key if he wants it.' I guess he spent a half a million dollars here, easy."

On July 27 Elvis set a record, for himself as well as for Madison Cadillac. He bought fourteen cars, including one for a woman he didn't know who merely happened by. She admired one of the cars he had just purchased. Elvis approached her and asked her if she liked

it. She said she did. Elvis said, simply, "I'll buy you one."
He then took her by one arm and courteously escorted
her into the showroom where he said, "Pick one out."
She picked a gold and white El Dorado, list price
$11,500.

Elvis then told Joe Esposito, who was at his side, to
write a check "to buy some clothes to go with the car,"
and on a whim asked Howard Massey if he still had the
station wagon he'd shown him a month before.

"Yessir, I sure do."

"Well," Elvis drawled, "back her out, I need somethin' to carry the chickens in."

Elvis began to realize his dream to own a fleet of airplanes when he made a bid of $1,500,000 and put down
a $75,000 deposit for a luxury Boeing 707 jet purport-
edly owned by exiled financier Robert Vesco. Another
party appeared claiming ownership and Elvis withdrew
and went to Nigel Winfield, who sold airplanes national-
ly from an office in Florida. From him Elvis bought a
Convair 880, a former Delta Airlines plane, paying
$1,000,000; he then ordered a $750,000 remodeling.
Elvis also bought a smaller, faster Lockheed Jet Star.
This was a four-engine jet, the type of aircraft popular
with big companies; in fact, he bought it from the
Amway Corporation, paying $850,000. Over the next
six months, as the big Convair was being renovated, he
used the Jet Star to shuttle his friends from Memphis to
Fort Worth to watch the progress.

"I'm building me the damnedest thing you've ever
seen," he told his friends over and over. "I'm building
me an airliner."

Flying them to Texas in the middle of the night, he
took them on a tour, at first through a skeleton of a
craft with all its seats and paneling ripped out. "It was,"
says T.G. Sheppard, "like walking into a tunnel."

"This is gonna be a little sitting area where I can
read my books . . . this is where the living room gonna
be . . . right here, gonna put me a little wet bar . . . right

here gonna put a dining room . . . then back here's
where the bedroom gonna be, then my makeup and
wardrobe."

He was going to paint an American flag on the tail
and under that paint his beloved "TCB" and lightning
bolt. The jet would be named after his daughter; *Lisa
Marie* would be written in script across the airplane's
nose.

Both of these planes got maximum use by Elvis and
his organization, and when you toured as much as Elvis
did, it made economic good sense to own planes rather
than charter them. Generally, the Colonel did his advance work in the sixteen-seat Jet Star and Elvis followed along behind in the *Lisa Marie*. These planes
would be owned—and used—by Elvis up to the time of
his death.

Elvis was still chartering planes for his tours to carry
his musicians and singers, so in July he decided to buy
a plane for them, at the same time buying a fourth
plane for the Colonel. The Colonel's gift was bought on
an egotistical whim; when he read that Elton John had
paid $40,000 for a Rolls Royce for his manager, Jerry
Weintraub—who was a friend of the Colonel's and who
promoted Elvis's concerts—Elvis laughed and said, "I'll
show that sonofabitch. . . ." Together the planes cost
Elvis $1,300,000.

"Elvis, I got to talk to you."

It was Vernon talking and Elvis knew what he wanted
and answered as he always did: "Daddy, I don't want
to talk about it."

"Elvis, you got to listen this one time. Son, you're
spending money faster than we're makin' it."

Elvis walked away from an argument with his father.
Then he said nothing when the Colonel refused his gift.
Nor did he say much when, soon after, two of the four
airplanes were advertised for sale in what was becoming

one of the Colonel's favorite publications for advertising about Elvis, *The Wall Street Journal*.

This may have been Elvis's most bizarre period. Besides the jewelry, Cadillac, and airplane spree, in 1975 there was the matter of his dog, a chow named Getlo. In her book about her boss, Graceland secretary Becky Yancey devoted three pages to the details of this story. It all started, she said, when the dog was flown in a chartered jet to Boston accompanied by Linda Thompson and Dr. Tom Miller of the acute kidney dialysis unit at Baptist Hospital.

At Boston it was determined that the dog was too ill to make the remaining 50-mile trip to the New England Institute of Comparative Medicine in West Boylston, Massachusetts, and accommodations were arranged in the swank Copley Plaza Hotel for two days.

An emergency mobile unit was brought in and doctors worked from the van, treating Getlo until she was strong enough to travel again. "The dog had a serious kidney problem," said the doctor in charge, Dr. S. Lynn Kittleson, director of the Institute. "Its blood picture was very bad. We were even thinking about a kidney transplant or dialysis."

Doctors decided to try a conservative approach first and administered fluid to the dog daily. She responded well enough so that a transplant and dialysis were avoided. She was transferred to Dr. Kittleson's home, where she had the healing companionship of a friendly Great Dane, and was given blood transfusions. Getlo's health improved sufficiently after two months for her to make the return flight to Memphis. Dr. Kittleson said the dog would continue to require daily fluid injections to prevent dehydration.

The doctor would not disclose the cost of treatment. She said only that "... this dog was treated very specially. I kept the dog home and kept it with me. He [she] really required intensive care." Dr. Kittleson and other central Massachusetts veterinarians collaborated with Memphis physicians and never had direct contact with Elvis.

Dr. Robert J. Tashijian, president of the Institute and a spokesman for the medical team, indicated that the dog's presence in West Boylston was kept secret until after its return to Memphis, partly because of kidnap fears.

"We didn't want to tell anyone because we were afraid the farm would be mobbed and the dog be stolen and ransomed," he said.

Getlo died a few months after her return home.

August, 1975–
September, 1975

One of the secrets to Linda's staying in Elvis's life for as long as she did was her willingness to share him with others. This was important. Women in Elvis's life—like most of the men—accepted a submissive role. Elvis also clung to the double standard, in which it was all right for him to see as many women as he wished, while the female (Linda) pledged absolute loyalty and took an oath of sexual exclusivity.

Elvis dated freely, and quite often it was his friend George Klein he called to find someone new to keep him company. George had graduated from Humes High School with Elvis, and was now a popular Memphis disc jockey, a position that gave him ample opportunity to scout the city's young women. One he provided was Melissa Blackwood, a former Queen of the Memphis Southmen. One day in July 1975 George called the 18-year-old Melissa and told her Elvis wanted to see her that night.

She fixed her hair and changed clothes four times and then waited until almost midnight, when she took off her makeup and dress, put curlers in her hair and went to bed. George called at 1 A.M. and told her to go to the Memphian. She said she couldn't, she was in bed. George said he understood and hung up, then started calling around for a replacement. In the meantime,

Melissa changed her mind, flew into her clothes, and drove her Cadillac that said "Queen of Memphis Southmen" on the side down to the Memphian Theater. By now it was two. She waited in the lobby.

After a while, Elvis appeared from inside the theater, greeting Melissa. She was shaking nervously and said, "How do you do, Mr. Presley?" He laughed. He said he was sorry, but he had made other plans. He thanked her for coming and she left.

The next day Elvis had one of his boys call Melissa and, with Lisa playfully disconnecting them from time to time by pushing down the telephone receiver, they talked for over an hour. After getting much of her life story, Elvis told her he was going on tour the next day, so it was a month before she heard from him again. This time she abandoned a regular boyfriend to return his call at 2 A.M. Elvis came on the line and said he wanted to see her right away. She said it was too late. Elvis said he understood and would send someone to pick her up at seven in the morning, for breakfast. One of Elvis's boys showed up promptly in a Lincoln Continental and finally Melissa was taken to Graceland.

"We entered the house and I was told, 'It's at the top of the stairs, through the big gold doors.' I was sent up there alone. I went through two sets of doors and Elvis was in bed, wearing blue pajamas. And he just looked so tired. I think he was sick. He looked tired and hot, like he had a fever. He'd been up all night, of course, and he said, 'Come here and sit beside me.' I think he could tell I was very nervous and he said, 'I want to tell you three things. The first thing I want you to know is that things may look a little odd, me in my pajamas in bed and all, but I want you to know I'm gonna be a perfect gentleman. I don't want you to think I'm a makeout artist. . . .' "

She sat on the edge of the bed and in her sweet, tiny voice answered his questions about her life. He called her Brown Eyes and he played with a lock of her hair that fell across her forehead. "After a while," she says, "he told me to get out of my clothes and put these pajamas on, these pajamas he had draped over a chair by the bed. I looked at him, shocked at the suggestion. He added, 'I don't mean anything by it. You have to understand I'll be more comfortable if you're wearing those and you sit here with me, both of us and just talk and spend some time together. I want peace and quiet. You won't get your clothes all wrinkled up and I'll feel more like you're at home.' So I went into the bathroom and put them on."

This apparently was not what some may think. The pajamas Melissa put on were Elvis's and so big on her they had to be pinned in the middle, creating an image more funny than sexy. Elvis's physical condition also was an inhibiting factor. He wanted to eat some yogurt, he told her, yet "he was so sick he couldn't even hold his head up and feed it to himself. So I held his head in one arm and tried to feed him."

They continued to talk and finally Elvis asked her, "What kind of car do you have?" She told him her father didn't think she was old enough to own one. "Well," he said, "if you could have one, what would you like to have?" She drove a Cadillac as Queen of the Memphis Southmen, she said, and it was too big, it was hard to park and felt like "it oughta be my father's car." He told Melissa she should drive a white car and then excused himself and went to the bathroom, where he telephoned the local Pontiac dealership and ordered a white Grand Prix to be delivered to Graceland in half an hour. Then, after talking with Melissa for a while longer, he took her down to the front porch to watch the car delivered.

"What did I do to deserve this?" Melissa said, after the squealing had stopped.

Elvis looked at her beneath heavy lidded eyes and said, "You came today."

"Then we went back upstairs," Melissa recalls, "and

he said he was really tired and wanted to go to sleep. That's when it got worse and worse. He took this bunch of pills and really started to sweat. They were all prescription pills and when he took them I had to hold his glass of water and just feed them to him. He was hot and uncomfortable, like a little child with a terrible fever. He was shaking and it scared me to death. I got mad and I took the pills away from him when he tried to take some more to go to sleep. He said, 'This is the amount I'm supposed to take, it's all right, I have the best doctors. . . .' Finally he said, 'Will you stay here and hold my hand?' And he wouldn't let me leave. It was the strangest thing. He would sit there in bed, silent, with his eyes closed for the longest time, and I would think he was sound asleep but when I got up to leave, he'd claw my arm, saying, 'Don't go!' He wouldn't let go of my hand until he was really sound asleep."

Melissa finally tiptoed out of the dark bedroom and, still worried about Elvis, confronted the young man who'd driven her to Graceland several hours earlier. She said, "There's something terribly wrong with Elvis and I want you to call a doctor."

He said, "Don't worry about it. He's like this every day. He has to have these pills. He's under a doctor's care. Don't interfere, because you just don't understand. This afternoon he'll wake up and he'll be fine."

Melissa then drove her new car home to show it to her mother, returning to Graceland about three in the afternoon. Elvis was awake and greeted her at the door: "I give her a car and she leaves me in it." He was joking, but Melissa knew he was angry, too. "I wish you hadn't left," he said.

That night, late, Melissa went with Elvis and several others to Fort Worth in his Jet Star to see how renovations were going on the big 880 Convair. Elvis was full of himself, practically strutting along the length of the airplane. "How nice that you named it after Lisa,"

Melissa said. "Yeah," Elvis replied, "I wanted to impress Lisa and when I showed it to her, she yawned."

"Then we went back to Memphis and to Graceland," Melissa says. "By this time I was really worn out, I hadn't been to bed in two days. He didn't want me to go home. He said, 'I want you to stay here. I don't mean staying with me. I just want you in this house. I don't want you to leave.'

"I said, 'I can't stay. I don't have my things. . . .'

"He said, 'Well, get your things. I have everything you need. You'll have your own place, your own bathroom, everything.'

"I said, 'No, I can't, this is too much for me, I want to go home and be in my own room and go to sleep in my own bed and then I'll come back. . . .'

"He said he and the boys were going to the movies and he wanted me to stay at the house. He said, 'I've given you the car and I've done everything and . . .'

"I got upset and said, 'Well, if that's why you gave me the car . . .' and I gave him the keys back and he looked so hurt. He gave them back to me and he said, 'That's your car, I want you to have it. If you don't take it, I'm gonna park it on the street until you come and take it away.' And then I left the room and sat in a chair and cried. He came and put his arms around me and I said, 'I care, Elvis, but I just can't move in here.'

"He said, 'I care, too, babe.'

"He walked me to the door and that was the last time I ever talked to him."

There were other women who came and went—a Las Vegas showgirl named Sandra Zancan, the actress Cybill Shepherd (who saw Elvis off and on while still dating director Peter Bogdanovich), and another Memphis Southmen hostess, Jo Cathy Brownlee. All were given big new cars or jewelry, or both, in much the same way Elvis surprised Melissa. All tell similar stories. And then it was Linda's turn again. However many women

Elvis saw—and he saw many after the divorce—it was Linda who returned again and again, it was Linda who was the closest.

Another reason Linda lasted so long was her vivacious personality, her willingness to do anything to get Elvis to laugh. In Vegas once after a show, she says, she was walking casually through the casino with Ricky Stanley, one of Elvis's stepbrothers, when someone who was visiting another of Elvis's bodyguards came up to her.

"The procedure was the guys would go around the casino trolling, go downstairs and invite girls up to the party after the show. That was a big line: 'Would you like to meet Elvis?' And it was used on me as I got on the elevator. He didn't know Ricky and he said, 'Hey, like to go up to the thirtieth floor, meet Elvis?'

"I went along with it. I said, 'Oh, you're kidding! You mean you could arrange that?' He said, 'Yeah, I know him, I'm going up there right now, to a party. You wanta go?'

"And I said, 'Oh, God, I'd be too nervous, I don't know what I'd say to him.' And Ricky was about to collapse laughing, but this guy didn't notice, he was so busy coming on to me and seeing his line was working, that he was oblivious to him. I said I'd love to meet Elvis, I kept it going all the way up to the thirtieth floor, when Ricky said, 'Do you know who this is?'

"He said, 'What do you mean?'

"Ricky said, 'This is Elvis's girlfriend.'

"The guy said, 'Oh, my God, are you Cybill Shepherd?'

"I said, 'Strike two, one more . . .' And then we went inside the suite. When Ricky told Elvis what happened, he died laughing. That became one of our classic stories. Elvis liked telling it."

Linda tells another story, one that recalls the time she blacked out her teeth to make Elvis laugh. This time it happened at a Vegas party, when Elvis and Linda entered Elvis's suite by a back entrance and changed before joining the large party elsewhere in the suite.

"We got all dressed up," Linda says, "and we'd blacked out our front teeth, but kept our mouths closed, sedate and stoic, and we descended the stairs and there was a hush. There were about fifty people there and you heard them say, 'There's Elvis, there he is! Oh my God, he's gorgeous! There's his girlfriend, isn't she pretty?'

"We got to the bottom of the stairs and people came up to us and we smiled. The funny thing was people were not sure if they should laugh or not, or pretend they didn't notice. It was dimly lit in the room and they couldn't tell, they didn't know if we took our teeth out and relaxed or were playing a joke. The people just had this quizzical look on their faces. And we just broke up.

"He told me I was the first girl he ever took on the road with him," Linda recalls. "Priscilla was the role of wife-mother, tucked away in the corner somewhere. She never went on the road with him. She came to Vegas at first on the weekends and after a while that stopped. Elvis told Priscilla, 'You don't take your wife to work with you.' That was his excuse for not taking her with him. She brought that up later, when Elvis and I were seeing each other. She said, 'You couldn't take your wife to work, but how come you take your girlfriend everywhere?' "

With Lisa back in Los Angeles with Priscilla, and Melissa and Jo Cathy driving new cars in Memphis, Elvis took Linda to Vegas for the annual "Elvis Summer Festival" on August 17. The way Red West tells the story in his book, they almost didn't make it when, after taking some unidentified pills, his breathing became labored. They were over Texas in Elvis's new airplane at the time, Red said, and Elvis suddenly yelled, "I can't breathe! Drop the oxygen mask, drop the oxygen mask!" When that didn't help, Elvis got down on the floor of the plane and put his head near an air vent, finally gasping, "I'm not gonna make it. *Land!*" An emergency landing was made in Dallas, where Elvis was taken to a motel to rest. Five hours later he seemed all right again and the flight continued.

In Vegas it got worse. Much worse. His pianist Tony Brown remembers that "everybody hated rehearsals because by now Elvis usually canceled them at the last minute, or he'd be in a bad mood or only do two songs and split. This time he came to rehearsals and tried to sing two sad ballads and they weren't sounding right, so he stopped. He started making jokes, fooling with Red and the others, while the string players and the rest of us just sat there, waiting.

"Suddenly he turned to the orchestra and said, 'You know what? I feel sorry for you sonsabitches have to live in this shitty town. I hate this place! Charlie, I hate it!' "

Charlie stared back at Elvis, who then curtly excused himself, saying he'd be right back. The long minutes dragged past as everyone waited for Elvis's return. Five minutes. Then ten. Finally someone called from backstage, "That's it. Rehearsal's over. The first show's at eight. Be in your places at the usual time."

The show that night was so-so and the second night was worse. In fact, Elvis didn't even want to go on the second night. He wanted to make this announcement after the audience was seated and the Colonel confronted Elvis, telling him he could cancel the rest of his engagement for all he cared, but he wasn't going to tell that night's audience that Elvis wasn't going on. "Tell your father to make the announcement," the Colonel said. Elvis muttered an inaudible reply and finally went on and did the show. But that was it. Immediately after the show, he was driven to the airport and he flew back to Memphis.

"It was incredible," says Tony Brown. "The next day there wasn't a picture of Elvis or a pennant in the whole hotel. By morning all the stuff was gone. All of it. Gone. The Colonel had his men taking it down all night and the next day Peggy Lee was moved over from the Flamingo Hotel to take Elvis's place. She pulled about ten people and then they brought in Bill Cosby, who did a lot better, but it wasn't like what it was when Elvis was there. When Elvis was in town you couldn't get into any restaurant; if you wanted to eat, you had to eat off hours. Then, when word got out he'd left town, the place was empty. The Colonel kept us around for a couple of days, because it was always possible that he'd come back, you just never knew. But he didn't."

In Memphis, the aluminum foil was back up on the windows of Elvis's suite in Baptist Hospital, where this time it was announced he was under treatment for "exhaustion." The truth was far more complicated, and serious. Elvis was suffering from an under-functioning liver and intestinal spasms caused by his enlarged colon. He was also forty pounds overweight and the huge quantities of uppers and downers he took had his metabolic system gravely unbalanced.

"Elvis was a junk food junkie," his doctor, George Nichopoulos, said, "and instead of helping him break his bad eating habits, the cooks at Graceland prepared whatever he ordered. They had diet sheets in the kitchen, but it was hopeless. They mothered him to death. They couldn't believe they were doing him harm by making a fuss over him. He'd say fix a hamburger and fries and they'd send up enough for six people."

Dr. Nick talked with Elvis about alternatives. There was an operation called an intestinal bypass, or "shunt," where a large part of his colon could be removed, permitting him to pass food through his body before it was totally digested. Dr. Nick said he didn't recommend the surgery, merely mentioned it as a possibility. Elvis, no stranger to rapid and extreme weight loss schemes, said he wanted the operation that night. When Dr. Nick went on to explain the difficulties Elvis would have afterward if he didn't adhere faithfully to a special diet, Elvis began to lose interest. That night he made his decision. He'd let 300-pound Lamar Fike have the operation, then buy him a little bitty sports car once he was down to a size that would fit into it. To celebrate the decision *not* to have the operation himself, he had one of his boys go to a fast food place in the neighborhood and sneak back with a sack of bacon cheeseburgers and fried potatoes.

Dr. Nick had also talked with Elvis about hiring private nurses to be with him at Graceland, to keep him on his medical schedule. Elvis said he wanted Mrs. Marian Cocke and a young nurse named Kathy Seamon to report to Graceland during their hours away from the hospital. They leaped for the jobs when they were offered and agreed between them that they wouldn't accept any pay.

Now, in the hospital, as Elvis's body detoxified, his mood leveled. People who were with him then recall the calmness, the normality, the laughs. Linda talks about how she and Elvis became absorbed by the afternoon game shows on television, and watched the babies in the nursery on the closed-circuit channel. "The nurses knew he watched," Linda says, "and sometimes they'd put a little sign on one of the cribs that said, 'Hi Elvis!' Sometimes they came up to the camera and waved."

This was also when Elvis took a telephone call from President Nixon. Elvis had called Nixon when the President was hospitalized some months earlier and now the Chief Executive was returning the courtesy.

Elvis's nurse, Mrs. Cocke—whom he had given a car soon after checking in—remembers Elvis's last night in the hospital. Good-naturedly he autographed a picture for her, marking it "To Mrs. Cocke, the sex symbol of the Baptist. . . ." That prompted Jerry Schilling to make a wisecrack about the last names of Elvis's nurses, Cocke and Seamon.

"I reached over on the bedside table," she recalls, "picked up a full pitcher of ice water, walked over to Jerry, pulled the neck of his shirt out, and poured the entire contents of the pitcher down his shirt. Elvis laughed until he cried and said I was going to work out just great at Graceland."

Elvis left the hospital September 5. It would be three months before he returned to work.

Once again the old "routine" was established. Movie theaters were rented for all-night screenings of *Dog Day Afternoon, West World* and *Towering Inferno.* He watched his favorite bunch of comedians in their first feature film, *Monty Python and the Holy Grail,* five times.

Other nights he flew his friends to Fort Worth to watch the *Lisa Marie* being readied for flight. A pilot with the unlikely name of Milo High was hired, along with a copilot and first officer. "His calls to warm up the plane usually came between 11 o'clock and 2 A.M.," Milo recalls. "And we'd be in the air an hour later."

Elvis continued to meet with Rick Husky and Ed Parker about his karate film, a project that was still limping along more than two years after Elvis had conceived it. Special costumes and patches were designed for a team that was sent to Europe and filmed, and later Elvis himself permitted a film crew to record him in demonstration, but there seemed to be no direction. "I remember when Parker and Husky came to talk about the film," says Jo Cathy Brownlee, who was still dating Elvis off and on. "They caught us as we were about to leave. We were sitting in Elvis's Stutz Bearcat with the mink rug when they came up. The motor was running as he talked to them. I sat there for almost two hours, watching the gas gauge go down."

The film also was being slowed by the Colonel's and Vernon's personal reluctance to spend money. Elvis, of course, had no such inhibition. Already well in the red for the second year in a row, a dozen automobiles and a small air force at his beck and call, still giving money and cars and jewelry away the way ordinary people send postcards while on vacation, surrounded by a staff of maids, cooks, gardeners, gate guards, secretaries, and round-the-clock nurses (not to mention the Memphis Mafia), in the autumn of 1975, Elvis devoted much of his time planning more ways to spend.

A recent convert to racquetball, he decided to build his own indoor courts at Graceland and traveled as far as Dallas to look at existing courts to get ideas. He also took possession of what probably was his most expensive ring, designed by Lowell Hays and nearly three months in the making. They woke Elvis up the day Lowell arrived at Graceland with it.

"He got up, one of the first times before dark," Lowell says, "came down and sat at the dinin' room table. He said, 'Where is it?' I gave it to him, he slipped it on his finger and looked at it and said, 'That's the most beautiful fuckin' ring I've ever seen in my life. God, won't Sammy Davis Jr. shit a brick when he sees this! How much do I owe ya?'

"I told him $55,000. He said, 'You got to be kiddin'!'

" 'No, Elvis, it's got an eleven-and-one-half-carat diamond in it.'

"Well, all right." Elvis smiled, then looked at Lowell with his lopsided grin. "I want to do something for you. What do you want?"

Lowell looked at Elvis blankly and someone in the room said, "He'll take your car, E."

Elvis said, "My car? You can't have mah car, 'cause that's a hoss and ain' nother one like it." Elvis was driving the first special edition Mark V with a brown and white interior. "I had to special-order this car," he said.

"But if you want a Mark V, we'll go get you one. Ricky . . . go get my car ready!"

Ten minutes later Elvis was in late-afternoon rush-hour traffic. As he looked around at all the cars on the freeway, one of the boys with him said, "Isn't it fun to get up before dark, E? Everywhere you look, man, there are real people. . . ."

December, 1975–
January, 1976

On December 2 Elvis went back to work, traveling with his entourage to Las Vegas to make up the twenty shows he missed when he canceled out in August. Once again he turned Las Vegas around, this time doing what no entertainer has been able to do before or since.

The vice-president of the Hilton hotels, Henri Lewin, says, "In December a Las Vegas showroom draws 20 or 30 percent of its capacity. That's the way it is. People stay home between Thanksgiving and Christmas and don't really come back to Las Vegas until after New Year's. Elvis Presley filled every show. You must understand that Tom Jones in the second week of December might lay an egg completely. Elvis sold out! Our slot machine revenue was *doubled*."

The shows were memorable only for their not being memorable. There were, for a change, no major incidents. It was, in fact, rather placid. The Colonel bought time on all the local radio stations to play a half hour of Elvis's hymns. In the hotel gift shops, Elvis's Christmas albums sold briskly. The fans came and went excitedly in the cold desert night and Elvis delivered the required number of performances that seemed to satisfy.

The Hilton wanted him back for New Year's Eve. Henri Lewin asked, but of course the Colonel said no. "The Colonel and Elvis, they are people who played obstacle courses," Lewin says. "First they played Las Vegas in December, which is insane for anyone else. Next, they go to Pontiac, Michigan, for New Year's Eve. I ask the Colonel to give me Elvis that night, but the Colonel says, 'Henri, how can you compete? Even if you gave me $100,000, I lose $50,000.'

"But it is not a sure thing," Lewin went on. "Pontiac, Michigan, on the last day of December, it could snow. There is a possibility you cannot go to the stadium. The Colonel gambles. If I'm a manager for a suntan lotion company, I don't open a branch in Alaska, right? If I sell ham sandwiches, I don't go to Jerusalem. This guy did. It didn't matter how big the obstacles."

This was the first time Elvis had ever worked during the winter holidays. In the 1960s it was always written into his contract that he was not available until after his birthday, January 8. Why did he break tradition? Why did he agree to perform in the huge Silver Dome that seated 80,000, when he knew it would be like the Astrodome—too big to give his fans the show they paid to see? The answer, of course, was money. Elvis needed money, desperately. His bank accounts were empty and he had *borrowed* money against future earnings, using Graceland for collateral. As difficult as it was to accept, Elvis was broke.

Of course his lifestyle didn't reflect this dramatic turn of events. Nor was Elvis the least bit worried. When the Colonel and Vernon confronted him with his bank balances, he growled that he didn't want to talk about it, and then began organizing one of the biggest road parties of his career.

"He even talked me and my wife into going to Pontiac with him," says T.G. Sheppard, "and I had to cancel a concert of my own to do it. He said he was nervous about the size of the room and wanted his friends with him."

Friends or no friends, the show was, every way except economically, a disaster.

The sounds of "Thus Spake Zarathustra" filled the gigantic space, echoing off a roof so far away a fifteen-story building could have been put on the stage next to Elvis. As he entered, he looked confused. Where were his sidemen? Where were his singers? Finally he spotted them below him, on another level. He was surprised, then angry. Why hadn't anyone told him he had to sing alone?

In the middle of the show, his pants ripped, splitting at the seams because of his extra poundage.

The temperature made it worse. It was so cold, the members of his band were playing in their overcoats. "The trumpet players, their lips were so cold they could barely blow their horns," says guitarist John Wilkinson. "It was so cold our strings kept changing key. Oh, we were glad to get out of there."

On the way home, Elvis exploded, cursing and blaming everyone and anyone he could think of for the show. So black was his mood, Linda just sat there and let it happen. Normally she would have made a face at him, or fed him some gooey sweet and cooed him back to serenity with baby talk.

A few days later a story appeared in the entertainment trade papers reporting a gross of $800,000 for the concert, believed to be a world's record for a single night by a single artist, beating out the Beatles' take at Shea Stadium in 1964. Elvis kept about half of it.

The Colonel pulled off another coup at about the same time, bringing much more money into the Presley —and Parker—coffers by selling to RCA Records all rights to all the material recorded by Elvis through 1972. Obviously this represented a huge body of product —more than 350 recorded songs, nearly fifty albums worth, almost all of it still in the catalog and selling slowly, but steadily.

One RCA executive claims that the Colonel's motivation for the deal was "greed, pure and simple," and says the record company went for it only because it figured that eventually it'd get its money back and the big price tag the Colonel attached to the property was worth paying to keep Elvis and the Colonel happy.

The price? A nice, round six million dollars.

Nineteen seventy-six began with little planned, and quickly turned chaotic. His forty-first birthday was January 8, and Elvis took Linda and several of his boys to Vail, Colorado, to celebrate.

"Elvis really didn't like birthdays," says Jerry Schilling, one of those who went along, "but this time he seemed to want company."

Jerry made arrangements for the rental of three condominiums, talking a family out of a vacation to make the largest of them available for Elvis. Linda baked a cake. President Gerald Ford's daughter Susan was vacationing in Vail, and when she heard Elvis was in town she invited him to a party. Elvis's hired hands started making arrangements.

What followed was, according to those present, a nightmare.

Ed Parker reports getting a telephone call from Elvis on the eighth. Elvis told Ed he thought he was getting old, was no longer worthy of his fans' love. Ed tried to reassure him, told him he had many good years ahead, was just now reaching his full maturity. Elvis said he didn't know and finally Ed changed the subject.

Elvis was also bothered by the ongoing lawsuits involving some of his bodyguards. Red and Sonny were among those with him in Vail and he turned on them, criticized them for getting so rough. They attempted to defend themselves.

"That's easy for you to say," Elvis shouted, "but I'm the one they sue!"

"Well," said Red, "they got our names on that lawsuit too, you know, boss."

"Damn right they do. It was you motherfuckers beat the shit outa that poor bastid."

And so it went. When the boys were present, he fought with them. When they weren't present, he told them to get their asses back on the premises. Susan Ford's invitation was trashed; if she wanted to meet him, he said, she could come to *his* condo. Then in the middle of the night he decided he wanted to move into the condominium that Jerry had gotten for himself and Myrna Smith, one of the Sweet Inspirations. He called Jerry and told him he was moving in immediately.

"Come on, Elvis," Jerry said, "can't it wait until morning?"

"Listen, Jerry, when I say jump, you jump. . . ."

Jerry said nothing in response, and after a minute Elvis barked another command that began, "Listen, motherfucker . . ." Jerry cut in, "Look, Elvis, you can have the condo . . . because I fucking quit." The next morning Elvis called Jerry and apologized.

Of course there were brighter moments, when the mood-altering effects of the drugs Elvis took subsided somewhat. In the days that followed, Elvis and his remaining entourage—after Jerry and Myrna had left—rented snowmobiles for noisy, 3 A.M. rides through the snowy woods. Wearing a white woolen ski mask and bulky snowsuit, he also visited a luxury automobile showroom in Denver, arriving three hours after closing time with a large party, telling three in the group to pick out the cars they wanted. These were Captain Jerry Kennedy, head of the Denver vice squad, and Detective Ron Pietrofeso, who had been Elvis's police guards during concerts in Denver months before, and Dr. Gerald Starky, a police physician who had treated Elvis a day earlier for a scratch he said was caused by his ski mask. The $13,000 cars he bought the three men were his way of saying thank you.

Before he left Colorado, while watching the television news, Elvis saw one of the local anchormen report on the car-buying he had done, then look into the camera and say, "Elvis . . . if you're watching, I wouldn't mind getting a car, too." Elvis had a new Cadillac delivered to the station the following day and then went home to Graceland.

Jerry Schilling's older brother, Billy Ray, had known Red West and George Klein "real well" while growing up, and met Elvis for the first time after he returned from Germany, when Billy Ray was a sergeant on the sheriff's staff. "I sent my squad cars down there to keep the girls off the property," he says. Later, Billy Ray served as a County Court Clerk, chairing the law enforcement committee, which put him close to the sheriff, Roy Nixon. This brought Elvis and Billy Ray together more frequently and sometimes Elvis requested favors.

"One time I was on the County Court and he invited me to one of his movies," Billy Ray recalls. "He called me 'Squire.' He come over to me and said, 'Squire, I need to talk to you.' We went to the back of the movie. He was going with Linda Thompson and he said Linda had a brother, Sam, who was with the Sheriff's department. Elvis said, 'They got him feeding the prisoners, Squire, and he's got a college degree. Here's a guy who got his college and you'd think he'd get something better than that. Can you do somethin'?' I went to the sheriff and said what Elvis said and Sam was transferred to the school detail, where he acted as a kind of liaison guy between the department and the schools, went to the schools and talked to the kids about law enforcement. The kids and the schools loved him. He cleaned up a lotta dope.

"A year later I went to another of Elvis's movies and he was in a bad mood, not talking to anybody. Elvis saw me and came over. 'Squire,' he said, 'I've got to see you right away. I've really got a problem. . . .' Now Nixon was still sheriff and I was still in charge of the law enforcement committee. Elvis was a special deputy under Nixon; it was Nixon that gave him his badge. So Elvis tells me he wants a traffic light outside Graceland

and he wants a blue light for his car. I went to Nixon and he said he didn't know about the traffic light, but then he reached under his seat (in his car) and pulls out his own blue light. This is the light you plug into the cigarette lighter and put it on your dash; it flashes and you can make cars pull over to the side of the road. 'Here,' says Roy Nixon, 'give him mine.' When I took it out to Elvis, it was like I gave him a Rolls. Royce. He was so happy. He took it right to his car and plugged it into his cigarette lighter and watched it blink on and off. I guess we musta set there for ten minutes and he never took his eyes offa it."

When Roy Nixon was elected mayor, Billy Ray was named by the County Court to take his place as acting County sheriff, to fill out the seven months remaining in his term of office. Two days later, Elvis called. "He said, 'Squire . . . I mean, Sheriff . . . this is Elvis.' I said, 'Yeah, Elvis?' He said, 'You know, Nixon made me chief deputy.' I said, 'No, I didn't know that.' He said, 'Yeah, I'm chief deputy, I got the badge and everything, I been chief deputy for six years. And I want a promotion.' I said, 'Elvis, you can't get a promotion. There's nowhere you can go from chief deputy except to sheriff of Shelby County and I been trying to get that for sixteen years.' He thought for a minute and said, 'Billy Ray? I been chief deputy for six years and I think I deserve a promotion. Would you like me to run against you when election time comes up?'

"I thought for a minute and I said, 'Okay, you can be sheriff.' And he said okay and that was it. I didn't think anymore about it. I went to bed that night and at one o'clock there's a banging at the door. There's Red and Elvis and some narcotics guy that was in town visiting. Elvis throws that chief's badge on the table and said, 'I want my sheriff's badge.' I'm thinking, Oh my God, what'm I gone do? I cain't go back on my word. I figured I could get another badge, so I got my badge and I gave it to him. Then I looked at his chief deputy's badge and it was full of diamonds and rubies. I refused to take it. I think Red took it. Later that day, Elvis left to go out of town and I got another call. He was at the airport. 'Need to talk to you, Sheriff. What about my card?' I said, 'You mean you want the card saying you're sheriff?' He said, 'Yeah.' I said, 'Elvis, I need to take your picture, we have to fingerprint you.' He said, 'I got all that up there already.' I said, 'Maybe when you get back . . .' He said no and sent one of the guys up to get the card. And he got it. I didn't want him runnin' against me."

February, 1976–
May, 1976

Elvis was losing control.

He hadn't recorded any new material in almost nine months and with RCA wishing to maintain its three-albums per year release schedule, new songs were sorely needed. In fact, the last album released, *A Legendary Performer, Volume 2,* and the one set for the next month, *The Sun Sessions,* both were repackaged anthologies of old material. Elvis had ignored pleas to go to Nashville or Hollywood to record, said he didn't want to go back to Stax in Memphis, either. So in the first week of February 1976, RCA began moving $200,000 worth of recording equipment into Elvis's Graceland den. If Mohammed wouldn't go to the mountain, then the mountain would go to Mohammed.

Elvis's road band came too, flown in from Los Angeles, along with a number of the top Nashville studio men—David Briggs on piano, Bobby Emmons on electric piano, Norbert Putnam on bass. J.D. Sumner and the Stamps were there and so were Kathy Westmoreland and Myrna Smith. Everyone was waiting for Elvis to come downstairs to sing.

Felton Jarvis was producing the sessions, as usual, and he kept moving nervously back and forth between the den and the big RCA mobile truck parked outside. The string of jokes never stopped, but by midnight everyone was getting quite anxious. Elvis sent word that he was sick and had a doctor in attendance. Red and Sonny West and Dave Hebler explain Elvis's behavior another way. In their book, *Elvis: What Happened?*, they tell a sinister story about a plan Elvis had to kill the city's top narcotics dealers and contend it was this that kept Elvis holed up in his upstairs bedroom.

Red says Elvis summoned him to his room, where he had a dozen rifles, at least two dozen pistols, several automatic rifles and machine guns (illegally owned), a handful of rocket launchers, and ammunition for all of it, strewn all over the floor. Most of this had been kept in his Los Angeles house, but once he sold the house, he had the arsenal moved to Graceland, where he liked to keep it handy in case he needed it. Now, he told Red, he needed it to wipe out all those "motherfuckin' drug pushers that got Ricky [Stanley] on heroin!"

Ricky was one of his three young stepbrothers, the sons of Vernon's second wife, Dee. Elvis doted on the boys, had spoiled them with lavish toys when they were younger and now had them on his payroll as valets, errand boys, and bodyguards when he traveled. When Elvis got heavily into pills, so, too, did they, as did many others on the Presley teat. Ricky caused the most trouble of the three. On five occasions he had run afoul of the police, the last time for forging a prescription for Demerol. Each time, Elvis bailed him out, got the charges dropped. In time, Ricky graduated to heroin, and Elvis was mad.

He handed a list of names and a packet of photographs to Red, given to him, Elvis said, by the Memphis police when he said he thought he and his guys could help get something on them if they knew who to look out for.

"Elvis had it all planned," Red wrote in his book. "He wanted myself and Dave Hebler and Dick Grob, the former cop [who had gone to work for Elvis some years previously], to go out and lure them, and he said he was going to kill them."

Not long before, Elvis had watched a similar plot in a film called *Death Wish*. In the movie, Charles Bronson carried on a similar vendetta, a one-man crime assassi- nation squad. Elvis identified strongly with the film, and Bronson's role, and told Red and Dave that he would use the recording sessions as his cover, or alibi. They'd set the target up—he told them—and he'd sneak out of the house the back way, make the hit, and then return swiftly to Graceland, where he then would go down- stairs and sing.

Red shook his head and said it was pretty heavy. . . .

"Hell," said Elvis, "the cops *want* them."

Somehow, Elvis was diverted, chemically or conver- sationally. His fantasy was pushed aside. And the re- cording session finally began.

In seven days Elvis sang a dozen songs, ten of which appeared on an album in May called *From Elvis Presley Boulevard*. The lyrics, as a lot, were sad, and Elvis's performance, though adequate, showed clearly his fail- ing strength and health.

The songs included Neil Sadaka's "Solitaire" ("There was a man, a lonely man, who lost his love . . ."); an old favorite of Elvis's, "Danny Boy" (". . . the summer's gone/roses dying . . ."); a song that said it all in the title, "Hurt" (his next single release); the old chestnut written by Fred Rose and recorded by Willie Nelson, "Blue Eyes Crying in the Rain"; as well as songs called, poignantly, "Bigger They Are, Harder They Fall" (by Larry Gatlin, one of Elvis's favorite contemporary com- posers); "I'll Never Fall in Love Again"; "The Last Farewell"; and "Moody Blue," a song written by Mark James, who had given Elvis "Suspicious Minds" several years before.

"Hurt" recalled, but weakly, the operatic drama of a much earlier hit, "It's Now or Never (O Sole Mio)." His reading of the hoary "Danny Boy" was uninspired;

he didn't even try for the high notes. On several others he insisted that the backup voices be allowed to all but bury his own. His voice remained rich, a worthy match for any sort of material, but there seemed to be a lack of concern or confidence. The performance sounded lazy, uncertain.

It wasn't easy to get even that much, as Elvis's moods continued to swing wildly. When he first saw the recording setup in his den, he said, "Let's leave it, I like it better this way than with the furniture." A few days later he stood in the den facing the huge playback speakers, his eyes glazed, pointing a shotgun. "The sounds no fuckin' good in those things!" he croaked. "I'm gone kill the motherfuckers and put 'em out of my misery." He cocked the shotgun and took unsteady aim. Some of the musicians got the gun away from him and a few minutes later the session was canceled. Other nights he didn't talk to his old friends in the usual way; he seemed remote, disconnected. Some nights he failed to show up at all. Finally, on February 9, RCA packed up its gear and returned to Nashville, happy to have what it had.

In the weeks that followed, Elvis tried to strengthen his loosening grip, tried to take control again. Of course, he'd been doing the same thing most of his adult life. Like so many millions of Americans, he worried about his weight obsessively. In this way, too, Elvis was the perfect American.

That's how the amphetamines had started big, back in the 1960s, when he wanted to lose weight quickly for a movie role. By the time he was making his first appearance in Las Veggas, he not only took appetite depressants, he wore five-pound weights on his wrists and ankles during long, active rehearsals. He went on yogurt and other "health" kicks. He fasted. He gobbled vitamin pills by the handful, drank mineral water by the gallon, and played racquetball even when he was exhausted. At one point he turned himself over to a doctor in Las

Vegas who promised him he would lose thirty-five pounds in two weeks if he moved into the doctor's home and followed the "Sleep Diet."

This one got Elvis into trouble.

The phone rang at the Hilton Hotel, where some of Elvis's guys were staying. It was Elvis. He said he was alone at the doctor's house on his belly, on the floor, unable to get back into bed. He'd managed to knock the telephone over and dial, but had no more strength. Would someone come and help him back into bed?

The way the diet worked, Elvis would be given medication to make him sleep during the periods when he usually ate. That way he could replace a caloric activity with inactivity, and literally snooze his pounds away. It was a faddish diet, one of many that gained some popularity in the 1970s and, according to most weight loss counselors, it seldom if ever produced lasting results.

One of Elvis's guys rushed to the doctor's house and lifted Elvis back onto his bed and, at Elvis's insistence, left him to continue the treatment.

On February 16, 1976, Elvis had the first four meetings with a Memphis hypnotist. Six months after Elvis died, the hypnotist told his story publicly (in the *National Enquirer*). As was usual in such personal matters, Joe Esposito had made the arrangements.

The hypnotist, William Foote, said Elvis slurred his words—a strong indication that he was under the influence of painkillers or tranquilizers. Foote quotes Elvis as saying he was taking morphine for pain, Quaaludes to sleep. He said people were taking advantage of him. He said he had emotional problems.

Foote taught him a simple relaxation technique to relieve the stomach pain he said he had.

The following visits were unrewarding. Elvis refused to say much and, although he seemed "straight" the second and third times, on the last office call Elvis was slurring his words again. Foote gave him a strong hypnotic suggestion to build self-respect, he says, and Elvis "awoke refreshed—but he also seemed anxious to leave. He didn't mention another appointment, and I didn't press him."

Just before Elvis left his office, Foote says, he turned and said, "Thanks, doc. I think I've got it now. I might be able to do it alone now. But I just don't know . . . if it will be enough to replace my medications."

In the midst of all this, Elvis went back on the road. This was the first of the really short tours—six shows in six days—that would characterize the remainder of his life. It was believed that this was as much as he could handle.

It was also his first with two new musicians in his backup band. Some time before he had lost Glenn D. Hardin on piano, a severe blow to Elvis, and when his replacement, David Briggs, also left, Elvis didn't know what to do. The loss of Ronnie Tutt, the drummer who'd been with him from the first show in Las Vegas, was an even greater jolt. James Burton also quit, but he returned, receiving a substantial jump in pay.

Why did they quit? They told Elvis they had better offers, offers they couldn't refuse. As much as Elvis was paying him—maybe more than any other pianist on the road—David Briggs could make even more at home in the studios. Both Glenn D. and James left to accept jobs with Emmy Lou Harris that offered them a percentage of the gate and a schedule that would allow them to pick up some of the same big studio dollars that David wanted. Ronnie Tutt said much the same thing, wanting to get back to the busy studios in Los Angeles.

"The short bursts seemed to work for a while, but it also screwed up the other guys," says guitarist John Wilkinson. "They were studio musicians and they lost too much work when they were always traveling. Studio time is booked a long time in advance sometimes and a lot of times for some reason they wouldn't tell us when the next tour was. We really griped and complained. They'd let us know a week-and-a-half ahead of time sometimes. I'd say, 'What! I've got a contract to sing in a hotel in San Diego. . . .' "

There were other reasons, of course. "The newness had worn off," says Larrie Londin, the drummer who took Tutt's place. "They weren't that impressed anymore. They didn't have the edge that it takes to drive that type of performer, like he was used to being driven. They'd been with him almost six years, most of them, and they wanted to try new things."

Worse—and some still won't talk about this publicly —they didn't enjoy watching Elvis slide. Already there was backstage talk not just about Elvis's mood, but his ability to function.

Habitual users of prescription drugs must be wary of several things. One, of course, is the law. But that is a problem only if the user gets his pills from an illegal source. All of Elvis's uppers and downers came from respected doctors, and by 1975 many of the prescriptions were ordered in the names of his hired hands, so Elvis's name wouldn't appear too frequently in the druggists' files. This was legal so long as the doctors first examined the employees, all of whom conveniently complained of something—back pain, insomnia, etc.— that resulted in their getting what they wanted. Thus, the law was not a problem for Elvis.

Another major concern is an overdose, either lethal or otherwise. There are thousands of deaths each year directly attributable to the use and abuse of "prescription" medicine. And there are many more instances of the users merely passing out, or getting so "stoned" they cannot function normally. For an entertainer who performed as often as Elvis, this was something to worry about.

The new band gathered at Graceland for a rehearsal before the March tour. "We just sat around and listened to records," says Larrie Londin. "Elvis came down about midnight or so, so we did about four bars of this song and he went back to bed. And we went back to the hotel and walked out on the stage the next day cold."

Nevertheless, the tour went smoothly, beginning a year of tours that would recall the crisscrossing of America of the Freedom Train. It was 1976, America's bicentennial, a time for a burst of national pride and Elvis was, miraculously, up for it.

First stop: Johnson City, Tennessee, where Elvis performed three concerts; was somewhat grouchy with his new band members; coaxed out J.D. Sumner from the Stamps and told him to hold out his "Elvis hand," the one with all the rings he had given him (worth more than $100,000), and told a joke about the bumper sticker on the Cadillac that said, "I paid for this—Elvis didn't buy it." After he left, the owner of the motel where he stayed cut up the sheets he slept on and the aluminum foil from his windows and sold them in one-inch squares.

And so it went. A girl rushed onstage in Charlotte and kissed him so hard she cut his lip. In another auditorium a small boy in a tiny Elvis suit that his parents made was lifted onto the stage and Elvis tried to get him to shake his little legs and sing "Hound Dog." Yellow-jacketed coliseum ushers were sent sprawling in Cincinnati by women rushing the stage.

Every city was the same on the April tour. He ordered the house lights turned on so he could see his audience. He joked about his road family, members of his band and backup groups. He accepted gifts over the footlights from fans and gave kisses and scarves in return. He sang patriotic songs, usually "America" or "God Bless America." He still entered the stage to the momentous "Thus Spake Zarathustra" from *2001: A Space Odyssey* and at the end, after singing "I Can't Help Falling in Love (With You)," he posed a final time, arms outstretched, smiling, smothered by the waves of energy rushing at him from the pounding band behind him to the roaring thousands at his feet.

There was a relationship between Elvis and his fans like no other in popular music. The writer in the *Los Angeles Times* put his finger on it when he described Elvis's Long Beach show (April 25) as "a combination of music and manner that often resembles more a visit among friends than a hard-edged concert performance."

Elvis was so good at doing this, he could do it in his sleep. And sometimes he did.

"Sometimes," one of his former sidekicks says, "he just hung on the microphone."

Elvis finished his tour of the West Coast in Spokane on April 27, and opened in Lake Tahoe four days later. During the engagement, he was visited by John O'Grady, the Hollywood private detective that Elvis liked so much.

Given Elvis's love for cops-and-robbers stories, there had to be people like O'Grady in his life. (His head of security, Dick Grob, the former Palm Springs policeman, was another in that category.) Meeting O'Grady was like reading Raymond Chandler. He was a tough former narcotics cop with a list of Hollywood stars for a clientele and, since helping Elvis with his paternity suit, O'Grady had performed many personal services. When Elvis showed some interest in a woman, for instance, O'Grady had the job of checking her out.

"I did an evaluation of the women," he says. "Background, that sort of thing. And I would make an absolute calculated determination about whether they'd hurt him or not. I was right about Linda. I told him she'd happily take the money, but she would never gossip."

Elvis also pumped O'Grady for information about drugs. The detective knew Elvis was using—"and probably abusing"—prescription drugs as early as 1970. "I was a narc for *twelve* years, and you can tell. I *knew*. I shared my knowledge with him. He carried the Merck manual around with him."

The Merck manual, produced for doctors and pharmacists, describes all prescription drugs—chemical makeup, recommended dosage, side effects. Elvis's favorites were in the book. Hycodan. Demerol. Percodan. Valium. Placidyl. Phenobarb. He memorized every sentence that had anything to do with whatever he took.

"You gotta remember one thing," O'Grady says. "He had real pain. He had blood clots in his legs. He had hypoglycemia. He had an extremely enlarged heart. He had glaucoma. He was susceptible to respiratory ailments. His liver was three times normal size. He had a twisted colon. . . ."

In May 1976, O'Grady's son, a graduate student, wanted to meet Elvis, so they went to Lake Tahoe. "He was bloated," O'Grady says. "His eyes were almost closed. He was fighting to make a good appearance. He was sick. I called Ed Hookstratton [Elvis's Beverly Hills lawyer, who first hired O'Grady] and I told him that I gave Elvis one year to live unless we got him into a hospital. We made quiet arrangements for a hospital in San Diego, the Scripps Clinic, which is known for drying out rich drunks and rich drug cases. He was to remain there for three or four months and then we were going to take him to a private estate in Hawaii on Maui, for the rest of the year, to recuperate. I had dinner with Priscilla and her sister, Michelle, and we presented the whole program. Priscilla agreed and she took it to Elvis and he rejected it. She flew to Memphis and he said he could handle it, he didn't need outside help. The next time I saw him, he said, 'I was okay in Tahoe. Really. It was the altitude.' "

May, 1976–
July, 1976

Only seventeen days after closing in Lake Tahoe, Elvis was back on the road again, moving into extremely loyal middle-American geography—starting in Bloomington, Indiana, on May 27 and going to Ames, Iowa (where the sold-out sign went up in forty-five minutes), then diving deep, to Oklahoma City and then to Odessa, Lubbock, Tucson, El Paso, and Fort Worth, closing in one of the true centers of deep-South Elvis fandom, Atlanta, on June 4, 5, and 6. There were a dozen shows in eleven days and Elvis was still hanging in there.

The pressure must have been awful for Elvis. The twisted colon, the nutritional imbalance, the side effects of several drugs, glaucoma, the kidney problem, the enlarged heart and a pulse that sometimes climbed to 180 beats per minute, the ongoing hypoglycemia, the hypertension, the arteriosclerosis, the lupus erythemtosis—if this weren't enough, now he had an extremely painful ingrown toenail. If it hadn't hurt so much, it would've been funny.

Add to this the psychological pressures attached to being Elvis Presley. The single best-known personality in the world—with the possible exception of Muhammad Ali (who was somewhat more popular in the Third World)—Elvis sold out everywhere he went, without real need for any advertising. Elvis was like the circus.

No matter what he did, he made news, and when he came to town, he made the front page. Knowing this, the Colonel would arrange to have local coliseum managers, where Elvis was to play, hold press conferences. Everywhere the event would be well-attended by all local media and orders for tickets were received for all seats in under twenty-four hours. Often matinees were added to accommodate the demand. Scalpers got $250 for front row seats.

There was so much he had to face, continually, good and bad, from his fans: the supernova caused by all the Instamatics when he walked onstage; the interminable fan magazine covers, and worse, the supermarket tabloids, prying into his personal life; the consistency with which his albums sold, even when there were no hit singles and the albums themselves were weak; the complete and utter devotion that lapped at his ankles from all those who surrounded him. There were fan clubs in dozens of countries; some were so loyal they chartered planes to come see him in Las Vegas and look at his Memphis home. The mail was enormous. Every time he appeared in public, women of nearly all ages threw themselves at him and showered the stage with room keys, underwear, and folded notes with their names and addresses, for when he came to their town.

Elvis had every damned thing he wanted. Over the years he had owned every kind of transportation, from horses, golf carts, motorcycles, sports cars, and limousines, to pickup trucks, tractors, motor homes, yachts, and airplanes. He'd had spacious homes in three cities, duplicate wardrobes in each of them. He had a faithful, loving girlfriend (Linda) and whenever he wanted someone else for a night or two, he had people on the payroll who went out and got them for him. On a whim he could meet a U.S. President.

Anything he wanted to eat, he could eat, any time he wanted it. Fried banana sandwiches for breakfast! Baconburgers by the sack at midnight! Ice cream, a spoon served with a quart. When he wanted to go shopping, stores and automobile agencies fell all over themselves to open at two and three A.M.

And Elvis hung in there—bloated and sometimes whacked out of his mind on prescription chemicals, but able to "maintain" nearly all the time, able to get out there and give the customers a show.

"The best show I ever saw him do was in Fort Worth in June," says pianist Tony Brown. "He was singing on pitch, no jiving around, singing entire songs, not a blown word. He was just great. That show was a killer."

And the next night he was stoned again, giving the folks another kind of show. Slower, shorter, somewhat disappointing when compared to previous performances in the same cities, but still "The King," performing for a constituency that wouldn't desert him no matter what he did or didn't do.

There was another tour in June and July, another twelve shows in eleven days. Every month now he was gearing up for another short run at the American heartland. It was then that the friction began.

"You can get along with someone very nicely when you're with them three times a year," says orchestra leader Joe Guercio, "but then when you're with somebody every two weeks, boy, then all those little faults they got absolutely like to kill you."

Even Guercio, who wouldn't have missed a show for anything in the early years, now was sometimes staying at home in Las Vegas to work in the hotels, sending the trombonist Marty Harrell out as conductor.

"He was surrounded by giants," Guercio says, "and if everyone there gave their all, it could be explosive. In the beginning that's what it used to be. It was great. As much smoke as would come out of the engine would come outa the back cars. It didn't happen so much later."

Yet Elvis was hanging in. He never lost his sense of humor. When he introduced Larrie Londin, who weighed 350 pounds, it was before he sang "God Gave Me a Mountain This Time," saying, "I got me my own little mountain right here in the band." His fans, knowing his quirky sense of humor, gave him funny hats to wear; in one city, Elvis was handed a loaded water pistol and he promptly began spritzing J.D. Sumner and the Stamps. On Marty Harrell's first concert conducting, Marty's friend Pat Houston, the trumpet player, got everyone in the orchestra to agree to sit silently when Marty gave the downbeat. "I was nervous as hell anyway," says Marty. "I gave the downbeat and nothing happened. I looked at my hands. What did I do wrong? I looked over at Elvis and he was doubled over laughing. I gave the downbeat again and they started the show."

"He was like a little kid," says Larrie Londin. "He'd stand out there and these thousands of cameras were going off and the girls behind us would holler, 'Elvissssssss . . . turn around!' He'd turn around and they'd squeal and he'd be lookin' at me and he'd get this boyish grin on his face, like, 'What're you gonna do?' And he'd go on with it."

Sonny West was in his dentist's office when he got the call from Vernon. Dave Hebler was by his Memphis motel pool when his wife said he had a call. Red West was at the office of a private investigator.

Vernon told each of the three that he wanted to see them in person. They knew something was afoot by Vernon's sober tone.

"I told him I was a grown man and could handle anything he could tell me on the telephone," Sonny said.

"Well," said Vernon, "things haven't been going too well and we're going to have to cut back on expenses. We're going to have to let some people go. . . ."

In their book, Red and Sonny and Dave say they were fired whimsically, a characteristic capricious decision of their former boss. "What pissed us off," Red says, "after all those years I had been with him, he never took the time to tell me himself. He just cut out and left it to his father to do. It was cold, man."

It *was* cold. Over the years, Elvis had "fired" Red and Sonny and Dave, along with all the rest, a dozen times or more apiece. "I'll fire your ass!" was a Presley cliché. Now, when it came time to fire three of his men for real, Elvis made the final decision, then ran away from it, holing up in Palm Springs.

But the decision was not whimsical or capricious. It came after much agonizing and advice from several of his most trusted associates. One of these, the former narc and private detective, John O'Grady, in fact, takes credit for being the first to recommend that the three be dropped.

"I also suggested they fire Jerry Schilling because he wasn't doing anything," O'Grady says (an action easily accomplished when it was discovered Jerry had quit several months earlier). "I recommended Red and Sonny be fired because they were too rough with the fans. Red had punched a guy while Sonny held him. That sort of thing was resulting in a lot of unnecessary lawsuits. Elvis was spending a lot of money on lawyers and it looked like he was maybe going to lose some of the lawsuits besides."

Elvis was getting the same advice from the Colonel and Ed Hookstratton, his Beverly Hills attorney (and a friend of O'Grady's), and his father. There was unity in the advice: The bodyguards were not just expensive, but dangerously so.

On July 23, ten days after the "Tuesday Massacre," Elvis went back on the road again. And soon after that tour ended, he was back on the road still another time. Three weeks off and one week on. It was a schedule they thought Elvis could maintain.

Yet on the other hand were the inevitable sold-out concerts and consistently successful records. On August 21, RCA distributed a press release announcing that sales of Elvis Presley records had passed the 400-million mark, a figure light-years ahead of any previous total for a single performer. Twenty years after his first million-selling song, "Heartbreak Hotel," through all the other various RCA greats (Jefferson Airplane, Waylon Jennings, John Denver, etc.), Elvis was far and away the biggest star the company had ever had, including Enrico Caruso.

"Elvis was always handled by the top executive and that top executive controlled it," says Joan Deary, the longtime RCA assistant who had graduated to a position of programming Elvis's repackaged albums *(Legendary Performer, Sun Sessions)*. "Nobody in the promotion department or the art department or in any other department could go off on their own. They could not do that! It was a hands-off situation. You want something on Elvis Presley, you see Harry Jenkins"—an RCA vice-president who, on his retirement, went to work for the Colonel—"and the same thing with Rocco Loginestra [the president] after that. Nobody in the company would go off on their own, *ever*. Only the top executives made decisions, and they made them in consultation and in continuing contact with Colonel Parker."

Colonel Parker. Inevitably it came back to him and his staff. Daily from the Colonel's seventh-floor office there were calls to Jerry Weintraub or Tom Huelett, or someone else working on Elvis's tours. There were calls to the William Morris Agency and elsewhere in the building to various offices of RCA. Other calls went to Graceland, or Palm Springs, where Joe Esposito would speak for Elvis to Tom Diskin, who spoke for the Colonel.

"The Colonel took the rap for being the heavy," says one of the Colonel's longtime associates. "That went with the title of manager. But it was Elvis who really called the shots. Elvis didn't do anything he didn't want to do. He didn't do anything the Colonel wanted him to do exclusively. Elvis had the power in that relationship, although it often looked the opposite. And Elvis would use the Colonel as his out. When someone asked Elvis, 'What about this or that?', Elvis always said, 'You got to talk to the Colonel.' Then he told the Colonel to say no."

And so it went back to Elvis again. The periodic friction between the talent and the manager continued through the years, right on up until Elvis died, but the synergistic relationship was always more positive than negative. In the 1970s, both were showing their years. The Colonel was in his middle sixties and Elvis was past forty. In the world of rock and roll, that was pushing it. Yet still they reigned, a sort of modern-day Louis XIII and Cardinal Richelieu. Seeming untouchable, unstoppable.

August, 1976–
November, 1976

The King went on the road again August 27, floating through the South from Hilton hotel to Hilton hotel, from one convention center or municipal auditorium or coliseum or sports arena to the next, $100,000 and more in the box office each night, several thousand more from the sale of pennants and picture books, sold-out houses everywhere, the same dazzling Instamatic flash.

Yet the image he projected to friends worried them. His pianist, Tony Brown, remembers a grim matinee in the Summit in Houston: "He was worse there than in Maryland. The sound truck turned over on the way to the gig and they had to hire a new sound company. He had more monitors than any group on the road. He was so loaded . . . I retract that. He was in 'one of his moods' again and mumbling through his songs. And the new guys had piled the monitors on the stage blocking the view of some people seated behind him. Elvis usually hung his monitors from the ceiling so they wouldn't block anybody. It wasn't the right microphone. The sound people were doing their best, they really wanted to impress Elvis, but he turned around and said, off mike, 'This is the sorriest sonabitchin' sound system I've ever seen.' The guys turned against him then. It wasn't much of a show. It was a sorry show. Every time somethin' like that happened, people started talkin' about the tour getting canceled. And the next night . . ." Tony snaps his fingers. "Okay again."

Up and down. Up and down. But mostly down. Joe Mescale, leader of the Imperials, crossed paths with Elvis a week later in Huntsville, Alabama. It was the last time he saw Elvis alive.

"He was fat and sick," Joe says. "I went to his hotel and when I entered the room, he cleared everyone else out. Sheila Ryan was with him. He was wearing a robe. I'd taken a *Living Bible* with me for him and I'd written something in the front of it. He held me by the neck, just put his forehead to mine and just hugged me. He said he was so sick. He said, 'I don't even want to be here.' "

The tour ended September 8 with a small incident that only made Elvis feel worse. Dissatisfied with his room at the hotel in Pine Bluff, Arkansas—because of the proximity of the noisy fans outside—he ordered a change of plans, canceled the floor of rooms and announced they were flying back to Memphis after the concert, rather than spend the night before leaving. Elvis was a perfectionist. He paid for his comfort and he expected to get it. He tolerated no mistakes, either on the stage or in the selection of his rooms. When he encountered these inevitable errors, he corrected them.

A month later, on October 14, his seventh tour of the year began, taking him deep into the Midwest (Duluth, South Bend, Madison, Cleveland, etc.); a month after that came the eighth, a rapid swing through the West (Reno, Portland, Anaheim, etc.) that ended with still another fifteen performances in Las Vegas. He had two weeks off for Christmas and then went on his ninth tour that year.

One city ran into the next. Elvis moved from the plane to the car to the hotel to the car to the stage to the car to the plane to the car to the next hotel, over and over and over again, until he rarely knew what city he was in, sometimes didn't know which state, usually didn't give a damn.

The windows of his rooms were always covered with aluminum foil. When he got into his limousine after a concert, a towel was ready for his neck, a bottle of Gatorade within reach for his thirst. His jeweler, Lowell Hays, was on call along with the men on his personal payroll, twenty-four hours a day. The constant praise protected him from the chill winds and damp of reality. The pills and, by now, injections wrapped him in another furry cloak.

The late summer and autumn months were really a disaster.

First came the dissolution of a partnership that Elvis had entered to build and operate a chain of fifty racquetball courts. Dean Nichopoulos, the son of Elvis's doctor, sometimes worked for Elvis on the road and was one of the fastest young racquetball players in Memphis. Elvis personally loved the game, so when Dean's father, Dr. Nick, asked Elvis if he'd like to be partners with him and Joe Esposito and a local real estate developer named Mike McMahon, Elvis didn't even consult the Colonel before saying yes.

Two months later Elvis suggested the name of the corporation be changed from Racquet Ball of Memphis, Inc. to Presley Center Courts, Inc. His partners were thrilled. To be able to put Elvis's name on the sign in front of the court was, they believed, to become rich. Elvis was named corporate chairman and agreed to be liable for 25 percent of the finances. Construction of the first court began in Nashville. Then Elvis pulled out, scattering his relationships all over the landscape. Lawsuits were threatened; lawyers were hired.

Meanwhile, Red and Sonny and Dave were striking back at Elvis in another way. They didn't sue their former boss; they "wrote" a book. First they went to Ricky Huskey, the television writer who was a friend of Jerry Schilling's, and asked him to help them. He said no, thanks. Then they asked Frank Lieberman, the one-time Vegas critic. He said no, too. But Steve Dunleavy, the Australian gossip columnist for the weekly tabloid *National Star*, said yes immediately, and a deal was quickly made, giving the three former members of the Memphis Mafia a hefty percentage of the book's earnings. They wanted to tell everything there was to tell, they said. They said they wanted to warn Elvis. "He will read it and he will get hopping mad at us because he knows that every word is the truth and we will take a lie detector test to prove it," Red later said. "But, just maybe, it will do some good."

The three began calling around, asking questions about dates, telling people they were writing a book and wanted it to be accurate. Many thought they smelled a rat and refused to help. Word got to Elvis and he was furious. He sent John O'Grady to say he'd had second thoughts about the firing, didn't know they weren't given any severance pay, and so was prepared to give them $50,000 apiece, if in return, O'Grady said, they wouldn't write a book. Red, Sonny, and Dave said no. Two days later, Elvis called Red at his motel in Hollywood. The conversation was tape-recorded and part was included in what came to be called "the bodyguard book."

PRESLEY: How you doing, man?

RED: I just woke up.

PRESLEY: I was just on one of those singing binges . . . I got a coupla new guitars and singing my ass off. . . . I'm by myself. Linda is in L.A. She's changing apartments. We had that apartment, the people found I was in back of it and raised the rent double. She got another one right down the street. . . . Charlie [Hodge] told me about the talk you all had. I guess I do owe an explanation.

RED: I wish you had come to me and told me.

PRESLEY: You don't do things like that 'cause that's my daddy's business.

RED: No, it's not.

PRESLEY: I was getting a lot of excess pressure . . . you know that *racquetball* thing? . . . Two courts for a million three hundred thousand dollars. My understanding was that we were just going to use my name. And that's all and that was the contract I signed. I did it as a favor for Dr. Nick [Nichopoulos] and Joe [Esposito]. I'm just trying to tell some of the things that led up to it . . . I was wrong about Hebler. Just a bad thing on my part. He was very undermining and sneaky. He hated all you guys and everybody else and I kept hearing this shit. It just burned into my ear . . . and those goddamn *lawsuits,* you know how them lawyers are. There were six lawsuits in two years. I don't know whether you heard it, but they were trying to prove us insane. . . . I'm talking about some influential people who were checking psychiatrist reports. . . . They were trying to prove us insane . . . the whole bunch.

RED: I could not believe it. You had left town. Your daddy called us and talked about cutting down expenses and giving us one week's notice. They give Chinese coolies two weeks.

PRESLEY: I didn't know anything about it. The one week thing.

RED: The bottom fell out. I got a little hurt at first.

PRESLEY: Well, I can see that. You know my damn voice is so low, I make J.D. Sumner sound like a tenor. My damn fingers are blistered. I'm not operating on but one cylinder. Well, you know what happened was a combination of a whole lot of things that piled up on me. . . . It was like a fuse burning. And maybe I did lose sight of a whole lot of things. Especially you, your family and everything.

RED: It was cold, man.

PRESLEY: I love Pat [Red's wife]. You got a good family and everything.

RED: Maybe sometimes I overprotected you. You have problems.

PRESLEY: Well, you know what it is. It's like that old guy said in *Cool Hand Luke,* a failure to communicate.

In November, Elvis had Joe call Jerry Schilling to say Elvis wanted to see him. He said he was at Linda's apartment.

"We talked at length about the bodyguard book," Jerry says. "He told me he really appreciated that I didn't get involved. I said, 'Jesus, that's no big thing. . . .' He said, 'It's a big thing to me and I'll never forget it.' He wasn't worried for himself. The concern he had for that book was the friends and family around him that could've gotten hurt. He told me, 'Jerry, everything that could possibly be written about somebody has been written about me already. But what about my family and friends, my doctor. . . ? There are good people that I don't want hurt.' He was extremely concerned about Lisa. If I'd 'a been in the situation Elvis was in, I'd 'a never been able to handle it as gracefully as he did."

If the firing of Red and Sonny and the collapse of the racquetball courts were stunning, what happened to Elvis's relationship with Linda put them in the shade. They had been drifting for months. To the outsider it became noticeable when Linda unglued herself from Elvis's side on the tours and in Las Vegas and began playing cards with the boys in the band. Hanging out. Breaking loose.

"The real thing that was most difficult to accept and probably the primary reason why I ultimately left," Linda says today, "was that there was no room for personal growth. Your life revolved entirely around Elvis's. It was not conducive to personal, individual growth. I couldn't be assertive as an individual. I felt like an appendage, which was not his fault. He had an overpowering presence. Not that he even meant to do that to people, but somehow when you were with him you knew how great his needs were and you were willing to give up yourself. I think that essentially I just grew up.

I think it amounted to that. I finally thought, 'Hey, I'm an individual entity, too. I have a right to my own feelings, my own desires, my own life.' And I wasn't having that. My life revolved around him. I felt stagnant.

"Wanting my own life came on slowly," Linda says. "It wasn't like I woke up one morning and said, 'I'm leaving.' It was a long time coming, it was a long, painful, drawn-out process. Because I loved him dearly, and still do. But there's a great tragedy sometimes in the realization that you can love someone and not be able to live with him, not be able to live their lifestyle and grow and prosper as an individual.

"After so many years being around the same people all the time, and then being together so much, it was more intimate than a marriage. He often used to say we had spent more time together in four-and-a-half years than a lot of married couples spent in twenty years. We were together twenty-four hours a day. I went to every concert. I never sat one out. I think that would have really hurt him if I had not shown an interest in every show. I was out there pulling for him. I had to give him critiques after the show. He would say, 'Did you see such-and-such?' He wanted that communication. He wanted to know you were with him. I was pulling for every high note and low note and watching every movement. That was ingrained with me. That was the kind of dedication you gave Elvis. He expected that of the others, too. Not just be there, but pay attention.

"From the very moment we met, we felt a true affinity for each other. We weren't just lovers, we weren't just mates, we were partners. I was his sister and he was my brother. I was his mommy and he was my baby. He was my daddy and I was his little girl. We were lovers, we were friends, we were everything to each other. It was an all-encompassing relationship for an awfully long time. There's a line from a Kim Carnes song: 'Sometimes the love that burns the brightest/burns itself right out in time.' There's so much highly charged energy sometimes within a relationship that it's almost too much. I really feel sometimes that I loved him too much, that he loved me too much.

"I never really left him and played cards with the guys until about three months before we broke up. I just had to start getting away."

Of course it wasn't so uneventful as that. There was friction. That much togetherness wears thin and as Linda rediscovered the assertiveness and competitiveness that made her a successful beauty queen, she began peppering her baby talk with criticism and advice. They also fought sometimes, over his demands for her fidelity when he left her at home to go on the road with other women, and over his subsequent sexual boasts. They also had what Linda describes as "horrible fights" about the pills he took, usually after she had stayed awake while Elvis slept so she could watch his breathing. More than once she had called for help from Joe and the others on duty downstairs when Elvis apparently took too many sleeping pills.

So finally she wrote him a "Dear John" letter, saying she still loved him and always would, but adding that she had to leave. Then, before returning the Master Charge card that Elvis had given her—with unlimited credit—she went out and charged $30,000 worth of stuff, a third of that in airline tickets.

Only Vernon was really upset. Elvis was somewhat amused and laughed.

November, 1976–
March, 1977

Linda left the first week of November and within a day
or two, George Klein was calling around Memphis for
a replacement. Ginger Alden was one of the names he
had on his list and he called her November 19. Ginger
was the daughter of a woman born in Arkansas and a
retired career army sergeant who had been present in
the Memphis recruiting office when Elvis was drafted
in 1958. Ginger was twenty when she answered George
Klein's call.

"When Ginger was growing up," her mother says,
"we'd go stand outside the Graceland gates when we
read that he was in town and watch him ride his horse
or his golf cart. We got invited to the Fairground when
Ginger was five and Elvis patted her on the head. We
stayed until four o'clock in the morning and Ginger
rode the roller coaster with him."

Ginger's older sister Terry was Miss Tennessee in
1976, the same year Ginger was named Miss Mid-South
and then went on to be first runner-up in the Miss Tennessee Universe contest. She also had won the Miss Traffic Safety title and was a Duchess in the Cotton Carnival.
She was a pretty girl, almost painfully shy, with long,
teased dark hair and dark makeup that made her look
very much like Priscilla did in the bouffant 1960s.

The first night she was taken to Graceland, she waited

for between three and four hours downstairs with the boys. She says George told her Elvis was upstairs practicing karate. "Finally," she says, "I was told to go upstairs and turn left into Lisa's room. I met him there. I stayed that night. We read some religious books. And then he had one of his aides drive me home. The next night he took me to Las Vegas for one night and on November 28 I joined him in San Francisco on tour. He had his personal pilot, Milo High, pick me up in the Jet Star for that. Then when he went to the Hilton Hotel in December, he flew my parents, my sisters and my brother and me out."

That was when Elvis bought his first big gift for Ginger, a white Mark V Lincoln Continental with white upholstery. How the giving of that gift was accomplished showed clearly what efforts were expended to follow the King's every whim.

"I got a call at 4 A.M. on a Friday," says Gerald Peters, the British-born limousine service owner in Los Angeles. "Elvis said he wanted a white-on-white Mark V delivered to his hotel in Vegas that night. I said, 'Tonight?' He said, 'Tonight.' I said, 'Well, the boss wants one, so we'll get one, right?' I called a friend at the Beverly Hills agency and he laughed. He said Lincoln was six months behind in delivery and white-on-whites are as rare as water in the desert. I asked if there was anyone else. He said no. So I called the Ford Motor Company in Detroit and asked where they'd delivered white-on-white Mark V's in Southern California. She said, 'We're not allowed to tell that.' I said, 'Honey, there's a fifty-dollar bill in it for you. Between me and you, it's for Elvis Presley.' She breaks the rule and tells me five different dealerships where they'd delivered them— Glendale, San Pedro, all around. The first four places told me they were sold already.

"The last call was Glendale. I said, 'I understand from Ford headquarters that you have a white-on-white . . .' Blimey, they hadn't sold it yet, but the boss was using it. I said I'd be there within the hour to buy it. Which I did, paying with a $17,000 personal check, although I didn't have any money in the bank. And then I drove to Las Vegas, arriving at 1 A.M.

"Elvis was on stage and they slipped me into a booth down front, so I could see the rest of the show. Then I went backstage. Elvis said, 'So, Sir Gerald, you've got it?' I said, 'Yes, whatever you want, you get.' Elvis said, 'Let's go see the car.' So we went through the laundry exit and he gives the car to this girl who was along, Ginger Alden.

"Now that should be the end of the story," Gerald says, "but it isn't. I went back to Los Angeles and Elvis called again. This time he said he wanted me to pick up the car in Las Vegas and drive it to Memphis. So my son and I flew to Las Vegas and drove nonstop to Memphis with the car. We arrived at 9 A.M. and he'd just gone to bed. We checked into a motel, got some sleep ourselves, took the car to a car wash, and then delivered it to Graceland. 'Here's the Lincoln,' I said. He said, 'That didn't take you long.' I said, 'We drove nonstop.' And he said, 'Well, you shouldn't-a hurried. I got her a Cadillac Seville.'"

Through the holidays Elvis's mood was good. The frequent short tours were exhausting and Elvis's reliance on the pills continued, but his weight was down slightly and the shows were for the most part good. There were no major incidents. With two weeks off for Christmas, when the group reassembled in Pittsburgh for a New Year's Eve concert, spirits were high.

"It was New Year's Eve day, a few hours before the concert," says Marty Harrell, the trombonist and sometime orchestra leader. "Four of us in the band were playing cards. We took a break as one of the guys—Howard Struble, one of the horn players—went down to get more booze. It was snowing and about five degrees, with at least eighteen inches of snow on the ground. There was a little park down below the hotel and Howard stamped out in twelve-foot letters a message to one of the other trumpet players, Pat Houston; FUCK YOU PAT. And then he came up to the room again. We called Elvis and Ricky [Stanley] answered the phone. He said Elvis was lying on the floor laughing. He'd watched Howard do the whole thing."

That night, Elvis put on one of his best shows ever. "He was bright-eyed and bushy-tailed," says John Wilkinson. "It was a great show. He never sounded better."

Taking care of business was his motto and there was little he liked to do more. So when Ginger's mother's father died, Elvis started making plans and issuing orders to get everyone to the January third funeral in Harrison, Arkansas. The Memphis sheriff took Ginger and her mother and sisters to Graceland at the same time a rented Lear jet was flown in from Nashville to accommodate those who couldn't be transported in the Jet Star. (The runway in Harrison was too short for the *Lisa Marie*.) Joe Esposito and Charlie Hodge and Ricky and David Stanley went along to drive the cars Elvis rented to take them to the church. He wanted to buy the fanciest coffin and didn't only because Mrs. Alden insisted that her father was a humble man, who had picked out his own before he died.

Two days later Elvis took Ginger and her sister Rosemary to Palm Springs, where they remained for more than a week. While there, one of Elvis's doctors from Beverly Hills, Max Shapiro, came to visit him, accompanied by his fiancée. Max was a dentist who later would admit that he had provided Elvis with prescriptions for some of his drugs, and over the years they had become friends. In fact, Max had designed an artificial heart and Elvis had talked about providing money to build the prototype, planning to give one to his father, another to Ginger's mother.

Max told Elvis that he had been planning to get married, but didn't know where or when. He already had the license, he said, and produced it for Elvis to look at.

Elvis suggested they get married right away at Elvis's house, so they did, with one of Elvis's friends, Larry Geller, performing the ceremony. Larry, once Elvis's hairdresser, had acquired a ministerial certificate by mail and for several years had been serving as Elvis's unofficial guru, suggesting and buying him books about spiritualism, religion, and philosophy.

A week later, back in Memphis, Elvis was planning his own marriage. The story of his proposal to Ginger is another that shows how those around Elvis dropped everything when he called.

Elvis had one of his guys call Lowell Hays about one o'clock on the morning of January 26. He said he'd consulted *Cheiro's Book of Numbers* and this was the day he was supposed to get engaged and he wanted a ring right away.

"Yes, sir," Lowell said. "Tell Elvis I can bring out a selection from the store. I can be there in . . ."

"Low'll . . . listen a minute. Elvis wants the diamond in the ring as big or bigger than the one you put in his TCB ring."

Lowell was aghast. "That's impossible! That diamond's eleven-and-a-half carats. I don't have any diamonds that size and there's no way of getting one in the middle of the night. Will you tell Elvis that?"

Five minutes later Elvis called back and said in an authoritative tone, "Low'll?"

"Yessir?"

"I've got to have this diamond and I've got to have it by tonight. If you don't have it, where can I get one?"

"I have no idea, Elvis, and you won't get one tonight."

Elvis shot back, "The hell I won't. Watch me."

Lowell went back to sleep, only to be awakened again an hour later. It was Elvis again. "Low'll?"

"Yessir?"

"What if you went to New York? Could you get me one then?"

"I doubt it, Elvis. They keep those things in bank vaults. No one's gonna have a diamond like that at home where they can get to it . . ."

Elvis interrupted: "Will you try?"

Lowell said he would and called "a couple of millionaire diamond brokers" he dealt with in New York, waking them to make his unusual request. Was there any way, he asked, to get such a diamond immediately? They said no, not even in New York. Then, just before Lowell started dialing a friend who had a diamond that size to see if he would let him "borrow" it, he thought of the TCB ring. He dialed the Graceland number.

"Elvis," he said, "I've talked to everybody I know in New York and there's no way to get an eleven-carat diamond tonight. What if you give her the diamond in the TCB ring and I'll put another diamond in your ring later?"

Elvis went for it and Lowell rushed to Graceland to retrieve the big ring, drawing a sketch of the suggested mounting. Then he rushed to his store and woke one of his employees, got him to come to work immediately, and the finished ring, worth about $70,000, was delivered to Elvis on time. Elvis then called Ginger into the big bathroom adjacent to his bedroom and proposed. When she said yes, he gave her the ring. Then they went to show it to Vernon.

Then Ginger said she didn't want to go to Nashville when Elvis told her he was going to record. He said she didn't have any choice about it; she was going and that was final. Normally shy and retiring, Ginger remained firm, telling Elvis that she didn't like Nashville and he was a gruff old bear for making her go. She questioned his love. Of course he loved her, he said; he didn't have to prove that.

This wasn't the first disagreement. Once, Ginger stalked out of the house and Elvis came running after her with a pistol, firing it into the nighttime Graceland air (where gunshots are the norm) over her head. Later the media would say Elvis was trying to scare her into returning. Ginger saw it another way. Elvis was just proving how great his love was. She turned around and walked to Graceland.

But she didn't go to Nashville, so Elvis went alone. Nashville was, in January 1977, the center of recording for America—not just the city where country and western records were made, but every other kind as well. Even most of the hot young studio musicians from Memphis and from the studios of Muscle Shoals, Alabama, had moved to Nashville. New studios were opening every month and it was to one of the new ones that Elvis's band reported.

It was his road band: James Burton, John Wilkinson, Ronnie Tutt, Kathy Westmoreland, and Myrna Smith from Los Angeles; David Briggs and Tony Brown from Nashville. For three days they waited for Elvis to show up.

"We waited for him at the studio," says Myrna Smith. "We'd wait and Felton would call and say Elvis hadn't left Memphis yet. . . ."

Finally, Elvis went to Nashville, flying with only a few bodyguards in his Jet Star. They checked into a motel. The musicians and singers continued to wait.

On the third day, Joe Esposito called the studio to make the arrangements to get everyone home, to arrange for cars and planes. Then Elvis flew back to Memphis to be with Ginger.

RCA was gravely disappointed. If the company was to maintain the output of Presley product they planned, they believed they needed more songs immediately. Only one album of new material had been released in a year and seven months, and that was the weak collection of sad songs recorded for the most part at Graceland in April 1976. RCA and the Colonel decided that again the mountain would go to Mohammed. A session was scheduled for Graceland for the first week of February, 1977.

Elvis hadn't forgotten the lousy sound he heard in his den, so this time the microphones and monitors and instruments and so on were set up in his big indoor racquetball court, which if anything was even more of an acoustical mistake than the den.

Again the musicians and backup singers waited, this time in their motel rooms. One, two, three days passed, just as they had in Nashville. Finally the call went out and Elvis appeared. Not to record, however.

"He didn't like the sound," says John Wilkinson. "He may've been using that as an excuse, because he didn't want to record. He told them to pack the speaker up and send it back to New York. He said, 'They're wrong! They're all wrong. Send 'em back. Get new stuff!' They tried to fix them and he still found something wrong. He finally called a halt to the whole thing. He gathered us around and he said, 'I'm really sorry about this. My throat doesn't feel right. We can't record with this kind of equipment. That mobile truck is no good. We'll do it again. No big thing. We need some other engineers and stuff.' And then he started talking about the bodyguard book. He just couldn't believe Red and Sonny'd do that to him. He had big huge tears in his eyes behind his glasses. He was visibly upset. He said he loved them like brothers and he couldn't understand why they'd want to stab him in the back. He'd bought cars for them, he'd bought houses for them, he'd given them jobs when they couldn't get jobs any place else. He went on and on and pretty soon he just stopped talking.

"Finally he asked how we wanted to get home. He was gonna take the *Lisa Maria* and fly all the L.A. people there on it and fly the others to Nashville on the Jet Star and have limos take everybody to their houses. Joe Esposito didn't like that and J.D. [Sumner] said he could have his wife meet him. Elvis said, 'Joe, give J.D. the keys to that white one out front.' A big white limousine went to J.D. Elvis flew us home, J.D. went and got in the car and drove off with the Nashville people. That was the last time we were in the house."

It was also the last time Elvis attempted to record.

On February 12, Elvis began one of his shortest scheduled tours—nine shows in nine days, about half of them in southern cities where he'd never appeared before: in Miami, West Palm Beach, and Orlando, Florida, and in Augusta, Georgia, and Columbia, South Carolina. It was as if the Colonel wanted a pin in every city on the U.S. map.

The tour was undistinguished. Elvis was overweight, nearing the 225-pound mark. Only a few of his costumes fit now, and often he wore the same one every couple of days. His performances were perfunctory, listless. By now he rarely learned the words to a new song, preferring to read them from a typed lyric sheet. Since splitting his pants, his movements were curtailed or abbreviated. The knee drops and high karate kicks were long past; now Elvis merely teased his fans with a slight shake of his beefy hips, his bay window noticeable as it hung over the top of his huge jeweled belt buckle. Elvis was bored, unable or unwilling to re-create more than a hint of the excitement he projected only a few years earlier.

So it was with great relief that the tour ended and he began planning a vacation trip to Hawaii.

Before leaving for the islands, however, there was one matter of business—the signing of his will. It had been drawn up by his Memphis attorney, Beecher Smith, and was taken to Graceland for Elvis's signature on March 3. In it, he named three principal beneficiaries—his daughter Lisa Marie, his father Vernon, and his grandmother Minnie Mae. The will also granted absolute control of the estate to Vernon, naming him executor and trustee. Vernon was to have discretion to provide financial assistance to other of Elvis's relatives "in need of emergency assistance." This generosity was to end with Vernon's death, however. No charitable organizations were mentioned, nor were Priscilla or Ginger or any of his longtime employees.

When the thirteen-page document was given to Elvis in his bedroom, he nodded his thanks and asked to have Ginger and Charlie Hodge sent up to witness his signing. A third witness, Ann Smith, wife of one of his cousins, tagged along and added her signature under Charlie's. Elvis then returned the will to his attorney and started talking about the vacation.

It was decided that Elvis and his party would leave from Oakland because it was two hundred miles closer to Honolulu than Los Angeles. He was taking the *Lisa Marie* and wanted every margin of safety in fuel loading. Not one to do anything by halves, however, Elvis took thirty-one others with him, and had Joe Esposito reserve more than a dozen rooms in the Hilton Rainbow Tower and rent a house on the beach.

The beach house, in Kailua, about half an hour's drive from Honolulu, was for Elvis and Ginger and her sisters, plus one bodyguard, the former Palm Springs policeman Dick Grob. The other stayed in the hotel and came over during the day or joined Elvis on his rare public forays. One evening, for instance, they were sneaked into the Polynesian Cultural Center to watch the Polynesian show. Other times, he took Ginger and her sisters and some of the others to one of the small shopping centers in Kailua, buying presents for everyone and, on one occasion, paying the bill for a stranger who was making a purchase for his wife.

Most of the ten days in Hawaii were spent close to home, sitting on the beach, playing Ping-Pong at the house, or touch football on the sand. Those who had been with Elvis for some time said later that his health improved during the vacation, said his color was better, his eyes brighter and clearer.

There was another observer who hadn't seen Elvis in some time, and he was shocked. This was Kalani Simerson, a onetime performer who operated a successful limousine service. He had known Elvis, and had worked for him, since the early 1960s, when Elvis made his first films in Hawaii. The last time he had seen Elvis was when he weighed a trim 170 or so for the satellite television show. As before, Kalani was again called to make some of the arrangements for Elvis's visit, and because of his long-standing friendship, he was invited to join Elvis on the beach socially.

"We played football," Kalani says, "and it was sad, very sad. Elvis was overweight and just unable to function normally. I guess it was all that medication they said he took. Somebody'd throw him the ball and he'd catch it and start running and he couldn't stop. He just wasn't able to control his own body. One time he ran right into a cyclone fence and cut his hand."

On the fourteenth day, Elvis got some sand in his eyes and abruptly the vacation was ended. Five days after that he was back on tour again.

March, 1977–
April, 1977

Elvis's small fleet of jets was aimed at the cities where his oldest and most loyal constituency lived—in Phoenix and Amarillo and Norman and Abilene and Austin and Alexandria. This was the territory he traveled when he drove from city to city with Scotty Moore and Bill Black ("The Blue Moon Boys"), to appear in noisy, crowded honkytonks and on the backs of flatbed trucks. This is where he was a young star on the "Louisiana Hayride" radio show. It was this region—in the panhandle of west Texas, in Arkansas, in north Louisiana—that gave little Sun Records an entire galaxy of stars besides Elvis: Carl Perkins, Roy Orbison, Conway Twitty, Charlie Rich, Jerry Lee Lewis, and Johnny Cash. It was a sound that defined the time and those whom it influenced went on to define the time to come. Buddy Holly and the Crickets, Buddy Knox, Leon Russell, and Mac Davis were only a few of the faces in his early crowds.

That was in 1955. Now it was 1977. More than twenty years had passed and, to the people who lived in the region, Elvis epitomized the American dream. They too were, or had been, poor; generally were part of the working class. And they wished to get out of their box, to live the fantasy life that Elvis had come to represent. He was what every woman wanted and every man wished to be, and it didn't matter that he was fat. They'd grown up with Elvis and weren't they fat, too? When you lived, or tried to live, the good life, wasn't fat one of the penalties?

At first the tour was like all the recent rest. Some shows were good, some were fair, and some were miserable. Elvis did his best, but nowadays his best was much less than it was when he played that city as a youngster. Some concerts, Elvis performed like an old man. At times it seemed he had only the loosest control of his voice and muscle coordination. He dropped lyrics, mumbled introductions, and very nearly *stumbled* around the stage.

On March 31, following a so-so show in Alexandria, Louisiana, Elvis's private plane took him to Baton Rouge for a concert at Louisiana State University. As was customary, the show started before he was to leave the hotel for the coliseum. All the usual acts performed. First the Sweet Inspirations; then J.D. Sumner and his youthful Stamps; then Jackie Kahane, with the predictable jokes. Elvis usually arrived during the intermission that followed Jackie's monologue. Tonight he didn't.

There was chaos backstage. Elvis's hotel room was called.

"Well, Joe?"

"I don't know, Charlie. Maybe . . ."

A half-hour passed. There were more calls. Finally it was decided to cancel the rest of the show, to say Elvis was too sick to go on, that he was under a doctor's care and was being flown back to Memphis to be hospitalized.

It wasn't untrue. Dr. Nick returned with Elvis to Memphis on the *Lisa Marie* and within hours of arriving, at six o'clock on the morning of April first, Elvis checked himself into his old two-room suite on the sixteenth floor of the Baptist Hospital. This time Maurice Elliott announced to the anxious press that gathered that Elvis was being treated for "exhaustion."

That wasn't entirely untrue, either. Elvis had been

taking so many uppers, he hadn't slept much. He ate poorly, he exercised not at all, and the performances, however listless, had taken what little he had. His old nurse, Marian Cocke, says she talked with him until eleven in the morning, when he was sedated and slept for thirty hours straight.

Dr. Nick watched Elvis closely. For a long, long time —for more than two years—Elvis's use of drugs had been daily, rather than occurring periodically. It was, in fact, *rampant,* in a runaway pattern that could now lead to a fatal overdose.

Elvis *had* nearly overdosed on several occasions. Linda Thompson recalls when she found him unable to get his breath, or unconscious on the floor by the bed. Red and Sonny West tell of a time when a girl Elvis took to Palm Springs actually was hospitalized after they'd spent an evening swilling Hycodan, a codeine cough syrup.

Elvis was an experimenter. Just as he wanted the newest automotive extravagance, he wanted the latest drug. The best and newest on the marketplace. Valium. Ethinamate. Demerol. Percodan. Placidyl. Dexedrine. Biphetamine. Amytal. Quaalude. Carbital. Cocaine hydrochloride. Ritalin.

He had once turned to Red West's wife and said, "Pat, I've tried them all, honey, and believe me, Dilaudid is the best." Dilaudid was a painkiller usually given to terminal cancer patients.

Elvis's attitude toward drugs was interesting. He, like so many other Americans, was putting one or more prescription drugs into his body on a regular, continuing basis. Many of these drugs were addictive—not just psychologically but physically, as would come out eventually. (Two years after his death, Congressional investigation of Valium use showed it to be highly hazardous, and Valium was one of the weaker drugs Elvis was taking.) At the time, many of these drugs weren't thought to be dangerous. They were an accepted part of modern life; thirty million were taking Valium alone.

Elvis regarded his many prescriptions as medicine. He had real problems—pains, insomnia, a tendency to obesity—and he had real medicine to take care of those problems. And that was it.

Except that wasn't it. Not all of it. He also knew that these drugs made him feel good in ways it was hard to explain. Dilaudid, he said, was best. That's the one that brought on that cushiony surfboard ride, that friendly blotto that wiped out all the psychic injuries, brought on a creamy somnolence. What was it that 1960s' poet Liza Williams called dope? Chewing gum for the mind.

Dope created pretty pictures, or turned them off. It dulled the sharp edges of life, or sharpened the blurry post-sleeping-pill downs and got you on your feet again. They made you talk rapidly and incessantly, made you outgoing and generous. The also made you stingy and mean and caused incoherent mumbling. What was the DuPont advertising slogan that became such a popular slogan? Ah, yes. Better living through chemistry.

Sometimes the drugs worked at cross purposes, and mixing them was tricky, indeed. The uppers—the Dexamyl, Biphetamine, and Ionamin—were cerebral stimulants, used in the treatment of obesity. Often, the psychic stimulation caused by these drugs was followed by depression and fatigue. Other side effects included restlessness, talkativeness, insomnia, and irritability. Elvis was often on uppers when he went on his car-buying sprees.

The downers were another trip. Valium was generally thought to be a minor tranquilizer, useful in the symptomatic relief of tension and anxiety; but side effects included drowsiness, fatigue, confusion, depression, and possible addiction. Placidyl, one of Elvis's favorites, was chemically unrelated to the barbiturates and used as a hypnotic to induce sleep. It was addictive, too, and side effects, in large doses, included respiratory difficulty.

Carbitral was a sleep-inducing agent that caused nausea and vomiting.

The painkillers added still another dimension. Hycodan, Demerol, and Percodan were narcotic analgesics that often caused lightheadedness, dizziness, nausea, vomiting, uncoordinated muscle movements, hallucinations, and irregular heartbeat. Quaaludes led to restlessness and excitement, accompanied by slurred speech, shallow and low respiration, weak and rapid heartbeat, possible coma, and death.

Elvis consulted the big, thick Merck manual regularly, checking recommended dosages and side effects. He mixed drugs the way bartenders mix drinks, the way chefs prepare an exotic dish. But drugs were different from food and alcohol. One drug affected perception and that, in turn, sometimes determined through confusion how much of a second drug was taken. And so on, while the side effects overlapped and contradicted each other and together the drugs did things that individually they did not do. It was almost as if the drugs were acting in conspiracy against the taker.

It was from a very peculiar position that Dr. Nick watched Elvis dry out in the hospital in April, because he knew that the pills Elvis was so strung out on had come from him. As early as January, Dr. Nick had become Elvis's primary supplier. It wasn't greed, or ego, that put this small, white-haired physician in that place. Up until January, Elvis had solicited his prescriptions from dozens of doctors, stretching from Beverly Hills and Palm Springs to Elvis's Graceland neighborhood. Dr. Nick, who had been one of them, figured that if he could become his patient's only source, he could gain control and with care and time could wean Elvis off drugs completely.

But the quantity and variety Dr. Nick prescribed challenged all credibility. Two years after Elvis's death a computer check of prescriptions in the Memphis area showed that in the final seven months of Elvis's life,

George Nichopoulos, M.D., prescribed 5,300 uppers, downers, and painkillers for Elvis. That's an average of about twenty-five pills or injectible vials a day.

As Dr. Nick watched Elvis's diet and medicine and put him through the customary battery of tests, what did he think about? Did he remember the first time he gave his patient a barbiturate to help him sleep, or an appetite suppressant? Did he remember January 20, the day he apparently gained control of Elvis's habit and prescribed twenty tablets of biphetamine, one hundred and thirty tablets of Dexedrine, fifty tablets of Dilaudid, and one hundred each of Amytal and Quaalude? Did he think about the bottles he carried in his black bag when he went touring with Elvis?

Elvis and his doctor had a special relationship. Every addict and his connection do. Yet, it was much more than that. Ask Elvis's closest associates and friends to name Elvis's other closest friends and nearly everyone puts Dr. Nick at or near the top of the list, up there with Charlie Hodge, Joe Esposito, and Billy Smith. Elvis had no secrets, really, when it came to Dr. Nick. Dr. Nick knew Elvis inside and out, literally. And Dr. Nick accepted Elvis as he was, totally; loved him. And Elvis loved Dr. Nick. Why, he even loaned him $225,000 when he wanted to remodel his big house on the outskirts of Memphis and join some other doctors in the construction of an expensive medical building, a venture that was slow to return any profit.

There was the glamor, too. Dr. Nick kept many of his older patients, but it was Elvis to whom he pledged his fullest attention, clearing his calendar completely whenever his patient went on the road, so he could go along. After a while, the hotels and airports must have gotten to Dr. Nick as they got to Elvis, but, still, how many other general practitioners lived such a glamorous lifestyle?

And what did Elvis think of Dr. Nick? He loved him, yes, and respected him, always called him Dr. Nick, never by his first name. Nick and his son, Dean, were family. Yet, there must also have been a little something else. For just as Elvis had his jeweler traveling with him in case he contracted a sudden case of diamonditis, he also had his doctor along in case he ran out of something. Best of all, the man who gave him the stuff that might one day cause him trouble could minister to his medical needs instantly and professionally. Elvis wasn't the only touring rock star who carried such a man on the payroll.

All of this was a part of Elvis's normalcy, a part of his everyday.

Elvis checked himself out of the hospital after five days and went home, where he resumed the regular routine of being handed a packet of eight or nine pills to go to sleep, another packet upon waking up.

Elvis wasn't always whacked out of his handsome skull, lying on his nine-foot by nine-foot bed semicomatose, dreaming of better times and space. And even when he was under the influence, say when the drug's effect was just coming on, he had learned pretty well how to cope, how to carry on though stoned. It was something every habitual user of any drug learned, whether the drug was marijuana, Valium, or alcohol. He learned how to pretend to be straight. To cope.

Elvis coped very well when, right after he left the hospital, Priscilla arrived for a visit with Lisa Marie. The three of them rarely were together; to Lisa Marie, having both parents together was an event, even if it only lasted a day.

Elvis also coped "normally" when one of his hired hands, Marty Lacker, called his attention to a story in the Memphis paper about an old woman who needed a new wheelchair. Elvis bought her one—of course it was electric, with all the trimmings—and then delivered it himself, picking the ancient black woman up in his arms and placing her into it. Then he pushed two hundred-dollar bills into the woman's hand and, wishing her a Merry Christmas, walked right back out of her life.

Elvis was the Lone Ranger, giving great gifts and then riding away in his Cadillac.

He joked with his maids back at Graceland. There was one named Maggie, a black girl who had dropped out of college to sit by the Graceland kitchen telephone and play with Lisa Marie when she visited. Elvis kidded her about the way her behind stuck out, said she could carry a pail of water on her butt and not spill a drop. Later, Maggie confided that she was pregnant. Elvis asked her, "Are you in love?" She matter-of-factly said, "No, it was all a big mistake." That made Elvis laugh. Then he asked if she liked being pregnant. Maggie said yes and pretty soon Elvis and Maggie were crying together.

His memory continued to amaze his friends. His buddy Bill Browder (T.G. Sheppard) remembers the first time he watched the 10 o'clock television news with Elvis. "I caught him repeating almost word for word what the newscaster was saying," T.G. says. "I said, 'Elvis, how you know what he's saying?' He said, 'Wull, I heard this part on the early news at six.' I said, 'You remember the words?' And he said, 'I just listened.' "

April, 1977–
June, 1977

The tide of favorable publicity had turned. In April, only days after he checked himself out of Baptist Hospital, a story appeared in the popular weekly tabloid, *The National Star*, that made Elvis appear foolish and over-the-hill. On the cover was his picture, sweating and overweight, a suspicious, spaced-out cast in his eyes, along with the provocative headline: "Elvis, 42, fears he's losing his sex appeal—psychologist explains Presley's tantrums and why, at 230 pounds, he craves young girls and jelly donuts." The housewives picked up the tabloid by the millions.

Then, only two weeks later, another unflattering photograph showing Elvis's double chin appeared on the cover of the *National Enquirer*. Now the come-on headline read: "Elvis' Bizarre Behavior and Secret Face Lift." Again a publication broke all previous sales records.

Elvis's name and face had sold two decades of wishy-washy movie fan magazines. In those days, the dirtiest it got was "The Night Ann-Margret Confessed to Roger Smith, 'I Can Never Forget.'" Now it was "Elvis—fat, feisty and 42 . . ." There were stories of how he fired guns in the air and how he talked about his mother's presence walking the Graceland halls at night. Motel keepers were interviewed about his diet; they said he ate like a family of four. His extravagances were reported disparagingly; once he dispatched his pilot and private plane from Memphis all the way to Dallas for a sack of hamburgers from an all-night snack bar he liked. Nothing, no matter how trivial or personal, was left out.

Nor did it get any better when Elvis went back on the road April 21 on a tour of thirteen performances in thirteen days. There'd been critical reviews in the past, but nothing to compare with these. It was as if the press, usually adoring of Elvis and his performances, or at least forgiving, had turned into a bloodthirsty pack of dogs, snapping at the singer's shaky legs.

A writer in Detroit was especially critical. Referring to Elvis as an "old idol," he said:

"Let me tell you something, gang; when I say old, I mean old. That turkey needs a feather transplant.

"It is damning Presley with faint praise to say that he stunk the joint out. If he appeared live and in concert tonight in my backyard, I wouldn't bother to raise the window shade.

"As it was we got stung $15 a seat to listen to his aging voice crack and to hear him stumble over lyrics he should have memorized 20 years ago.

"I couldn't get close enough to see his eyes or smell his breath, but the dude had to be either high or stiff when he came on stage—late, of course.

"Presley is old, fat and virtually immobile. At best, he is a parody of himself. At worst, a bad imitation of Burl Ives.

"It was a merciful gesture when Presley left the stage following his brief and disappointing performance and refused to make a curtain call."

And so on.

Because Elvis still moved on to the next city immediately following a concert, he continued to miss seeing such reviews. Not so the members of his backup band, however. They read the reviews and were hit with the force of a blow. "The Green Bay paper and the

Detroit paper were vicious and nasty," says John Wilkinson. "The *Green Bay Chronicle,* April 29, 1977, I'll never forget it. It was sick."

"There was one guy, he panned it so bad it was like he was pissed off," says Tony Brown. "We got panned nine times out of ten. He was still packin' 'em in, but we got panned anyways, because he was overweight: 'Elvis ain't like he used to be, blah blah, blah.' The really bad one was in Detroit. We were staying way out in the country, forty-five minutes from the auditorium, and on the bus Jackie Kahane wrote an answer to the review: 'Dear So-and-So, I was reading your review, sitting in the john, and it stunk up the place worse than anything I was doin'.' At the end he says, 'Well, that's all I have to say about your review. There's no toilet paper and I guess there's only one thing to do with it. Signed: Jackie Kahane.' It was a masterpiece."

Why had the press turned so completely? It was true that Elvis didn't look his best and that many of his shows were lethargic or cut short. But there had to be more to it than that. Perhaps the mood of the national press had changed. This was, after all, what *Esquire* magazine called "the age of gossip" and, thanks to Watergate, newspapers had learned they could be brutally honest and get away with it. In toppling a president, reporters had scored their first big kill. After Nixon, who was big enough to attract these game hunters?

Perhaps, too, it was the old story about those who come to power through the media shall fall by the same hands. The old I-made-you-and-I-can-break-you routine.

More legitimately, many began to think they'd been deceived all these years. Apparently Elvis hadn't been quite so innocent and pure after all. It was like discovering that Jack Armstrong was a Communist.

It was, simply, a good story—somewhat trivial, taking a cosmic view, but fascinating nonetheless. It was what sold papers, and in the spring and summer of Elvis's last year, sold them by the millions.

Two weeks on, two weeks off, and in May it was time to go back on tour. This time Elvis faced fourteen shows in fourteen days, starting May 20 in Knoxville, then working his way north and east into Maine, finishing in the deep South. The first part of the tour was uneventful, but it was clear that Elvis's health was not good.

His eyes hurt. He used eye drops to protect them from the glare of the bright stage lighting, but when the sweat ran into them, they stung. He'd pulled a hamstring muscle and it hurt to strike any of the karate-style poses that once were such an important part of his choreography. The enlarged and twisted colon, the high blood pressure, the ravaged liver, the shrinking arteries and enlarged heart—none of it went away.

His eyes were lidded during most performances, his speech slurred. In one city he forgot the words to a song. Everywhere he looked tired. He complained aloud about his intestinal problems and a sprained ankle. A crisis was approaching. It arrived in Baltimore's Civic Center in front of 13,000 people on May 29.

Later there were reports that he collapsed onstage and had to be carried off by two of his bodyguards. This wasn't true, although he did leave the stage for nearly thirty minutes. The early part of the performance was rough. His voice was weak and he mumbled the lyrics, or dropped them. He also dropped his microphone and had one of his aides hold a microphone in front of him while he played at his guitar for a few minutes. Then he introduced one of his favorite singers, Sherrill Neilson of the Stamps, and asked him to sing "Danny Boy." While he was singing Elvis left the stage and, leaning on friends for support, he went to his dressing room. Right behind him was Dr. Nick.

"Bodyguards stationed themselves and nobody was allowed inside," says Larry Collins, the Civic Center's publicist, who rushed backstage, worrying about whether he'd have to refund the $200,000 box office. "The doctor came out, then went back inside with his medical bag. Thirty minutes later, Presley reappeared looking refreshed, went back on stage and sang four or five songs. . . ."

John Wilkinson remembers: "He asked J.D. and the guys to sing a couple of numbers and Charlie Hodge emceed while he was gone. I got the impression he had to go to the bathroom. When he came back, he thanked everybody and apologized. He said, 'But when you gotta go, you gotta go.' And then under his breath I could hear him over the microphone. He said, 'Sometimes it hurts me so fuckin' bad. . . .' It was like his insides were just being torn up. I also saw him wince as he walked a couple of times, as if it was hard for him to move. Hence no more stage movements. It was tragic to see."

From Baltimore the plane flew to Baton Rouge. "The show started," John says. "Jackie and the Sweets and the Stamps did their thing and the intermission went on and on and on. All the bigwigs were talking: 'What do we tell the audience?' Because you could have yourself a riot. Elvis never left the hotel." The Colonel had to refund the money for that show, and for the one scheduled the following day in Jacksonville. By the time Elvis limped back into Memphis a couple of days after that on June 2, following listless appearances in Macon, Georgia, and Mobile, Alabama, his concert promoters on the West Coast were talking about Elvis dying.

"How many more times," they asked, "can Elvis be pointed onstage and be expected to perform? How many more times can he even be expected to *find* the microphone?"

It was a cold description, almost seeming cruel at the time, but it was accepted as the truth. So seriously was it taken, in fact, that I was called by the radio syndicator for whom I had adapted my first Elvis book. He'd talked to Elvis's concert promoters and wanted me to start thinking about coming to Los Angeles (from Hawaii where I lived) to begin lining up interviews so we could update the series when he died.

It was so ironic. As Elvis's health slid rapidly, and even as the gossip mongers and critics closed in for the kill, in many ways his career seemed unaffected, his great success remained untouched.

The same week Elvis lay recuperating from his tour in Memphis, his records were selling in greater numbers than they had in several years. In England, for example, RCA Records had reissued sixteen Elvis Presley singles simultaneously. All had been number one hits in Great Britain at the time of their initial release and included such songs as "Return to Sender," "Jailhouse Rock," "It's Now or Never," and "All Shook Up." All sixteen went onto the British charts again.

In the U.S., his new single was the prophetic "Way Down," a song from the Graceland sessions a year before.

The record was a hit on the Easy Listening, Country, and Popular charts, and was followed by the album *Moody Blue*. The press release from RCA for the trade publications showed the Colonel was still at work:

"The album will initially be released as a limited edition, pressed on blue, translucent vinyl with a sticker calling attention to the fact that 'Way Down' is contained in the album.

"RCA's blitz campaign on the single and album began in the trades and will continue there and in consumer publications through the months of June and July with special emphasis in cities Elvis will be visiting on tour and where the single is having the greatest market impact.

"Marketing aids will include two radio spots, one featuring 'Moody Blue' and 'Way Down' and the other featuring 'Moody Blue' and Elvis' entire

RCA catalog on which a special program will be running throughout the summer.

"A five-foot standup display of Elvis will be the chief accessory among the merchandising items. Others will be a 'Way Down' streamer, a 'Moody Blue' poster featuring a blowup of the album cover, Elvis calendars and a die-cut display.

"Heavy advertising, window and in-store campaigns and other special localized promotions, are planned throughout the campaign."

It was as if nothing had changed. As ever, the Colonel was the master of the "tie-in" campaign, the guru of the market blitz.

That's not to say the Colonel was callous in his control of the Presley empire, willing to kill the golden goose. Not at all. In fact, following the tour that was to begin June 17, the Colonel had nearly two months set aside with nothing for Elvis to do but rest. And it should be noted that most of the promotional activity involved with any Presley campaign—whether it was to sell a movie, a record, or a concert tour—was handled not by Elvis but by publicists, record distributors and retailers, concert hall managers, and hundreds more whose incomes came all or in part from the Presley mint. At no time was Elvis ever required, or even asked, by the Colonel to do anything more than a rare press conference.

Still, it was clear to the Colonel that Elvis needed more than rest. He also needed a new challenge and however much he may have wondered if Elvis was up to meeting one, by late spring of 1977 the Colonel was planning not one, but two "events." One was another documentary film, this one for the CBS television network. This was to be filmed—in concert—when Elvis went back on tour in June. Elvis also was scheduled to open the Las Vegas Hilton Hotel's new Pavilion, a convention hall and sports arena that seated 7,000. This was to be Elvis's only Las Vegas appearance in 1977. The regular showroom engagements were canceled to further whet the appetite.

"We did not put Elvis in the hotel before that," says Hilton vice-president Henri Lewin, "because we wanted it to be the greatest opening ever. It was to open in October. The sound system was assembled by Elvis's concert promoter and Colonel Parker. It's still there. We considered him so great that what we replaced him with was the Ali–Spinks fight. When we lost Elvis, we knew we had to get Ali no matter what it cost. No one else was big enough."

First came the CBS documentary. The Colonel had Elvis's agent, Larry Auerbach at the William Morris Agency, call CBS rather than NBC because the Colonel wasn't happy with NBC. In the past, NBC had loomed large in Elvis's career, with the "comeback" Christmas special in 1968 and the satellite show from Hawaii in 1973. Ratings for both shows were extremely satisfying, but when the satellite show was rerun, the audience was much smaller and subsequently NBC went cool on suggestions to do some follow-up specials. Auerbach called Bill Harbach and Gary Smith, two seasoned television producers, who were also represented by the Morris Agency, sending them to Las Vegas to meet the Colonel.

"The Colonel told us Elvis wasn't interested in doing anything that required anything special of him," says Gary Smith. "He said Elvis would do it while touring rather than in a studio. He also said Elvis didn't want to attend any meetings. So we flew to Chicago in May to see him in action. He was overweight and his voice was only fair, but the electricity in that audience was something."

Gary and Bill returned to their Hollywood offices to begin logistical planning that eventually involved their own production team of twelve, a six-man film crew, and about twenty more from CBS. They surveyed the cities that Elvis would visit during his June tour, starting in Springfield and Kansas City, Missouri; going on to Omaha and Lincoln, Nebraska; Rapid City and Sioux Falls, South Dakota; Des Moines, Iowa; Madison, Wisconsin; Cincinnati, Ohio; finishing in Indianapolis, Indiana.

"We picked Rapid City for filming because it was Elvis's first concert in that hall," says Gary. "He'd never been to Rapid City before. We wanted to avoid any possible audience disappointment over his being overweight."

How did Elvis feel about appearing on television overweight? Reports are mixed. So, perhaps, were his feelings. Tony Brown says, "It didn't seem to bother him that he was overweight. He seemed to be excited about being on TV again. He said, 'People want to know what I'm doing.'" In his book, Ed Parker saw another side: "As we drove to the auditorium where Elvis knew that the CBS cameras would be waiting, he turned to me and asked, 'How come I get placed in these situations?' He looked out of the window, bit his lip and said, 'Ah . . . hell, I guess it's show business.'" A few days earlier, a fan handed Elvis a caricature that emphasized his bulging waist and Elvis held it aloft and asked, "Do I look like that?" It was Ed's opinion that he'd been shaken by that incident and was experiencing "controlled white knuckle panic" about the bright lights and unblinking cameras of CBS.

Whatever his feelings, the Omaha show was just so-so. They were staying in Lincoln and on the drive back to the hotel after the show, Elvis slumped quietly in the right rear seat of his limousine, staring into the midwestern night. A few collected in his room to go over what they'd done and not done. Elvis sat on his bed in his pajamas. His cousin Billy Smith and Charlie Hodge were nearby.

Elvis asked Joe Guercio, his orchestra leader, "Well, what'd you think?"

Joe said, "It was a fair dress rehearsal."

Elvis said, "Yeah, you're right."

Elvis went on a crash diet, fasting and consuming greater than usual quantities of his favorite appetite depressant, Ionamin. Gary Smith says that when he saw Elvis again two days later in Rapid City, "It looked like he'd lost ten pounds." Elvis also put on a much better show. One reason may have been that he was under the influence of stimulants now, rather than staggering under the weight of painkillers and sedatives, which were responsible for wrecking so many of his recent shows. Another reason was that Elvis rose to what little challenge he saw in being on TV again. So he tried harder. As a result, only one song from Omaha, "My Way," appeared in the edited, hour-long show and all of the rest of the music came from Rapid City.

"I thought the show in Omaha was very bad," says John Wilkinson. "He was pale and unsteady. I don't even know if he knew where he was. Maybe he did. And yet the other show, which made up most of that special, it was pretty good. His voice was strong. Physically he looked awful, but he was steady on his feet, and in Omaha he was not."

The finished show, broadcast after his death with a tacked-on message from Vernon, showed John's appraisal correct. Elvis *did* look awful, and much of what could be said positive about the performance had to be couched in phrases that hinted at how much worse he could have been. His movements, however steady, were slow, restricted. His voice, however strong, was never daring.

Yet the show caught a special moment in Elvis's time. Drooling fans were interviewed about how much they had sacrificed to make the trip (of sometimes hundreds of miles) to see Elvis; car mechanics and postal workers and their overweight, spray-haired wives told stories about emergency surgery and house fires, yet still they came to see their King.

There were scenes showing the aging, gray-sideburned Al Dvorn selling Giant Photo Albums and Portraits on Portrait Paper for $5, Elvis Forever Lapel Pins for $2, the same price for a twelve-inch by fourteen-inch color photograph. Binoculars went for $5, a popular item because so many sat so far away.

Elvis wore his white suit with the Mayan calendar design. He had two of them and alternated wearing them every night of the concert tour, sending his staff scrambling to clean them between shows. They were the only two of the more than fifty he'd had made that still fit. His eyes bulged slightly, slitted under puffy lids. His face was swollen. His cheeks melted right into his neck. There was no chin line. His hair was sprayed. In close-up it looked as if someone had stuck the distinctive wide, flat nose and bee-stung lips onto a balloon face.

The camera followed him up the stairs and onto the stage. He moved slowly, like an older man, as if he were fragile, feeling his way almost a step at a time. He was breathing heavily while singing "C.C. Rider." Occasionally he hefted his wide belt over his midsection, calling attention to his bulk. Throughout his performance, sweat rolled off his face in sheets. Still, it wasn't a bad show. He sang "Jailhouse Rock" and "How Great Thou Art" and "Early Morning Rain." A little something for everyone. He introduced his father, mentioning how sick he had been. He introduced Ginger. He gave away scarves and kissed his fans. At the end of the show he held out his beefy arms in a Christ-like pose for another Instamatic flash. It really did appear that he was having a good time.

His next-to-last concert was in Cincinnati where, at three o'clock in the afternoon, the air-conditioning unit in his room stopped working. Elvis liked his rooms as cold as it was possible to get them. Angry, he stormed out of the hotel and started off down the street in search of another. One of his stepbrothers, David Stanley, saw him leave, raced along behind Elvis and half a block from the hotel was joined by Ed Parker, who was returning from a late lunch. Then the Colonel spotted Elvis and, according to Larrie Londin, "like to swallowed his cigar." Because Elvis never did anything like that. He didn't like the hotel, so he left. "And the Colonel was runnin', hoppin' along after him."

Elvis was wearing a jogging suit. His black hair was askew, his tinted glasses sliding down his nose because of his heavy sweating. People on the sidewalk stopped to watch him pass. The clerk in the next hotel was startled, too, and as a crowd began to gather in the lobby, Elvis was taken into the manager's office while another of his security aides, Dick Grob, arranged to book two rooms, one for Elvis, the other for his bodyguards. Shortly after that, Elvis announced they would return to Memphis after the show and not stay in Cincinnati at all. Which is what they did, flying on to Indianapolis the following day for Elvis's final performance.

The Market Square Arena in the Indiana capital is an ugly building that looks as if a flying saucer (or a pregnant pancake) had landed on a multilevel parking garage. It was the last of ten shows in ten days and it was one of the best. In retrospect it sounds corny or maudlin to say so, but it did seem even then that Elvis was determined to make it a better-than-usual show.

In the beginning, after the *2001* opening and "C.C. Rider," Elvis did what he often did, teased the audience, played it like an instrument. "Wull, wull, wull . . ." he'd say, amused by the screams his silliest grunts returned, sliding into "I Got a Woman" and from it directly into a prolonged chorus of "Amen" with the ten backup singers he had with him. After that, Elvis joked with the audience for five minutes, using J.D. Sumner's voice as a toy, getting him to sustain long low notes to the crowd's amusement. He sang a final chorus of "I Got a Woman." Then came another few minutes of offhanded small talk and goofing around with the audience and his real oldie of the evening, "Love Me."

And so it went for an hour and seventeen minutes. He sang a handful of his early hits, including "Jailhouse Rock," "Teddy Bear," "Don't Be Cruel," and the inevitable "Hound Dog." There were dramatic renditions of "I Can't Stop Loving You," "Bridge Over Troubled Water," and "Hurt," songs that had worked in the past as records and in performance, with Elvis stretching for and reaching the high notes. He tossed the customary dozen scarves to the bleating, writhing women who clamored at the lip of the stage throughout the show. No matter what he sang or said or did, or didn't do, the frenzied response was constant, sounding exactly like the one he got when he first shook his hips at the Overton Park Shell in Memphis more than twenty years before.

He introduced "the guys in the back, the number one gospel quartet in the nation," the Stamps, flattering each one individually, and then featured each member of his band in a song, and then Joe Guercio and the orchestra. He introduced his daddy (did Mick Jagger or Paul McCartney or Bruce Springsteen or the Bee Gees ever take *their* parents on tour?) and "my girlfriend, Ginger," and her mother and sister, and Dr. Nick and three cousins, several sound engineers and his producer Felton Jarvis. It sounded like an Academy Award acceptance speech.

"Most of all I'd like to thank you and I'd like to say this is the last day of our tour. And we couldn't have asked for a better audience. And you've really made it worthwhile."

He closed with "Can't Help Falling in Love," the song he always sang last, and finally held out his arms, strutting around the stage for a final time, disappearing into the darkness as the band began its thunderous vamp. The voice of one of the Stamps came booming into the big arena.

"Ladies and gentlemen, Elvis has left the building. Thank you and good night."

There was a slight pause and the voice continued. "We'd like to remind you that following this evening's concert the Elvis Super Souvenir Concession Stands will be open for a short while. If you didn't get your souvenir of your evening with Elvis, be sure that you do so before you leave. We thank you for coming. Be careful driving home. Good night."

"We played Indianapolis three times," says John Wilkinson. "The first time the sound wasn't right and the audience was rude and the second time it was much better. But the last one was really good. The place came unglued, like they were really glad to see him. It was a dynamite show, rock and roll all the way. But he looked whipped when he came around the corner to get off the stage at the end of the show. He really looked tired."

June, 1977–
July, 1977

Elvis returned to Memphis immediately at the end of the tour, arriving in the pre-dawn hours of June 27, and went into virtual seclusion, a bear in summer hibernation, asprawl on his image-sized bed, two television sets in the ceiling, Ginger at his side, often going several days without seeing anyone else, except when the regular meals and packets of medicine arrived, brought by his maids and hired hands.

Elvis had exactly seven weeks to live. Forty-nine days.

If Elvis reflected on his recent years—his final years—he had much to be proud of. In 1968, after years hidden away in Hollywood making lightweight musicals, he had climbed into a black leather suit and in a single television special launched a comeback that really never stopped peaking. His return to performing in public in 1969 in Las Vegas and the following year on the road were significant musical events. In 1971 he won the prestigious Bing Crosby Award. In 1972 he filled Madison Square Garden four shows in a row, breaking all attendance and box-office records. In 1973 he did his "Aloha from Hawaii" satellite show, ultimately reaching a billion or more people . . . won a Golden Globe for his documentary, *Elvis on Tour* . . . and won his first Grammy (after nearly fifty albums and almost ninety singles) for his gospel album, *He Touched Me.*

272

The awards and events came less frequently after that, but came nonetheless—as in 1975 he played to a New Year's Eve crowd of 80,000 in Pontiac, Michigan, walking away with the largest box-office take of all time. And still the records sold and sold. Every year with the inevitability of the seasons and tides, it was his name that appeared in the *Guinness Book of World Records* for selling more records than any other artist in the history of recorded music.

If Elvis was in a reflective mood, he might also have looked back on more than a thousand personal appearances in eight years. Where hadn't he been in America during that time? Surely he must have visited everyone's hometown. Perhaps that was what made Elvis such a superstar. Here he was, the most isolated star of our time, on view in everyone's neighborhood, year after year after year. Inaccessible, yet accessible, too, yours for an hour and a kiss for only fifteen dollars.

Elvis's sky began to darken at the end of July when the first copies of *Elvis: What Happened?* by Red and Sonny West and Dave Hebler went into the supermarkets and drugstores and airports of America, and simultaneous with the book's release, lurid excerpts appeared in *The Star,* the tabloid whose entertainment editor, Steve Dunleavy, had written the book. The first installment told the story of Elvis's mad wish to have Priscilla's boyfriend killed.

Suddenly through much of the Western world big headlines and dripping prose chronicled Elvis's abuse of drugs and guns, told of late-night conversations he had with his mother, said he was a man obsessed with religion and psychic powers (his own) and law and order and probable life after death. The overall picture a reader got was of a fat and stoned-out aging rock star locked away in a southern mansion, venturing forth only on rare occasions to a movie theater kept open from midnight to dawn for his personal use, living his life by the numbers in his numerology book, a machine gun cradled in his ample lap. Not even Howard Hughes seemed so colorful, so eccentric, so sick.

The book was a distortion, a bitter diatribe without perspective or compassion, motivated by a wish to get even and rich. It was perfect for its gossipy time and perfect in its timing. The book probably wouldn't have attracted so much attention if Elvis hadn't died within a fortnight of its release. Then it sold like hotcakes—nearly three million copies in all.

But there was truth in the book—however narrow its scope—and sometimes the truth hurts. Elvis was wounded by it. For hours, day after day, he talked about Red and Sonny and Dave. Dave he could forgive, or forget, he said, because he hadn't been around long. But Red and Sonny were *family!* He called Priscilla and said he was worried about what Lisa Marie would think if she ever read the book, or heard her friends talking about it.

Elvis told Priscilla he was going on the road soon and asked, "Would it be all right if Lisa Marie comes to visit first?"

Priscilla thought it would help take Elvis's mind off the book and agreed happily.

At the end of July Elvis sent one of his hired hands in the *Lisa Marie* to Los Angeles to collect his daughter for what would be her longest visit at Graceland since Elvis and Priscilla split up. During the three weeks left to him, he spent time with her nearly every day, leaving her to amuse herself or be entertained by Ginger and the maids and cooks when he remained in his room, sleeping long hours or too sedated to move around.

In Lisa's room nearby there were dolls and toys and a television set (one of sixteen in the mansion) and behind the house in the garage she had a miniature electric golf cart that Elvis had bought for her. Always accompanied by one of the help or bodyguards—Elvis feared for her safety always, terrified of a kidnapping—she often took the cart down the sloping driveway to the gate, whooping with laughter as her adult companion ran breathlessly along beside her.

On August 7 Elvis planned a special treat. A year earlier the old Fairgrounds amusement park that he had rented so often in earlier years was reopened as Libertyland, a theme park. It was here that he had ridden for hours in the fifties on the Dodgem bumper cars and in the sixties on the roller coaster, standing up, always riding without holding on. It was a slower, fatter, less daring Elvis who rented the park on this night. His friends remember him as a proud father, somewhat solemn but fun-loving as he accompanied her from ride to ride with the other children and adults he had invited to go with him.

On August 10 he took a group of friends to the United Artists Southbrook 4, renting the theater and paying the projectionist for an after-midnight showing of the latest James Bond movie, *The Spy Who Loved Me*. Elvis loved James Bond, usually took his gold-plated PK Walther with him; that was the gun Bond usually carried.

The final week was memorable only because it was the final week, otherwise not extraordinary. Elvis saw friends occasionally, or talked on the telephone when they called. He played racquetball in the court behind his house with his cousins and stepbrothers and Dean Nichopoulos, who almost always let Elvis win, no matter how hard it sometimes seemed for Elvis to move around the court. He watched the gospel shows on television. He talked with Joe Esposito about the tour that was to begin on the seventeenth in Maine and invited his father to go along; Vernon had stayed home on some of the tours this year to rest and to be with his girlfriend, a warm and generous nurse named Sandy Miller, but this time he said yes. Ginger says they continued to make wedding plans, claims he was going to make an announcement at a concert at the end of the tour in Memphis in two weeks. He read in his Bible and in his numbers book. He ate his cheeseburgers and took his pills.

On August 14 he started a fast, something he often did to lose weight quickly before going on tour. Oddly, he didn't take any Ionamin, the appetite suppressant that he had favored for so long. Perhaps he believed the racquetball and fasting were enough. Besides, what difference did it really make? At 250 pounds he was grossly overweight and in two days how much could he lose? Five pounds? Be truthful, how good could he look in his bathroom mirror at 245? He'd still have sixty pounds he didn't want to see.

On August 15 he awoke at four and after breakfast played with Lisa on the grounds, laughing as she ran around and around in her electric cart. She was going home to Priscilla the next day.

In the early evening, some of his guys reported to him that they were unable to get the projectionist at the Ridgeway Theater to stay past midnight that night, so he'd have to see *MacArthur* another time. Soon after that Elvis called his dentist at home and, apologizing for the time of his call, he asked if he and Ginger could see him. Dr. Lester Hofman had been the subject of Elvis's generosity many times; he drove a Cadillac that Elvis gave him. He told Elvis that yes, 10:30 that night at his office would be fine.

Elvis arrived in his customized Stutz Bearcat with Ginger and Billy Smith and Charlie Hodge jammed into the small rear compartment. Dr. Hofman had never met Ginger. Elvis introduced her, using his pet nickname "Gingerbread," and after the dentist X-rayed her teeth he turned to Elvis and filled an upper right first bicuspid and an upper left molar. As was the custom, the fillings were porcelain. Elvis had many fillings and he didn't want a flash of gold when he opened his mouth to sing.

There was a lot of Elvis-styled small talk. Elvis invited the doctor to come out to Graceland to see his new Ferrari, and the doctor said the next time Elvis went to California he'd like to go along so he could pop in on his daughter and surprise her. Elvis said sure, there was always room on the *Lisa Marie*.

Three hours passed. It was now Tuesday, 1:30 A.M. and Elvis was back at Graceland, where he called one of his security men, Dick Grob, and handed him a list of songs he had decided to add to his concert repertoire. He told Grob to locate the words and music and chord changes for the new material, so he could brief his band before they went on (and would have the lyrics for himself onstage in case he needed them). Grob later said he and Elvis talked about public reports of his health and reaction to "the bodyguard book." This was his first public appearance since the book had been published and this must have worried Elvis much more than he allowed friends around him to see. Grob says that as he left the room Elvis said, "Dick, we'll just show 'em how wrong they are. We'll make this tour the best ever."

By two or two-thirty Elvis had changed into a striped workout suit and was on his racquetball court with Ginger and Billy Smith and Billy's wife Jo. They played loosely, without much enthusiasm, as if Elvis were merely warming up. Then Ginger and the Smiths drifted away to one side as Elvis began clowning around with the ball. Ginger says she was hoping the play would help Elvis relax enough to fall asleep easily. Elvis called it quits about four and after working out leisurely for a few minutes on the exercise cycle he had positioned at one end of the gym, he and Ginger retreated to his bedroom.

There is disagreement over what happened next. Ginger says they merely talked about their wedding and when the tour was mentioned, Elvis reportedly grabbed his flabby midsection in his hands and said, "The boy's not in shape, Gingerbread, the boy's not in shape. It's been too long since the last tour. Too long. . . ." Others who were in the house say Elvis and Ginger fought over whether or not she would go with him on the tour; reportedly he wanted her by his side and she wanted to stay in Memphis to spend some time with her family.

Whatever the truth, Ginger soon fell asleep, leaving Elvis alone, reading a book on the bed beside her.

Between eight and nine o'clock in the morning of the sixteenth Elvis's Aunt Delta Mae Briggs knocked on his door, delivering the morning newspaper and a glass of ice water he'd requested. Elvis told her he was going to sleep until seven that night, then leave for Portland, Maine, about midnight. Between getting up and leaving, he said, he wanted to see Nurse Cocke to say goodbye; would Aunt Delta call the nurse and ask? Aunt Delta did and soon after that Elvis called Marian Cocke himself. She said she'd come to the house when she finished work.

At nine, Ginger awoke to find Elvis still reading. She says he told her he couldn't sleep and was going into the bathroom to read. Ginger knew that meant he was going to take some of his medication. Elvis's syringes were in the bathroom and so was some of his personal pharmacy.

"Okay," Ginger said, "just don't fall asleep." And with that, she rolled over on the big bed and went back to sleep herself.

Elvis went into the bathroom with a book, his finger stuck into it as a marker. He may've glanced at himself in the mirror. Blue pajamas. Puffy eyes and face. Bad color. No one knows, but it's likely he helped himself to something from his pharmacy, because as the autopsy would later show, he now had as many as ten different drugs coursing through his body, taking control of his brain, his heart. Four of the drugs were in what the medical examiner would describe as "significant amounts." These were codeine, an addictive opium derivative, commonly prescribed for severe pain; ethinamate and methaquaalone, two strong sedatives; and unidentifiable barbiturates, which are depressants. The others were also "downers." He had taken an unidentified number of Placydil and Valium capsules, both tranquilizers, and unknown quantities of Demerol and Meperidine, both painkillers. Bringing the amazing total to ten were morphine, which is an illegal substance and probably was the natural result of the body's absorption of codeine; and chlorpheniramine, an antihistamine which by itself would make its user sleepy.

Elvis sat staring at the open book in his lap, his eyes glassy, his body motionless. Then his chin dropped to his chest, the big body slumped imperceptibly, then shifted and toppled out of the big cushiony chair, the noise of the fall muffled by the thick brown shag carpeting.

The room was silent except for the sound of his final breath.

Ginger slept on the other side of the bathroom door, and downstairs in the mansion the rest of the household, which included three maids and two cooks, went about their daily routine. Joe Esposito was present, along with Al Strada. Charlie Hodge was in the kitchen drinking coffee. Uncle Vester Presley was at the Graceland gate. Vernon was in his home less than a hundred yards away.

The Colonel, meanwhile, was in Portland, Maine, where it was by now Tuesday afternoon and he was meeting with the auditorium manager and watching Elvis's sound crew move equipment into the backstage area. Members of his band and orchestra were in Los Angeles, Las Vegas, and Nashville, packing or waiting for the *Lisa Marie,* which would take them to Portland. Elvis was to follow along behind in the Jet Star. The thirteen-city tour was a sellout. The crates of posters, pennants, and picture books were on the way by truck. The local record stores had been serviced by RCA to accommodate the certain demand for Elvis's records that followed all his concerts. Elvis's limited wardrobe of his bigger costumes was packed, along with several hundred scarves. Dick Grob had the music together, except for one song, which was driving him nuts.

Ginger awoke sometime between one and two in the afternoon. Seeing the bed empty beside her, she walked quickly to the bathroom door.

"Elvis?" Ginger called timidly. "Elvis, darlin'?"

There was no answer, so she entered, finding Elvis on the floor. She ran gulping from the room and called downstairs. Al Strada answered the phone and came rushing up, with Joe Esposito right behind him. Together, and with some effort, they rolled Elvis onto his back. The flesh was stiffening and cold and when Strada saw that Elvis wasn't breathing, he leaped for the phone in the bedroom and called the nearest doctor to Graceland, Dr. Perry Holmes, while Joe started pounding on Elvis's chest, suspecting a heart attack brought on by an overdose of drugs.

"They sent me out of the room," Ginger says, "but I went back in and I tried to beat on his chest, too. I was praying: 'Oh, please, God, don't let Elvis die!'

"Mr. Presley arrived and they pried open Elvis's mouth with something. He'd bitten down on his tongue. Mr. Presley was on his knees and saying, 'Elvis, speak to me! Oh, God, he's gone!'

"Lisa Marie came in. She said, 'What's wrong with my daddy?' I pushed her away and closed the door. I said, 'There's nothing wrong, Lisa,' and she ran around to the other door into the bathroom and saw Elvis on the floor."

The doctor Al Strada called wasn't in and Al hung up abruptly. One of the doctor's associates was in, however, and when he was told that Strada seemed extremely upset, he called Graceland, reaching Elvis's Aunt Delta. She said her nephew was having difficulty and asked the doctor to make an emergency house call. The doctor suggested that Elvis be taken to a nearby clinic.

Meanwhile Sam Thompson—Linda's brother, still on the payroll as a bodyguard—had arrived to take Lisa

Marie back to Los Angeles on a commercial airliner. On the way up the drive, he passed David Stanley, one of Elvis's stepbrothers, on his way down to the gate. David hollered something unidentifiable as he passed. Sam continued on up to the house and was met at the front door by Lisa Marie.

"Sam!" she cried. "Sam! My daddy's dead! My daddy's dead!"

Joe was now administering mouth-to-mouth resuscitation. Dr. Nick was on the way and so was a fire department ambulance. Vernon was in the bedroom with Ginger, who was sobbing uncontrollably. Someone took all the syringes and pills out of the bathroom. Graceland was in panic.

Finally Ginger and Vernon and Aunt Delta retreated into Grandma Minnie Mae's room to pray, as Dr. Nick and Joe and David Stanley went off with Elvis in the ambulance.

Resuscitation attempts continued all the way to Baptist Hospital without result. At the hospital Elvis was wheeled into one of the emergency department's "trauma rooms." A call went out on the hospital intercom, ringing through every hallway and room: "Harvey Team report to E. R. [Emergency Room]. Harvey Team report to E. R. Harvey Team report to E.R." This was the signal for the hospital's team of resuscitation experts, who literally ran through the corridors when they got the call. When the heart stops beating, only eight minutes remain before there is irreparable brain damage.

"Whenever Elvis was admitted to the hospital," says vice-president Maurice Elliott, to whom fell the job of press relations again, "there always were rumors that he was dead. It got so I took it with a grain of salt. I was in my office and I got a call from Miss Bingham, the nursing supervisor in the emergency department. She said, 'We're doing a Harvey Team on Elvis and it doesn't look good.'

"I went to the emergency department. He was in the

first trauma room, which is a small operating theater. There were several doctors in attendance, a respiratory therapist, a nurse-anesthetist, a number of people. They were working at both ends of the table. Elvis was nude and his head was over the edge of the table. My first impression was that he was dead. His head was blue.

"I went into the Number Two trauma room and waited with Al Strada, Charlie Hodge, and two or three others. They worked on him for about thirty minutes and then Dr. Nick came in, his head down. He said, 'It's over. He's gone.' You could see tears come to his eyes and everybody there started crying.

"Joe came to my office to make some calls. He didn't want anything said to the press until Dr. Nick had gone back to Graceland to tell Vernon. So for thirty minutes we had to hold the press off. They were there before Elvis was, because they heard it on the fire rescue radio. So what we did was say he came in in severe respiratory distress and that they were working on him right now. And that was true. At least I rationalized it was true. He was obviously in severe respiratory distress. He wasn't breathing."

After Joe called the Colonel in Maine and the tour organizers in California, and after he got word from Dr. Nick at Graceland, he went to meet the press. He choked up, unable to say anything. "You do it," he said to Maurice Elliott. "I can't do it. You do it."

Within minutes, thanks to the media that had aided Elvis so greatly in his meteoric climb, it was known throughout the world that the king of rock and roll was dead.

Several of Elvis's band members and backup singers had been picked up in Los Angeles and Las Vegas, and were on the way to Maine when the pilot got a message to return. No explanation was given. The fuel level was low and it was decided to continue on for refueling in Pueblo, Colorado, where Marty Harrell called the Presley office to find out what was happening.

"We'd all gotten out of the plane and were wandering around when Marty came back," says John Wilkinson. "Marty stood on the stairs of the plane, everybody gathered around and he said, 'I hate to be the one to do this, but Elvis died this morning.' Marty was crying. He was hanging onto the rail. We were all just wandering around in a daze. The band and two of the Sweets, Kathy [Westmoreland], the Las Vegas guys, nine or ten of them, twenty or twenty-five people altogether. I've never been through anything like that before. Myrna broke down and cried as hard as I've ever seen a woman cry. We were all so shocked. Elvis Presley doesn't die. I die, you die, but he doesn't. And he damn sure did. Someone asked, 'Marty, what happened? Car wreck? Suicide?' It could've been anything. Marty said, 'Something about respiratory failure combined with a heart attack, I don't know. All I know is we're going home for the last time.' "

In Nashville, the rest of the musicians were at the airport waiting for their flight to Portland when Felton Jarvis got a page to come to the courtesy phone. All he said when he rejoined the others was, "Tour's off. We may call you later. You know how Elvis is." Tony Brown hung around for a while and heard someone in the airport say, "Elvis is dead!" He found Felton and told him. Felton said yes, he knew.

On the *Lisa Marie* returning to the Coast, James Burton said to no one in particular, trying to brighten the solemn mood, "Well, I guess I'll have to call and see if John Denver needs a guitar player."

It was a sick joke and no one laughed.

Elvis's body was moved onto a gurney and taken to the hospital pathology department for autopsy under the direction of the department chief, Eric Muirhead. A representative of the coroner's office was present when they began.

Says Maurice Elliott, "Our pathologists were concerned, without it being said, that with the controversies that surrounded John and Robert Kennedy's autopsies, they wanted to be sure that the hospital wasn't embarrassed and that this was done very thoroughly and professionally. They were very detailed and the autopsy took three or four hours and then the body was released to the funeral home."

At eight o'clock that night, the coroner, Jerry Francisco, and Elvis's physician, Dr. Nick, held a press conference to disclose their preliminary findings. Some said later that this is when "the whitewash" began.

Death was due to "an erratic heartbeat," the medical examiner said. "There was severe cardiovascular disease present. He had a history of mild hypertension and some coronary artery disease. These two diseases may be responsible for cardiac arrhythmia, but the precise cause was not determined. Basically it was a natural death. It may take several days, it may take several weeks to determine the cause of death. The precise cause of death may never be discovered."

Francisco was asked to explain "cardiac arrhythmia." It was just another name for a heart attack, he said; it meant Elvis had an irregular heartbeat and it stopped beating. This explanation was subsequently endorsed, and given credibility, by Elvis's great aunt, Vera Presley, who told reporters, "The Presleys all had such bad hearts. . . ." No one contradicted her, recalling Elvis's mother's death by heart attack and the recent attack that put Vernon in intensive care.

There were questions from the press regarding Elvis's use of drugs, prompted by the garish headlines running that week in *The National Star* and by the stories in the "bodyguard book." Francisco denied that there was any indication of drug abuse. The only drugs found in his body, he said, were those prescribed by his physician for the hypertension and a long-standing colon problem.

The next day, tissue samples from several of Elvis's organs were sent to laboratories in California to determine exactly which drugs Francisco was talking about.

That report, two months in the preparation, ultimately would play a significant role in a major controversy over Elvis's death. In the meantime, most chose to accept the "cardiac arrhythmia" version. Why even the way the word "arrhythmia" sounded, it was somewhat comforting.

August 17-19, 1977

The days that followed were as strange as any in Elvis's life.

Tuesday night the body was taken in a long white hearse from the Baptist Hospital to the Memphis Funeral Home, where the body was to be prepared for an open-coffin viewing the next day at Graceland. Already the fans were gathering. Less than an hour after the death had been announced Tuesday afternoon, a crowd formed outside the mansion gates. Many carried portable radios, all broadcasting a constant parade of Elvis's record hits, interrupting with news bulletins whenever another bit of information or another interview was obtained. By now, the media was covering Elvis's death the same way it covered his life—in great and lurid detail.

Hundreds of daily newspapers sent reporters. All the television networks scheduled instant specials and assigned their best feature men; Geraldo Rivera was there for ABC, and so was Charles Kuralt, whose popular "On the Road With" series had run for so many years on CBS. The wire services, *Time*, *Newsweek*, and the *National Enquirer* sent teams of reporters. (The *Enquirer* alone had twenty on the story.) Caroline Kennedy was there for a women's magazine. *Rolling Stone* sent people not just to Memphis, but to Tupelo, and two days before going to press threw out half of their pages and started filling it with Elvis material, calling upon writers on three continents. All over Memphis anyone who had known Elvis or who had been near him when he died was being interviewed.

All over the Midwest and deep South fans began traveling to Memphis to pay homage to their king. Hour by hour the crowd grew, right on through the night. By lunchtime Wednesday, there were thousands standing in a slow mist, waiting for the hearse that would bring Elvis from the funeral home to Graceland, where the informal, open-coffin service for family and friends was scheduled for 2 P.M. Shortly after noon the caravan of police motorcycles and the long white hearse, lights flashing, sirens blaring, swept past the Graceland gates and entered the estate by a side entrance to avoid the milling crowd.

Vernon decided to let mourners file past the open casket from three until six, and literally miles of Elvis's fans lined up. The sun returned and in the 90-degree heat and high humidity, dozens fainted, to be tended by doctors dispatched to the scene, along with platoons of police. Eventually, National Guardsmen were called out, as the crowd swelled to an estimated 75,000.

Inside the high rock walls a press compound had been established with telephone lines and tables with typewriters. Next to it was the medical area and farther up the hill, closer to the big house, were all the flowers in Memphis. Every florist in the city ran out. Eventually 3,166 floral arrangements were sent by everyone from the Soviet Union to Elton John to the Memphis Police Department, many of them in the shape of guitars, crowns, hound dogs, and hearts.

Inside the house, just past the National Guardsmen standing at stiff attention at the door, at the end of the foyer, Elvis lay at rest inside a 900-pound copper-lined coffin, beneath a crystal chandelier. He wore a white suit, a light blue shirt, and white tie. As is true with most corpses laid out in such a manner, there was too much makeup and hair spray, creating a sort of mask grotesque.

For more than three hours the fans filed past, thousands of feet scuffing over the white linen spread on the Graceland rug. Across the street, opportunists were selling out of the trunks of their cars Elvis "memorial" tee-shirts and lapel buttons that they'd had made up overnight.

When Priscilla and Vernon and the others inside the house watched the ten o'clock news that night, there was an outpouring of tributes from entertainers and politicians alike. "We lost a good friend," Frank Sinatra said. "There's no way to measure the impact he made on society or the void that he leaves," said Pat Boone. Even President Carter issued a statement, saying the death "deprives our country of a part of itself." Elvis's music and personality, Carter said, "permanently changed the face of American popular culture." Flags were lowered to half-staff throughout Mississippi and Tennessee.

Outside the Graceland gates the crowd thinned, leaving several hundred to settle in restlessly for another all-night vigil on the lawn and behind police barricades that'd been placed along the highway for a half a mile in either direction. Then at 3:30 A.M. came tragedy, when a speeding car plowed into the mourners, killing two women instantly and critically injuring a third, tossing them into the air like bundles of rags. Police stopped the driver and charged him with two counts of second degree murder, drunk driving, public drunkenness, reckless driving, and leaving the scene of an accident. Everywhere lay the heavy blanket of mystery, a sense of the weird, or bizarre.

For four hours starting at 9 A.M. a hundred vans— from nearly every flower shop in Memphis—transported the thousands of floral tributes from Graceland to the Forest Hill Cemetery three miles away, where Elvis was to be entombed later that afternoon following a private service for family and close friends.

There were about 150 gathered in the Graceland music room at two o'clock for a service that was scheduled to last half an hour and went for nearly two. Priscilla sat in the front row, flanked by Vernon and Lisa Marie. Linda and Ginger sat farther back and in between were the Smiths and Presleys and dozens of former employees and friends, along with actor George Hamilton and Ann-Margret, the actress. Colonel Parker, sitting at the back in his shirtsleeves, was making his first public appearance since the death was announced.

First, Kathy Westmoreland sang "My Heavenly Father Watches Over Me" and then a singer Elvis had claimed was a major influence on him, Jake Hess, stood up with two members of the Statesmen gospel quartet to sing "Known Only to Him." James Blackwood sang with the Stamps the title song to one of Elvis's albums, "How Great Thou Art," and finally the Stamps alone sang "His Hand in Mine" and "Sweet, Sweet Spirit." This was followed by remarks from C. W. Bradley, pastor of the nearby Whitehaven Church of Christ, a longtime friend of the Presley family; Rex Humbard, the television evangelist from Akron, Ohio; and the comedian Jackie Kahane.

"We are here to honor the memory of a man loved by millions," Bradley said in the main eulogy. "Elvis can serve as an inspiring example of the great potential of one human being who has strong desire and unfailing determination. From total obscurity Elvis rose to world fame. His name is a household word in every nook and corner of this Earth. Though idolized by millions and forced to be protected from the crowds, Elvis never lost his desire to stay in close touch with humanity.

"In a society that has talked so much about the generation gap, the closeness of Elvis and his father, and his constant dependence upon Vernon's counsel was heartwarming to observe. Elvis never forgot his family. In a thousand ways he showed his great love for them.

"But Elvis was a frail human being. And he would be the first to admit his weaknesses. Perhaps because of his rapid rise to fame and fortune he was thrown into temptations that some never experience. Elvis would not want anyone to think that he had no flaws or faults. But now that he's gone, I find it more helpful to remember his good qualities, and I hope you do, too.

"Thus, today I hold up Jesus Christ to all of us. And challenge each of you to commit your heart and life to Him. May these moments of quiet and thoughtful meditation and reflection on Elvis's life serve to help us also reflect upon our own lives and to reexamine our own lives. And may these moments help us to reset our compasses. All of us sometimes get going in the wrong direction."

It was an honest eulogy, franker than some might have expected, alluding to Elvis's "temptations," asking those present to remember the positive side but also to learn from the more troublesome side.

After the last words were spoken, friends and family gathered in small groups, talking softly, moving toward the door. Then the caravan, led by a silver Cadillac followed by the white Cadillac hearse with Elvis's body and seventeen white Cadillac limousines, rolled slowly down the curving drive and onto Elvis Presley Boulevard to the cemetery. A brief ceremony followed in the white marble mausoleum where Elvis was entombed. The huge coffin was slid into place. Vernon stood quietly by it for a moment, then walked slowly away, as workmen entered to cover the opening with concrete and cement.

The following morning, Friday, an estimated 50,000 fans visited the cemetery, each taking home a single flower at the wish of the Presley family.

* * *

That, of course, should have been the end of it. But no. It was just another beginning. Back in Los Angeles, Colonel Parker already had a slogan—ALWAYS ELVIS—that would say it clearly. But not even the wily Colonel could foretell the strange turns events would take in the following years.

Epilogue

It was a classic moment of truth. George Klein, who was president of Elvis Presley's high school class and remained a friend for life, was the guest lecturer at Memphis State University two years after Elvis's death. He was telling some of his favorite Elvis Presley stories to a class in popular music when he noticed one of the two professors in charge taking notes. George stopped talking.

"What are you doing?" he asked.

"Taking notes." The professor looked perplexed.

"Well, stop it. I don't want any note-taking in here."

Like so many of Elvis's friends, George didn't want to give his stories away. Already a movie company had paid him for them. Now he was planning a book. And he didn't want anybody to steal what he now regarded as his *property*.

George wasn't alone. Within two years of his death, almost everyone who had been close to Elvis was selling his or her memories. In death, as in life, Elvis Presley was product and industry, and it was as never before *gelt* by association.

Within two years there were more than a dozen books, several movies and television specials, and dozens of assorted other projects, all launched by Elvis's friends and relatives, they said, to set the record straight or pay tribute to The King. This group was led by Uncle Vester Presley, Vernon's brother at the guard gate all those years, who published a slender, trivial volume himself that he sold (and autographed) by the thousands to fans who trekked to Graceland each week.

Ed Parker, the karate instructor and sometime bodyguard, wrote an answer to Red, Sonny, and Dave, defending his former boss; he said there was no use of drugs, said Elvis was the single most generous man he ever met, etc.

Charlie Hodge sold his advice to Dick Clark for a television movie that captured the Presley character in Kurt Russell's acting, but lost something in the script, which stressed severe separation problems over the loss of his twin (at birth) and the later death of his mother. After that, Charlie designated Dick Grob, who was still head of Graceland security, as his "manager" and began (1) working with an Elvis imitator, (2) selling subscriptions to a newsletter at $10 a year, and (3) appearing at Elvis fan gatherings—a new phenomenon, sometimes attracting as many as 10,000 in a weekend. At these, Charlie sold copies of a little picture book he put together about Elvis's last vacation, in Hawaii, and then posed with the fans for a Polaroid snapshot. Dick Grob took the picture and then sold it for $5. Of all those associated with Elvis, it was Charlie Hodge who got the biggest hand when he was introduced. He was, in his peculiar field, a star.

Even Elvis's nurse at Baptist Hospital, Marian Cocke, cranked out what passed for a book. (Lots of pictures, big type, and not many pages.) She called it *I Called Him Babe—Elvis Presley's Nurse Remembers*. Behind that sensational title there lay 158 pages of treacly adoration.

Other of Elvis's "best" friends weren't so generous. Marty Lacker was one of the Memphis Mafia for ten years, who had left in the late sixties to pursue what turned out to be an up-and-down career in the recording industry. In his book, also privately published and titled, oddly, *Elvis: Portrait of a Friend,* he and his wife and their collaborator took turns gossiping. The picture they painted revealed more about the authors than the subject, but that is the way it often is with such books.

So, too, with *Elvis: We Love You Tender* as told to another hired writer by Vernon's ex-wife Dee and her three sons, Ricky, Billy, and David, who had lived and traveled with Elvis through their teen years. They received $100,000 from a New York publisher and after some problems with the first writer assigned to them, they produced a manuscript that, in Dee's words, "made the West [bodyguard] book look like a kindergarten class." David also began coaching one of the dozens of Elvis impersonators who began filling clubs and lounges, and Ricky became a lay minister, preaching about the life of sin he led while living with his stepbrother.

Still another longtime hired hand, Lamar Fike (the fat one Elvis bought an intestinal bypass for), hooked up with the author of the sensational Lenny Bruce biography, Albert Goldman. Because of Goldman's name, they got $225,000 from another New York publisher and then set out to write a book that told even more of the "truth" than the others did, and to imply that Elvis committed suicide.

And so it went in publishing. Other friends and relatives staked out other portions of this rich mother lode. J.D. Sumner, the gospel singer, began renting the "stretch (elongated) limo" that Elvis had given him, for $1,000 a weekend (big in southern flea markets and shopping center openings). Ginger Alden became, overnight, an "actress," starring in a movie about a pop singer who has trouble with success. (Her mother, meanwhile, sued the Presley estate for $40,000, claiming he had promised to pay off her mortgage.) James Burton produced an album of his former boss's songs by members of the Elvis stage band. Sam Phillips,

Elvis's original record producer, changed the call letters of his radio station to WLVS. When a Memphis promoter named Buddy Montesi bought Elvis's old ranch in Mississippi and began selling seven-inch pieces of the board fencing, it was Billy Smith, Elvis's cousin, who authenticated the origin of every piece on a certificate bearing his signature. (Billy also promised to donate all his cars and furniture and guns, and so on, gifts from Elvis, to a museum that Montesi was planning for the property; in return, Billy would get a lifetime job working in the museum.)

Montesi is one of the "entrepreneurs," the second category of Elvis privateers. These are the "free-lancers," free agents in private enterprise who look for the quick buck wherever they can find or promote it. The first two years following Elvis's death there must've been several hundred of them. Montesi was one of those few who didn't make money fast. When he and some partners bought the ranch soon after Elvis's death, he says, "My plan was to sell it an inch at a time to the fans. We made up certificates of transfer, individual deeds, the whole shot. If we sold an acre at five dollars a square inch, we coulda made a bundle." He said he was selling portions of the fence to make payments on the property until the "bundle" came in.

Others were more successful. The body wasn't in the ground before several singers began recording musical tributes. One of these, "The King Is Gone," established Ronnie McDowell as a star in Nashville, earned him a job singing for "Elvis" in the Dick Clark television movie. Paul Lichter, an Elvis collector in Pennsylvania who had written one book about his hero—a picture book called *Elvis in Hollywood*—immediately began cranking out another, also produced a calendar, and watched his Elvis Unique Record Club, a mail-order operation, double in size to 200,000 members. Within a year, Paul was the largest retailer of Elvis records, as well as the biggest merchandiser of pre-1977 Elvis memorabilia. His wife, Janice, admitted that Paul "has a lot of guilt feelings—all of a sudden he feels like a whore, to cash in like everybody else." Still there was that $30,000 a month in the mail. And soon Paul had signed a contract with an outfit called National Media Marketing. "They now own the rights to my name, my likeness, the whole bit," he said at the time. "People know me. I'm a commodity."

Paul sold records by mail. Steve Goldstein did it with television. He recalls that as soon as he heard about Elvis's death, he took an album that had been selling for $2.98 in the stores, increased the price to $6.98, bought a $100 telephone order ad on a New Orleans television station at 3 A.M. Next morning, he says, "There were 150 orders. I told my people, 'Buy every market in the U.S.! Buy the world!' Orders were so heavy we shorted out phone systems in Little Rock, Cleveland, Memphis, and Nashville."

The next couple of months, Goldstein picked up another four albums, charged $10.66 for each—although all were available in stores for $7.98—and using the same advertising techniques, moved 665,000 records. Goldstein also quickly published a newsstand picture magazine, selling 270,000 copies in under a month, and bought a Cadillac Elvis once gave a girl in Denver and started taking it to Elvis fan gatherings, charging $3 to have a picture taken at the wheel.

"We were making $3,400 a day," says Goldstein, who is still in his twenties. "Those people are sick, man, sick!"

Some believe that Goldstein was operating outside the bounds of decency, although inside the limits of the law. Others ignored the law, however, and manufactured and marketed "bootleg" or unauthorized, albums. Within a year, there were more than fifty of these records. One of the leading bootleggers, Dave Toledano (not his real name), was a lab technician in a West Coast hospital, making records from unreleased tapes, pressing only 500 copies at a time. "That was before Elvis died," he says. "After he died I started ordering 10,000 at a time. There are fans who have to have one of everything. That's the market I went after. Some stores carry my records. Mostly I solicit the fans by mail, and sell at the conventions."

The first year there were dozens of these "conventions," featuring a weekend of nonstop Elvis movies and videotapes, visits by authors of Elvis books or Charlie Hodge, auctions of Elvis memorabilia (his earliest records, on the Sun label, generally brought $300 apiece), and a wide range of new Elvis product, legal or illegal.

In Memphis, Elvis exploitation verged on the ridiculous. By the second anniversary of the death, there was an entire shopping center of stores directly across the street from Graceland, offering more than seventy different Elvis products—ashtrays, coasters that looked like the original Sun record labels, guitar-shaped hairbrushes, pennants, pillows, picture books, replicas of the TCB pendant, lapel buttons, postcards, bumper stickers, candle holders, Christmas tree ornaments, key chains, posters, plastic drinking cups, trash baskets, wall clocks, wristwatches, scarves, pencils, statuettes (four sizes), belt buckles, pen knives, pocket mirrors, etc. One shop gave away a replica of Elvis's driver's license with every purchase. Another allowed visitors to punch up their favorite Elvis song on a jukebox in the foyer. Even gas stations nearby and the Howard Johnson restaurant carried a full line of Elvis tee-shirts.

By mail from Memphis it was possible to order a "Complete Elvis Memorial Package" that included copies of the last will and testament, marriage certificate, and medical examiner's final report, along with a handful of cheap jewelry, $9.95 plus $1 for postage. Gray Line Tours was running an Elvis Memorial Tour, taking busloads of fans to see the renovated Sun Recording Studio, Nathan Novick's Pawn Shop on Beale Street where Elvis bought some of his early clothes, Humes

High School (now a junior high school), Loew's Palace where he worked as an usher, Graceland, and the Crown Electric Company where he drove a truck—$7.50 for adults, $5 for children. All up and down Elvis Presley Boulevard, shops and motels and restaurants were using the address as their name (*i.e.,* Elvis Presley Boulevard Inn; 3765 Elvis Presley Blvd. Souvenirs). The Memphis newspapers combined all the stories about Elvis published the week following his death into a single special edition and sold more than 250,000 copies.

Newspapers and magazines everywhere made millions of dollars trading on the Presley name. Some were negative in their appraisals, including the *Village Voice* ("The World's Most Beloved Solipsist Is Dead: How Long Will We Care?"). Others, like the movie magazine *Photoplay,* collected a "treasury" of articles ("The Day Priscilla Became His Dream Bride!" "God Spoke to Me When My Mother Died!"). The tabloids virtually "made up" stories to fit some of the strangest headlines ever written: "While Giving Away Cars & Jewelry to Strangers . . . ELVIS NEGLECTED CLOSE KIN LIVING IN POVERTY" *(National Enquirer),* "I AM ELVIS' SECRET DAUGHTER" *(Midnight Globe),* "Christmas Without Elvis" *(The Star),* "UFO's Hover Over Elvis' Tomb" *(Modern People).*

In England a 22-year-old former computer operator recorded an album using the name Elvis Costello (and turned out to be an impressive talent anyway). In Manitowoc, Wisconsin, foundry worker Herbert Baer, 41, a longtime Presley fan, went to court and got permission to change his name to Elvis Presley. In Orlando, Florida, Dennis Wise, 24, underwent plastic surgery to look like his idol. Back in Memphis, in the grisliest turn of all, three men were arrested fleeing the cemetery where Elvis was entombed. One of them said their plan, aborted by police, was to steal Elvis's body and deliver it to an unidentified man who would then hold it for $10 million ransom. (The body was moved by Vernon Presley to Graceland shortly thereafter, where the gravesite was put under 24-hour armed guard.)

And on and on and on it goes.

Of course the Colonel wasn't asleep at his desk. He, too, was taking care of business. The difference was, he didn't try to steal the body. He still owned it. Or, in some areas anyway, nearly fifty percent of it.

The Colonel was at the auditorium in Portland, Maine, making his preliminary security check and looking at the dressing rooms for Elvis's first concert in over two months when he got the message to call Memphis. For the rest of his life, he'll remember that date as well as his own birthday. His Golden Goose was dead.

The Colonel was stunned, but not surprised. Already he had taken Elvis into his company, Boxcar Enterprises, and had been talking with an East Coast promoter about the merchandising rights that in death would become worth millions.

Rather than return to Memphis, the Colonel flew to New York, where he met with Harry "The Bear" Geissler, the 47-year-old owner of Factors Etc., Inc. Geissler, who took his nickname from the town where he had his factory, Bear, Delaware, was a third-grade dropout and former steelworker and just the man for the job, the Colonel decided, because he already had a multimillion-dollar operation and the experience to handle something big, yet he wasn't so big he wasn't still hungry. Geissler had made it into the big leagues earlier that year when he put up $300,000 for the Farrah Fawcett-Majors tee-shirt rights. By the time Elvis was dead, he'd earned enough to pay over $400,000 in royalties to Farrah's agent as well as purchase merchandising licenses to *Star Wars* and *Rocky*. (Later he would sign *Superman* and *Grease*, too.)

The second thing that attracted the Colonel to Geissler was his slightly more distant past. He'd started out hustling Little League decals, moving into the entertainment field when he had questionable legal right. Before taking on Farrah, Factors paid $100,000 to companies that claimed Geissler was a bootlegger. This, the Colonel figured, rightly, gave the Bear and his aggressive 27-year-old son Lee an edge when it came time to go after the bootleggers who were sure to characterize the Presley market in the years to come.

And so they have. In fact, Geissler claims he filed 400 lawsuits the first two years, while working with the Memphis Merchants Association to get several anti-huckster ordinances passed to keep the unauthorized product off the streets. Geissler also won two key federal court rulings, in New York and Tennessee, establishing the idea that a performer's merchandising rights go to his heirs. Previously, this "right of publicity" ended with death.

"People want to be aware of a celebrity," says the Bear. "They want to wear him on their chest. They want to have souvenirs and that is a valuable commodity. We are the only protection against people dancing on Elvis's grave."

If anybody was dancing, of course, it was the Bear and his authorized licensees, plus the Colonel and his longtime lieutenant, Tom Diskin. Boxcar Enterprises—named for double-sixes in the game of craps—was owned 56 percent by the Colonel and 22 percent each by the Presley estate and Diskin, who was president. Royalties were divided fifty percent to Boxcar, twenty percent each to the estate and to the Colonel and ten percent to Diskin. This meant that of all the money that came in from the nearly one hundred Elvis souvenirs being marketed the Colonel pocketed half and Diskin got twenty percent of the rest.

Making the deal even juicier was the fact that Geissler was paying to file those hundreds of lawsuits, just as RCA was paying lawyers to go after all the record bootleggers. This was the Snowman's credo. The Colonel was Chief Potentate of the Snowmen's League, a gag organization whose membership included presidents and hundreds of media people. The successful Snowman, he said in his membership brochure, must show a "willingness to see the other man's problem and show the greatest understanding without financial involvement."

Back in his office, following the funeral, the Colonel lived up to another credo, the one his client emblazoned on his airplane's tail and hung around all his buddies' necks: "Take care of business (with a flash)." It was like being in a war room the first few days . . . as orders went out to RCA and staggering sales reports came back . . . as the Colonel demanded the return of all rehearsal tapes sent over the years to Elvis's backup musicians (a move aimed at stemming the bootleg tide) . . . as hundreds and hundreds of calls came in from promoters wanting the rights to this or that. The Colonel also had a rubber stamp made that said ALWAYS ELVIS, and over the next few years this slogan would go onto all that funky old stationery he still used, as well as decorate a number of commercial ventures.

"It's still Elvis and the Colonel, but now it's Elvis and Vernon Presley and the Colonel," he told people on the telephone that week. "Elvis didn't die. The body did. We're keeping up the good spirits. We're keeping Elvis alive. I talked to him this morning and he told me to carry on."

Still, it was the body that the fans wanted and when the Colonel announced an "Always Elvis" extravaganzà in Las Vegas on the first anniversary of Elvis's death, with the unveiling of a lifesize statue outside the showroom where he'd performed so long, attendance was disappointing. The magazine writers attacked it viciously, saying it was tasteless exploitation and the fans, after opening day, stayed away in droves. They preferred to go to Graceland. By 1979, in fact, so many preferred this they were spending an estimated three million dollars a year in Memphis and Elvis, as a tourist attraction, was, in the words of one local citizen, "bigger than the Mississippi River."

Of course, the Colonel, acting on behalf of the Presley estate, was doing well enough, too. After Elvis's death, RCA tied up every record pressing plant in the country to keep up with orders, clearing every record store in the nation in 24 hours, selling an astonishing 200 million records the first year. Royalties from this, along with the percentage of every guitar-shaped hairbrush and musical fifth of bourbon sold (the bottle played "Love Me Tender") brought the estate more than five million dollars during that same period, a similar amount the second year.

Meanwhile, intimate and sometimes embarrassing snippets of information were revealed. Elvis's stepbrother David Stanley said his job when Elvis was alive was to carry an attaché case full of pills and rolls of $100 bills, said he and Elvis prayed together just hours before he died. His head of security, the ex-cop Dick Grob, copyrighted an outline to a book that swore Elvis was dying of bone cancer, then admitted he'd made the story up. ABC television called the heart attack story a cover-up, demanded an investigation. As it happened, an investigation was already under way, and Elvis's doctor, George Nichopoulos, faced the possibility of losing his medical license for prescribing more than 5,000 pills for Elvis the last seven months of his life. Following a computer check of all prescriptions filled in Memphis, state health officials said that on the day before Elvis died, he received 150 tablets and 20 cubic centimeters of the painkillers Percodan and Dilaudid, 262 pills of the depressants Amytal and Quaalude, and 278 tablets of the stimulants Dexadrine and Biphetamine. Apparently he was stocking up for the new road tour. No one knows how many of those pills Elvis took. ABC-TV mentioned the $225,000 Dr. Nick borrowed from Elvis and quoted Rick Stanley as saying Max Shapiro, the Beverly Hills dentist, gave Elvis anything he wanted;

said there was no police investigation, no search of the house trailer behind Graceland for drugs; said the internal organs were discarded; said there was no coroner's inquest. ABC wanted the body exhumed.

Long before ABC-TV made its noisy demands and charges, Baptist Hospital spokesmen were claiming "polypharmacy" as the probable cause of death. What this means is that the cumulative effect of several drugs acting together is greater than the effect of the drugs individually. Or: two plus two equals not four, but five, or six. This is a position held by Maurice Elliott, a hospital vice-president, and it is believed that it explains why the hospital's chief of pathology, Dr. E. Eric Muirhead, refused to sign the original autopsy claiming death due to cardiac arrythmia.

For months the controversy raged and finally Dr. Nick had his wrists slapped; his license was suspended for three months and he was placed on three years probation.

In the meantime . . .

RCA continued to release "new" Elvis albums; all went on the bestseller lists.

A nine-and-a-half-foot statue of Elvis went into the Orpheum Theatre in downtown Memphis, admission $1 for adults, fifty cents for children. In Nashville there was a "memorial" exhibit that featured a ninety-foot cyclorama; visitors got a twenty-minute recorded "tour" for $4 and for another $2 could autograph the wall.

Vernon died, leaving the bulk of his estate to his girlfriend Sandy Miller. Control of the Elvis estate was then transferred to Priscilla and her lawyers. The Colonel's influence was diminished somewhat, because he didn't get along with Priscilla as well as he had gotten on with Vernon, yet when the Colonel made the deal for the authorized feature-length documentary, Priscilla happily contributed all her home movies.

An $80,000 Elvis Presley chapel was dedicated in Tupelo, Mississippi, Elvis's birthplace.

The new product got pretty weird. Besides the replicas of Sun Records labels that served as drink coasters, and an Elvis Presley wine (Elvis didn't drink), there was a lifesized Elvis doll that actually perspired. This incensed a filmmaker in Seattle, who whipped up a satirical six-minute movie in which the King's decaying body was exhumed and brought back for one final concert tour. The corpse was trotted out for record store autograph sessions and it released an album, *Necrophilia Hawaiian Style*. Finally, slices of rotten flesh were hacked off and sold in "Piece-O-Presley" packages.

Who knows where or when it will end?